WINSTON FIRST

WINSTON FIRST

The unauthorised account of
Winston Peters' career

Martin Hames

RANDOM
HOUSE
NEW ZEALAND LTD

Random House New Zealand Ltd
(An imprint of the Random House Group)

18 Poland Road
Glenfield
Auckland 10
NEW ZEALAND

Sydney   New York   Toronto
London   Auckland   Johannesburg
and agencies throughout the world

First published 1995

© Martin Hames 1995
Printed in Australia
ISBN 1 86941 257 5

Contents

Acknowledgements

Numerous people have assisted in the writing of this book, giving generously of their time, their ideas, and their encouragement. Without them the book would have been considerably poorer, if it could have been written at all. There are far too many to thank individually. Many of those whose assistance was most valuable would not want to be named. You know who you are.

There is one person I would have liked to thank by name for his co-operation — Winston Peters himself. Sadly, my request to meet with him was turned down.

Introduction

MUSIC and speeches from the stage have warmed up the audience, but the one they are waiting for has delayed his entrance. The air is thick with expectation, with an almost religious fervour; and every minute that passes heightens the tension so that when he arrives they will be ready to stand and cheer him all the more. Suddenly he is among them: good-looking, powerfully built, impeccably dressed in a double-breasted suit. A strong-looking man. A man on whom the audience is placing its disappointed hopes and baffled feelings. A man drinking in the oxygen of their adulation.

When the applause has died away he begins to speak. That dark, familiar voice is charged with strength, sincerity, moral protest. He speaks the words his audience feel instinctively to be true. A betrayal has taken place. A small élite has stolen New Zealand from its rightful owners, the people. There can be no doubt who the enemies are: Treasury, the Business Roundtable, the government, monetarists, the Reserve Bank, multi-nationals, foreign investors, the people who are selling our assets to foreigners, and sinister sounding international organisations like the OECD and the IMF. All have lined their pockets while ordinary New Zealanders have been sold short.

It is a powerful image, this lone battler engaged in a conflict of good against evil. Though it is a small élite he is battling, they seem to be everywhere. Little is said — little *needs* to be said — about how the speaker would right these wrongs. Faith can move mountains. When you behold the way, the truth and the life there is no need to ask for its manifesto. It is enough that when the man is leaving the hall they can crowd closer to him and to his aura, reach out their hands, touch the hem of his robe.

1

The man is Winston Peters — politician extraordinary and one of the most vivid presences in our national life. The scene could be taking place in 1989, or 1993, or as you read these words. No politician in a generation has stirred greater fervour among his supporters. Yet no politician has been a more wholly negative force in New Zealand politics, or wreaked greater destruction. Peters came into Parliament through an electoral petition that he was lucky to win. For a time he was a small-time bovver boy who specialised in personal attacks. In the late eighties he grew into a red-blooded populist with a remarkable gift for self-publicity. In 1992 he brought the grisly tactics of Senator McCarthy to these shores, not once but repeatedly. The party that brought him to prominence cast him out. But he is still alive politically, still young and still revelling in the tactics of fear, denunciation and intimidation.

This is a book that takes sides: against Peters, and against the cynical style of politics that he stands for. But the fascination of the man and his strange career is compelling. If Peters wanted power, he has almost wholly failed to achieve it. If he had a policy agenda he wanted to implement, his failure has been almost as great. On his return to Parliament by the electors of Tauranga in 1987 he stated a goal: to be the first person his colleagues would turn to when any important economic or social issue arose. It did not happen. He soon became almost the last person his colleagues would turn to. Even when he sat in Cabinet, his contributions were at best fitful. After he was cast out of Cabinet, it soon became a question not of what he could contribute, but of how much of the temple he could bring down with him.

If Peters wanted attention, if he wanted adulation, he has been more successful than he might ever have dared hope. He has pulled crowds that would be the envy of any other politician. He has topped the Prime Minister of the day in the opinion polls. He has done this despite never being leader or deputy leader of a major political party, despite never ranking higher than eight in the National line-up. He has experienced the warm inner glow of a very public martyrdom. He has been praised and adulated time and again for being the one honest man in politics, the one prepared to 'tell it as it is'. If adulation is what he was looking for, Peters has received it many times over.

No demagogue exists in a vacuum. No McCarthy goes on a rampage and is alone to blame. The conditions had to exist in which a Peters would flourish: social and economic stress. A mood of cynicism. Large numbers of people who felt excluded by the process of government. A media who often preferred to highlight each new 'revelation' rather than soberly examine whether the last revelation had even been worth running. Too few people prepared to stand up and be counted. Too few people prepared to defend a free society and the rule of law. The conditions for a Winston Peters were here in New Zealand. The story of Peters is the story of our times.

CHAPTER ONE

The Road to Parliament

April 1945–May 1979

THE tiny coastal settlement of Whananaki is a long way from the centres of power and influence in New Zealand. It is a long way from anywhere. Even today the drive north from Whangarei takes you over a winding metal road, through wild and attractive country. These days many of the houses in Whananaki are holiday homes. It was not so at the end of the war, when Winston Raymond Peters was born, the sixth child to Len and Joan Peters. The couple were to have five more. Len was a Maori from the local Ngati Wai tribe, Joan a McInnes from Scotland. Several wrong dates have been in the public arena for Winston's birth. His *Who's Who* entry gives 11 April 1946, but according to the official record he was born on that same day one year earlier in 1945. Interestingly, his first name is spelt 'Wynston' in the birth entry held by the Registrar-General.

The large Peters family was poor by the standards of the time, and still more so by today's standard. Yet Len and Joan did not fail as parents. The Peters clan was, and remains, a tight knit family. The amiable Len, who died in 1991, was regarded with a sometimes patronising affection by the children. It was Joan Peters who was the driving force in the household. She brought to the family the Scottish belief that the route to improvement lay in education and hard work. Despite growing up in the provincial isolation of a depressed rural area, most of the children were academic achievers and went on to professional careers. Jim Peters, the eldest, became a

4

secondary school headmaster, David a farmer, Marie a dental nurse and then a Maori issues consultant, Ian an insurance salesman and later an MP, Lynette a nurse and social worker, Ron a schoolteacher, Heather a training college lecturer, Beverley a dental nurse, Alan a prison officer and Wayne a lawyer.

Often Len was away from the farm working as a carpenter or in the freezing works. In his absence the sons milked the cows before going to school in the morning, and then again in the evening. It made for long days. Getting to school was a walk along the beach and estuary; if the tide was up they rode horses. Winston's acquaintance with horses dates from his earliest years. When he was three years old, Len would place him on the saddle to show a prospective buyer how docile a horse was. Later the family moved about between sharemilking jobs, but Winston was 11 before he saw Whangarei, and much older again before he saw Auckland.

There is little about the bare facts of Winston's childhood that explains the strikingly unusual political personality he was later to become. He clearly had huge respect for his mother and absorbed a great deal from her. In culture and outlook she was the one who proved a lasting influence. Joan Peters was the first person to interest him in British history and he also absorbed from her his lifelong addiction to neatness and cleanliness.

At first Winston appeared to be not the most favoured by nature of the Peters sons. He suffered from asthma which prevented him from participating fully in sport until the age of 13. He also worked to overcome a stutter. He was to suffer a disappointment over his secondary schooling. The elder brothers had all been sent to Wesley College, the Methodist boarding school in South Auckland, but when it came to Winston's turn the money had run out. So he attended Whangarei Boys' High and Dargaville High, sometimes doing his homework in an upturned corrugated iron tank in a paddock.

It is possible that those aspects of Winston's early life hardened him in his determination to prove himself. It is said that from early on Winston had three ambitions: to be an All Black, to be Prime Minister and to own a racehorse. Something,

5

either in nature or in nurture, marked him out from his brothers and sisters. He had more ambition and more determination than the others. While very much a member of the family, Winston is also one apart. Today the other family members share his charm but are notable for their sheer normality. Their brother is different: he is a man driven.

Winston may have been ambitious to get on, but in the decade after he left school there was little evidence of a carefully worked out career plan. His first step was to Auckland Teachers' Training College, which led to one year of teaching at Te Atatu Intermediate. Then he promptly gave up teaching and enrolled at Auckland University where he successfully completed a Bachelor of Arts degree, majoring in history and politics. For his compulsory language unit he took Hebrew, not having done one of the more common language subjects at high school. One of his closest friends at this time was fellow student Bruce Cliffe, who later became a Cabinet minister in the Bolger administration. It was Cliffe who in 1967 signed Peters up for the National Party, and who took him along to his first Young Nationals meeting. Cliffe was then chairman of the Auckland Division of the Young Nationals. Another of Peters' friends at this time was Paul East, who was also to become a Cabinet minister under Jim Bolger.

Peters at this stage showed little interest in active party politics, but he did take part in student forums on political issues. On one of those occasions he had his first confrontation with Richard Prebble. Neither man knew at the time that two decades later they would be clashing repeatedly across the floor of Parliament. A forum had been called to discuss whether New Zealand should insist on its right to take Maori players on All Black tours to South Africa. Peters took the conservative line that New Zealand should respect South Africa's wishes not to host Maori, whereupon Prebble shouted from the back that Peters was an Uncle Tom. Afterwards Peters came storming up, demanding to know who had called him an Uncle Tom. He had a fair idea who it was. Prebble's response: 'Whoever said it, Winston, was wrong. Uncle Tom was a good Christian gentleman.'

Along with brothers Ron and Alan, Peters played rugby for

6

the Auckland University Club. For several seasons he was in the senior team, then one of the best club sides in Auckland. He could play in the midfield or on the wing, and was a talented — if sometimes erratic — player. He was an individualist on the field, able to do very good things but not noted as a passer of the ball. He was competitive by nature and said to be fond of talking to the referee. Peters never came very close to his ambition to be an All Black, but he did captain the Auckland Maori side.

On completing his arts degree, Peters spent a short time in Australia, where the money was good, working in a variety of labouring jobs. He returned to Auckland just in time to enrol in law school. He was never a brilliant student, but he had an extremely good memory and an ability to work hard when he needed to. However, he did not possess outstandingly strong analytical abilities for a subject like law. Most of his pass grades were Cs. Law associate professor Bill Hodge recalls a well-written Peters essay that, unusually for the time, argued for the constitutional importance of the Treaty of Waitangi. But Peters was no sixties radical. Nor did he look like one. With his immaculate appearance he made a studied contrast to most around him.

In 1973 Peters married Louise, a primary school teacher and, in the following year he graduated and took a job with Russell McVeagh, one of the most prestigious law firms in the country. He was there about three years and during that time he became more heavily involved in politics. His first taste of political campaigning came in 1975, the year Robert Muldoon swept on to the Treasury benches in a landslide victory over Bill Rowling's Labour government. Muldoon that year stomped the country with charts, told New Zealanders they needed to tighten their belts, and came up with one of the biggest election bribes — national superannuation — ever dangled in front of the New Zealand electorate. Peters stood as the National candidate for Northern Maori — a lost cause, if ever there was one, but an opportunity for him to gain some exposure within the party. He ended up doing well in the circumstances: he clocked up almost 2000 votes against his Labour opponent Mat Rata, becoming the first National candidate in a Maori seat for some years not to lose his deposit.

Despite the relatively good result, Peters seemed to take the defeat personally. He told a friend he would never again stand for a Maori seat, since Maori had rejected him. The following year Peters became a member of National's Dominion Council, the body at the top of the party organisation. With his experience as a candidate, and his service at a high level with the party organisation, he was building the type of record that could help him win selection in a winnable seat.

That chance came in 1978. The latest redrawing of electorate boundaries had created the new seat of Hunua. A strange mixture of urban and rural, poor and affluent, it included part of the wealthy urban suburb of Howick, a section of working-class Otara (with its large Maori and Pacific Island population) and a large expanse of South Auckland farmland. On balance Hunua looked winnable for National, but it would clearly be no pushover.

There was no shortage of candidates chasing the Hunua nomination for National. Among them were Pat Baker and John Tremewan, both long-time officials in the party's Auckland Division, Neville Wallace, husband of Judge Augusta Wallace, and Barry Hutchinson, who managed Beltons Real Estate. And there was Clem Simich, who was to enter Parliament 14 years later as Muldoon's successor in Tamaki. Others too were tempted to put their names forward. One of them was Winston Peters.

None of the candidates in the field looked unbeatable, which may well have been why Peters was persuaded to enter. Peters had also been encouraged by some in the Hunua electorate. He was seen as a man who had risen in the world in praiseworthy fashion with no inherited advantages. He was young and presentable. And he was perceived as coming from the private enterprise wing of the party. Some in the Auckland Division of the party were less impressed with Peters' credentials. They thought he was lazy, and that other candidates in the field had more substance.

Peters made it through pre-selection, the process by which the field of prospective candidates is whittled down to a shortlist. Peters then worked hard on the delegates who would be voting in the final selection meeting. He received valuable support from influential figures in the electorate, and by the night of the selection meeting he had the contest won, barring a spectacular accident at the podium. None was to occur. Peters gave the best speech of the five candidates. One future Cabinet minister who was in the audience recalls Peters' speech as coming from the John Marshall/Hugh Templeton side of the party — the urban liberals. Peters won on the first ballot.

The very next morning Peters was heading to Wellington. At the airport he met for the first time Don McKinnon, who earlier that week had won the Albany selection. As newly selected candidates, they were flying down to receive their first riding instructions. Peters was far from impressed by the name on his airline ticket: it was Pat Baker. The ticket had been purchased before the selection meeting and Baker was the candidate the Division thought — and probably hoped — would win. Peters was convinced Baker's name on the ticket meant the Division had been plotting against him. It was an early manifestation of Peters' suspicious nature, his inherent tendency to prefer the conspiracy theory to the cock-up theory.

Peters told his Hunua party workers that he would campaign full-time from August until the election. He did not in fact do that, offering the excuse that Muldoon had asked candidates to keep their heads down. Peters believed he would win Hunua without too much trouble, a misjudgement he shared with many others in the electorate. Nationwide the government was well ahead of the Opposition in the opinion polls, and most commentators were expecting National to win the election comfortably. Peters' confidence was increased when he was selected to front National's television advertisements for the campaign. Someone, even at that early stage, had put their finger on Peters' potential as a television performer. He was chosen to conduct a series of interviews with none other than the Prime Minister himself, a man Peters held in awe. The candidate for Hunua was over the moon. 'I'm going to become the David Frost of New Zealand,' he told some of his party officials.

Peters did not end up becoming the David Frost of New Zealand. The advertisements turned out to be rather poor, though that was not Peters' fault. The format was stilted. The theme of the advertisements was National 'keeping its word', carrying out the commitments in its 1975 manifesto. There was no genuine interviewing: Peters would ask a sycophantic question, there would be a response from Muldoon or another senior minister, along with relevant images on the screen, then Peters would come back at the end to wrap things up and remind New Zealanders that in yet another area National was keeping its word. Peters looked like a glove puppet, and not one with too much independence of thought. It did not make for riveting viewing.

Probably the television advertisements did Peters little harm in Hunua. But they did him little good either, and there were some in the electorate who believed he would have been better off spending time on the ground rather than playing at being David Frost. As it turned out, Peters was to need every vote he could get in the fight against his Labour opponent, Malcolm Douglas. By election day National was still expected to win the General Election comfortably, but election night told a different story. There was an unexpectedly strong swing towards Labour. The two main parties polled almost exactly the same percentage of the total vote. In terms of seats, however, National was comfortably ahead of Labour on election night. In view of the number of seats that might be overturned once the special votes were counted, Rowling was not yet conceding defeat. But it looked all but certain National would remain on the Treasury benches.

The contest in Hunua turned out to be extremely close. At the end of the night Douglas had a lead of 236 votes. It was a lead that would stretch to 301 once the official count, including special votes, had been made. But Peters on election night was in no mood to concede. National Party scrutineers in the Otara polling booths had reported a large number of voting irregularities. Already both Peters and Muldoon were telling the media that National might lodge a court challenge in Hunua. Douglas for his part was complaining about the constant challenging of Pacific Island voters by National scrutineers in the course of the day.

Lodging an electoral petition to the Supreme Court (as it was then called) is an expensive and hugely time-consuming exercise. Peters soon decided he wanted to proceed with a petition. To do that he needed to persuade the National Party to give him financial backing. He had far more to gain from a successful petition outcome than the party at large — National did not need to hold Hunua to be able to govern effectively. Nonetheless, Peters was successful in persuading Muldoon to give him party backing. There followed six months of hard slog, not only for Winston and Louise, but also for a large number of Hunua party workers. A good deal of detective work was required. The task was to provide documentation to back a court challenge to almost 1000 votes.

Some time into this exercise Peters confided to one of his key electorate people that his own vote in Hunua had been invalid. Peters had not been entitled to cast a vote in Hunua because he had chosen to be on the Maori roll in the 1976 census. The reaction from Peters' electorate official was volcanic. Why, he demanded, had Peters left it so late to tell anyone about it? A shamefaced Peters said that if he had mentioned it before, he would not have received the go-ahead from Muldoon to launch the petition.

In March 1979, four months after the election, the hearing began in Auckland's Supreme Court. The presiding judges were the Chief Justice, Ronald Davison, Justice Speight and Justice Sinclair. Peters was challenging votes on a large number of grounds, including voters not meeting the residency qualifications, voters being on the Maori roll and thus not eligible to vote in Hunua, double voting, non-existent voters, dead voters and voters who were overseas. Douglas filed in reply a list of objections to the petitioner's case. Among the objections was a challenge to Peters' right to stand as a candidate. It was this issue which took up the first day of the hearing, providing an uncomfortable moment or two for Peters in the witness box.

The facts were these. Peters had chosen in 1976 to be on the Maori roll, and was correctly registered as an elector of Northern Maori. As the law stood, once Peters had chosen the Maori option he could not switch over to the general roll until the next census in 1981. In April 1977 Peters had moved to a Howick address which was in the Hunua electorate, and in

Western Maori for the purposes of the Maori roll. In May 1978 Peters then shifted to another address in the Hunua electorate. This time he filled out a change-of-address form for electoral purposes. He did not state on that form that he had chosen the Maori option in the 1976 census, but neither did he assert that he was on the general roll; he simply put down the details of his change of address without ticking either of the option boxes for Maori or General. On the basis of that change-of-address form it was assumed by the electoral office that Peters was on the general roll. He was placed on the roll for Hunua, a mistake that only became apparent after the election. The fact that the previous address on Peters' change-of-address form did not match the address given in his 1976 census return, when he had chosen the Maori option, may have been a factor in preventing the electoral office from correctly placing Peters on the Western Maori roll.

Under cross-examination on the first day of the hearing, Peters said that in hindsight he had not made himself as familiar with the Electoral Act as he should have. He agreed some familiarity with the Act was required to be a Parliamentary candidate. He was not quizzed on why he had not ticked either of the options Maori or General when filling out his change of address form. When asked if he did not think it strange when he received a form acknowledging he was registered on the Hunua supplementary roll, in view of the fact that he had previously chosen the Maori option, Peters at first made no reply. When the question was repeated Peters said it had caused him some apprehension. His recollections, distant though they were, were that he had exercised the Maori option in the 1976 census. But when he had received notification that he was on the Hunua roll, he had assumed he must have left that section blank on the census form.

No doubt Peters *had* suffered a memory lapse. However, for a lawyer and a Parliamentary candidate, and for a man regarded by friend and enemy as having an extremely powerful memory, the lapse was uncharacteristic. If Peters had been lying about his memory lapse, he would, of course, have been committing perjury. When asked whether he had done anything to check whether his misgivings were misplaced or well-founded, Peters said he had not given it a thought until December when he had heard Labour were challenging his nomination on the basis of the 1976 census.

The counsel for Douglas argued Peters was not entitled to be a candidate because only people registered as electors in an electoral district were entitled to be candidates under the Electoral Act. Fortunately for Peters, there was another section of the Act that appeared to give him an out:

> The nomination of any person as a candidate for election, or his election as a member of Parliament, shall not be questioned on the ground that, though entitled to be registered as an elector of any district, he was not in fact registered as an elector of that district but was registered as an elector of some other district.

Even though Peters was not *validly* registered as an elector in any electoral district, the court ruled that Peters was both registered as an elector of Northern Maori and *entitled* to be registered as an elector of Western Maori, and was thus in terms of the Act entitled to be a candidate. On the second day an oral judgment was delivered to that effect, disposing of Labour's challenge to Peters' candidacy.

It was a long and complex hearing lasting eight weeks. Many witnesses were called on both sides. Many examples of votes that should be disallowed were clearly demonstrated by Peters' counsel. At first the focus was on which votes were, or were not, valid votes. However, in the course of the hearing a great deal of evidence emerged on the poor state of the electoral rolls. Already the state of the rolls had been subject to wide and justified public criticism. Now the counsel for Douglas developed a submission that the roll was so defective in terms of the Electoral Act that the court should order a by-election in Hunua. Had that submission been successful it would have been a good outcome for Labour: by-elections usually go against the government and Labour would probably have secured Hunua.

In calling for a by-election, the counsel for Douglas brought up a number of reasons to support their contention that the rolls were defective. There was the controversial fact that, contrary to the Electoral Act, the compilation of the rolls had been centralised in Wellington rather than in each electorate. There was also the curious case of a Labour Party worker who had been involved in the registration of voters. She gave evidence that around 490 people, whose application forms she claimed had been posted off in good time, never appeared on the Hunua roll. Around 290 of the cards were later located in Wellington in the national alphabetical collection, having been received in time; the other 200 were never located. However, the argument for holding a by-election was not accepted by the judges.

In its judgment the court ordered a recount to be undertaken, and gave its rulings on the wide range of issues that had come up during the case. The judgment was good news for Peters. It disallowed almost 500 votes out of the 900 he had challenged. The disallowed votes fell into a large range of categories. Eleven of the disallowed votes were of people found to have voted twice. The judges stated that double voting was aided by the common Polynesian practice of employing more than one name, and that there was little doubt others had voted twice but had not been detected. The judges suggested ID cards would help prevent abuse of the voting system. Douglas would later claim that most of the cases of double-voting were simple clerical errors. Special voting was another area where the court found dubious practices, stating that often no adequate enquiry was made of applicants for special votes to establish their eligibility. In its report to Parliament the court would state that formalities were not always complied with, and that one person who witnessed many special vote declarations was 'less than scrupulous in her observation of the law'.

In the 50-page judgment there were two crucial areas where Labour seemed unfairly treated. One was the issue that became virtually synonymous with the Hunua electoral petition — informal voting.

The instructions on ballot papers had asked voters to strike out the names, not party affiliations, of the candidates for whom the voter did not wish to vote. In Hunua there were hundreds of voters not complying with that instruction. All sorts of permutations and combinations of ticks, crosses (the method used in local body voting), lines, underlinings, circlings and other markings had been applied to names and/or party affiliations by the voters of Hunua. While some of these votes were ambiguous as to their intent, most did show a clear voting preference. For instance, more than half of the informal votes — 354 — were informal merely because party affiliations rather than names had been struck out. Yet the great majority of informal votes had been rejected by the returning officer.

It was no secret that the bulk of informal votes would have been cast by Polynesians living in Otara, many of whom were semi-literate at best. This area was heavily supportive of Labour. Counsel for Douglas had submitted during the hearing that all votes should be allowed where the intention of the voter was clear. However, in what seemed a curious reading of the Electoral Act the court held that a voter needed to follow the exact instructions on the ballot paper if his or her vote was to be valid.

The court's ruling out of all informal voting methods was a bitter blow to Labour's chances. A schedule detailing the various types of informal voting would subsequently be provided by the court as part of its special report to Parliament on the Hunua electoral petition. By this author's count, 451 out of the 560 informal votes expressed a clear intention, and thus on a correct reading of the Electoral Act would have been accepted as valid.

The other ruling Labour were entitled to feel unhappy over concerned non-Maori who had placed themselves on the Maori roll. Most of these non-Maori were Polynesians who had mistakenly taken the Maori option in the 1976 census. The court ruled that, having made that mistake, they could not validly vote in Hunua. That meant these voters could not validly vote on *either* the general or the Maori roll. The ruling was based on a complex and highly literal reading of the Electoral Act. It can hardly have seemed the intention of Parliament to disenfranchise a large group of voters in this way.

After the judgment there was a two-week wait while the recount was undertaken. It was plain to Labour that a loss in Hunua was well on the cards. Already there was talk of applying to the Court of Appeal for a declaratory judgment on the issue of informal voting. A judgment overturning the Supreme Court decision would not affect the result in Hunua, or in Kapiti, which was going through a similar electoral petition. But it could play an important role in all subsequent elections.

Eventually the day came for the Hunua result to be announced. Peters had travelled down to Wellington; Douglas sat in the chair he had occupied for just one week, as he listened to the Speaker read out the results: Peters 7507, Douglas 7315, Morell 2346, Robinson 271, Informal 560. The seat had gone to Peters by 192 votes. There were protestations from the Opposition benches. Douglas sat, seemingly impassive, as the formal procedure got under way for erasing his name from the Hunua writ. Then he was led out of the House by his brother Roger. Outside Parliament Douglas was close to tears. He said 700 voters had had their democratic rights taken away from them on technicalities, and he challenged National to fight on the streets of Hunua and not in the court.

The losing margin of 192 was indeed a slim one. If two-thirds of the 450-odd disallowed 'informal' votes had gone to Labour (a fairly conservative assumption), with the remaining third going to the other parties in proportion to their total share of the vote, Peters and Douglas would have been neck and neck. Add to that the ruling on non-Maori who had chosen the Maori option, and the case of the application forms that never ended up on the electoral roll, and Douglas appeared desperately unlucky.

By the time Peters entered the House the Opposition were vainly trying to force a snap debate on the Hunua verdict. A buoyant Peters was led in by the Chief Government Whip, to applause from government members. No more dramatic entry into national politics could have been imagined. The Opposition members were less than impressed. As Peters stepped forward to take the oath, one called out: 'Mind you don't choke'.

CHAPTER TWO

Hunua MP

May 1979–July 1984

WE can be sure Peters was nervous when he rose to make his maiden speech in Parliament. The debating chamber was new and unfriendly territory which he would have to confront and conquer. Major public appearances have always appeared to take a large physical and mental toll on him. Like many politicians, Peters' carefully controlled public facade is one thing, the inner man quite another. And like many politicians, the inner tensions still have a way of breaking the surface. Peters possesses a nervous blink and a facial rash which expands and contracts as a barometer of his stress. Those who have worked closely with him know how tense and jumpy he grows before major media events. If that is true today, it can be no less true of the young Maori from Whananaki back in 1979.

To those who imagine they know what Peters stands for, what he said in his maiden speech comes as quite a surprise. The speech was not a hymn to economic pragmatism. He did not condemn the theorists of the free market or slam the Treasury for its academic excesses. What Peters said was something very different:

> I believe the most effective government the country can have is one that believes in free enterprise, encourages hard work, keeps control and regulations to a minimum, carefully controls state spending, and sets taxation rates that are an incentive, not a disincentive, to work.

It could be Roger Douglas speaking, or Ruth Richardson. But it was not: it was the young Winston Peters. There was a good deal more in this vein. He went on to say:

> When I say I believe in private enterprise, I extend that concept to workers, for they are entitled to a free market for the services they render.

This was a radical thought in the days before even voluntary unionism. Peters also warned against letting the welfare state grow too large, and against letting government spending take up too large a proportion of national income. There was praise for community initiatives in the Hunua electorate that did not rely on government handouts.

The maiden speech is where a new MP traditionally sets out his or her political philosophy. Peters' stated philosophy was plain. It was freedom, independence and enterprise. He believed in small government and a minimum of regulation. Some who knew Peters during that first Parliamentary term think that deep down, perhaps very heavily buried, he still believes it.

In 1979 there was something of a new wind blowing in the National caucus. The 1978 election had seen the entry into politics of a new group of MPs who did not feel they owed their seats to Muldoon. Some of them even felt they had won their seats despite him. They wanted more free enterprise and less government regulation. This group included Michael Cox, Doug Kidd, Ian McLean and Don McKinnon. Peters, at least in rhetoric, was happy to be one of them. He would comment, speaking of the 1978 intake, 'I think we reflect in a purist sense the philosophy of the party — private enterprise, but without the clichés.'

In light of his later career Peters' maiden speech is a most revealing document. There is more to it than just the philosophy of a free marketeer. Towards the end of the speech he identifies a certain type of critic of society. According to Peters this critic is not motivated by a desire to remedy specific abuses, but rather 'his criticism is a goal in itself', he preaches a doctrine of 'despair, guilt and pervasive unworthiness'. This critic:

Sets out to exploit every tremor and spasm in society, the economy or race relations, seeking to use every such event as a vehicle to project his own public personality. This critic never joins the ruck of human existence; his opinions are never put at risk. His non-participation is a fail-safe device.

The picture is so instantly recognisable that one cannot help wondering if Peters felt any sense of premonition. Can his feelings have been completely pure at his condemnation of the self-promoting populist; or did one part of him, even then, feel drawn to the black arts of the demagogue even as he was denouncing them? Whatever his feelings, Peters was describing with uncanny accuracy the type of politician he would one day become.

That was far into the future. For the moment Peters was finding his feet as a very junior backbencher in an administration where backbenchers were expected to be seen and not heard. They tend to work together, socialise together, even flat together. Peters flatted for his first three years in Parliament with Hamilton West MP Mike Minogue. If he did not know it already, he soon found out that life for a government backbencher was far from glamorous. At the best of times backbenchers have little real power. They also have little chance of carving out much of a public profile unless they choose to be mavericks. That was especially so under Muldoon, to whom backbenchers were lobby fodder and little else. In his first term Peters stuck by these rules. He never rocked the boat publicly. He never became a maverick like his flatmate Minogue. And, despite attempts at self-promotion, he did not stand out from the general ruck of government backbenchers. For a politician whose later career would be so tumultuous, Peters would have a surprisingly uneventful first term.

It seems such a long time ago now, Peters' first Parliamentary term. So much has changed that it takes an effort of the imagination to think yourself back into that political landscape. It was a landscape completely dominated by Muldoon. Belligerent in rhetoric, cautious in action, Muldoon was much more of an interim figure than he seemed at the time. He did not know, though he may have dimly sensed, that almost everything he stood for would soon evaporate. He stood for a whole set of social attitudes that were dissolving even as he tried to stem the tide. He stood for a pro-American foreign policy which would change abruptly on his departure. Most famously of all, he stood for a heavily controlled and regulated economy.

Though there was general unease about the performance of the economy throughout the Muldoon years, few people at the time realised just how deeply in trouble we were as a country. Even fewer correctly saw what would eventually need to be done. Our relative economic performance had been in decline for decades. The cause was bad economic policies — the policies of regulation and protection. The Fortress New Zealand strategy pursued from the late 1930s onwards made the country into the most controlled and regulated economy in the western world. Fortress New Zealand was designed to build up New Zealand's manufacturing sector; but it created the most inefficient manufacturing sector of any developed country. Very high levels of import protection meant there was almost no incentive for manufacturers to innovate and add value. Business efficiency was further compromised by a chronically inflexible industrial relations system and by numerous other regulations. Skill levels slowly languished. Quality research and development was not pursued. Gradually the rest of the world began to pass us by.

We carried on exporting unprocessed primary products, still earning for a while a first world standard of living from what was essentially a third world economy. In the early seventies, when our vulnerability as an economy should have been obvious, we were still making grandiose new additions to our welfare state. Then an oil shock hit us, along with Britain's entry to the EEC. It was then that, quite suddenly, a large gap appeared between the material aspirations of New Zealanders and the capacity of our economy to deliver on those aspirations.

The response of Muldoon, just like that of the Labour government before him, was to bridge that gap with borrowing. It was a temporary response; it could not be a long term response. Muldoon was cautious about economic reform. He waited for something to turn up. He may have seemed at the time an activist Minister of Finance: changing tax rates; giving an incentive here and taking it away there; boosting and contracting the economy by turns. But really Muldoon was shuffling just the same old pack of cards. In the end the logic of New Zealand's position was inescapable. We faced two basic options. Either we reconciled ourselves to becoming the Ireland of the South Pacific and adjusted our expected living standards accordingly (there was no sign of New Zealanders wanting to do that) or we opened the economy much more to international competition — and that would be painful.

Not enough New Zealanders clearly appreciated at the time that this was the choice we faced. Even fewer articulated it. Partly this was due to Muldoon's vigorously combative political style: few wanted to make themselves the target of a Prime Ministerial personal attack. But the real reason was deeper. All societies live by myths, and New Zealand was no exception. We had many myths, and we preferred our myths to reality. There was the myth that New Zealanders were enterprising people, when in reality we had the most incubated economy outside of the third world. There was the myth that New Zealanders were independent, when we had put in place one of the world's most comprehensive welfare states. There was the myth that we were a well-educated society. And there was the myth that we had excellent race relations.

New Zealanders, then, were only dimly aware that big changes would one day be in store for them. Not even the second oil shock, which came right at the beginning of Peters' first term, jolted New Zealanders out of their complacency. The government's response was Think Big, which poured billions of dollars into deadbeat energy projects in a misconceived attempt to lessen New Zealand's dependence on imported fuel. Think Big was one of the dominating debates of the day. For the rest of Peters' first term it was the usual catalogue of scandals, infighting and political soap operas. Duncan MacIntyre was found to have acted 'very unwisely' in the Marginal Lands Board scandal. He was rewarded with the deputy leadership when Brian Talboys stepped down. There were two sensational public inquiries. One was held into the Arthur Alan Thomas case, and was damning on the police. One was on the Erebus disaster, and was damning on Air New Zealand. There were two failed political coups. Muldoon was almost toppled, and would have been if Talboys had shown a desire to be Prime Minister. In the opposite camp Bill Rowling survived by one vote in a coup attempt organised by David Lange's supporters. There was a great deal of industrial strife. And there was the long trauma of the Springbok Tour.

The Hunua judgment had created another explosive issue — electoral law — and Peters was right in the middle of it. Labour were convinced democracy had lost out in Hunua, and there were bitter attacks on the unfairness of the result. For months Peters had to put up with the accusation that he was not the democratically elected member for Hunua. To Labour, Peters was the 'court-appointed member'.

A few weeks after the Hunua verdict Labour at last got the chance to debate the issue in Parliament. In a stormy all-day debate the Opposition slammed both the Hunua judgment and the general state of the electoral rolls. The government defended the judgement and used the trial transcript to claim electoral malpractice by Labour in Hunua.

When it was Peters' turn to speak he added some spice of his own:

> In 1977 Labour Party members in Hunua left the Party with a sense of grievance because they stood for nomination when a member of the selection panel for that electorate — totally against Labour Party rules — was a person in the employ of the man who later became the Labour Party candidate for Hunua.

This brought an interjection from Roger Douglas — 'Stick to the truth. That's a bloody lie.' Douglas was forced to withdraw, but challenged Peters to repeat his remarks outside the House, where Parliamentary privilege did not apply.

The man Peters referred to was one Hugh McCarthy, who worked as a chemist in Red Seal Laboratories. Malcolm Douglas held a small percentage of the shares in Red Seal

Laboratories. These facts hardly amount to McCarthy being 'in the employ' of Malcolm Douglas. It was the first time Peters had used Parliamentary privilege to launch an unwarranted attack on someone outside Parliament. It would not be the last.

In August the Labour Party made their expected application to the Court of Appeal for a declaratory judgment. Labour sought a judgment on the issue that had proved so crucial in Hunua: whether the voter must strictly comply with the instructions on the ballot paper, or whether it is sufficient that he or she expresses a clear preference. Also in August, in response to widespread dissatisfaction with the handling of the last election, the government set up a special Parliamentary select committee to look into a host of issues concerning the voting system. Peter Wilkinson chaired the committee, while Peters was made a member by virtue of his Hunua experience. The select committee's brief was wide. It covered all the issues that had proved controversial in Hunua, and even the question of whether the first-past-the-post voting system should be retained.

Shortly afterwards came the report of a committee, headed by Sir James Wicks, which had been set up some months previously to look specifically into the handling of the election. The committee identified major shortcomings in procedure and performance and it had some telling criticisms of the way in which the electoral rolls had been compiled. Despite its detailed criticisms the Wicks committee pronounced the rolls to have been 'adequate' for the election. This was perhaps surprising in view of the committee's own comment that in some seats there was doubt over the result. Had the committee declared the rolls 'inadequate' for the election, the political fallout would have been very considerable. As it was, the committee recommended a complete re-registration of all voters. Its report went to the Wilkinson select committee.

The select committee spent some months on its deliberations. Peters was not an influential member, nor did he show any interest in changing the first-past-the-post electoral system, an issue which, later in his career, he would take up so strongly. There was, however, one area where he had very strong views and which happened to correspond with his self-interest. That was whether voters who had opted to be on the Maori roll in the 1976 census should have the opportunity to transfer to the general roll for the 1981 election. The Wicks Committee had recommended that Maori have that opportunity. That was also the advice of the inter-departmental officials committee advising the select committee. But Peters was instrumental in persuading his colleagues on the select committee not to grant Maori the right to transfer. The self-interest was clear. National MPs in marginal seats were vulnerable to Maori switching from the Maori roll back on to the general roll to make their votes count. National MPs like Peters.

It was not until May 1980, shortly before the select committee was due to report, that the Court of Appeal brought down its declaratory judgment on voting methods. All five Appeal Court judges rejected the interpretation of the Electoral Act in the Hunua judgment. All held that if a voter clearly indicated a preference on the ballot paper, their vote should not be rejected as informal simply on account of some informality in the way they had filled out the paper. In this author's view the Appeal Court verdict was undoubtedly the correct reading of the Electoral Act. Although it could not reverse the result in Hunua, the verdict came as bad news for Peters. If the Appeal Court ruling had applied in his own case, Peters would probably not have been elected to Parliament.

There were immediate calls from Labour for Peters to resign his seat. Barry Brill, who had held Kapiti with a majority of just 23, was also in the firing line. Peters claimed then what he had claimed before — that the informal voting issue had not been crucial to the outcome. Peters had no intention of resigning. But on balance he was lucky to be in Parliament.

Soon afterwards Wilkinson's select committee reported its findings to the House. Many of the recommendations were non-controversial. Some were extremely controversial, especially the recommendation that informal methods of expressing a voter's intention not be allowed. Wilkinson stressed that this recommendation had been arrived at before the Appeal Court had brought down its judgment. In the end, the government decided to bow to the Court of Appeal. When electoral legislation was finally introduced into the House, it was the voter's intention that counted. It has continued to be the case ever since.

If the Hunua electoral petition reinforced Peters in anything, it was in the assumption that life was a battle. A provincial Maori from a remote corner of the country, Peters had had to overcome poverty, a stutter, an insecurity about his status. Then he had had to fight a six-month battle through the courts to get into Parliament. Having arrived he was still being challenged as the 'court-appointed member'. The lesson was that you had to fight your battles if you were to make your way. The pugilistic streak in Peters already ran deep. One day he would even be photographed for a feature article sitting in a boxing ring and wearing boxing gloves. There was also a picture of a boxer which Peters, as a young lawyer, hung on his wall and afterwards took with him into his office in Parliament buildings. In a revealing interview, Peters one day described that picture:

> It's just of a boxer standing in the corner of the ring. He's got a towel over his head. The fight is over. But, you see, the towel is not hanging on the ropes. You can tell he's in pain — but he's not throwing in the towel. So you don't know if he has won or if he has lost. Everyone who came into my office hated that picture. They thought it was terrible. But I don't mind because it's mine . . . it is all about how I feel sometimes.

Peters' early speeches in Parliament clearly show him as a pugilist who felt he had a point to prove. Right from the beginning there was a pronounced tendency for him to play the man, or woman. A certain amount of attacking the previous speaker, or attacking someone who interjects, is part of the normal cut and thrust of the debating chamber, but Peters scarcely made it through a speech without an *ad hominem* element — often a very strong one. One of his frequent lines of attack was to criticise Labour members for being academic and unacquainted with working people. For some reason Michael Bassett and his 'pristine hands' seemed especially to get Peters going. He made no secret of the fact that he for his part had done manual jobs.

25

In that line of attack, as in much else that he said, there was a bravado that seemed to mask a certain defensiveness. Whatever was being discussed, there was a good chance Peters would claim that he personally knew more about it than Labour members. His frequent refrain was 'I know a damn sight more about farming/the law/working hard/Maori/the poor/etc., than the member for x'. Too much of this sort of thing sometimes made him look simply absurd. The general impression was of an insecure person trying to boost himself by drawing attention to himself and attacking others.

Peters also talked a great deal in Parliament about his electorate — something he was rarely to do in later years when member for Tauranga. At this stage of his career Peters' greatest interest was in promoting himself to his Hunua constituency. There were periodic scraps between Peters and neighbouring Pakuranga MP Pat Hunt over who had the right to ask questions in the House on issues falling on the border between the two electorates. At times constant references to Hunua could descend into bathos, as the Hansard record shows:

Peters: I represent a large number of town milk suppliers in my electorate. Also in my electorate are consumers who drink as much milk as those in other electorates — probably no more and no less.

Ralph Maxwell: Shattering!

Peters: I tell the member for Waitakere, who has never been weaned, and who has a mind to match, that I have more town milk suppliers in my electorate than he has in his — probably 20 times as many . . .

Peters was always looking for speaking opportunities. By the end of his third year he was making the occasional good speech, showing that he did have promise as a political performer. But he had not achieved the *gravitas*, the air of authority, that would come later in his career. Philosophically Peters remained a free enterpriser all through his first term. One of his better speeches came in 1981 when he got the chance to second the motion in the formal address-in-reply debate, a keenly sought platform for a backbencher. This is how he summed up his speech:

> This address is about freedom in its more powerful sense — economic liberty; not that freedom of which Janis Joplin sang 'Just another word for nothing else to lose'. We have turned our minds tonight to acknowledge that wealth and wealth alone creates jobs, enables men and women to combat taxation, and
>
> enables governments to overcome inflation. Seen that way, this address is a defence of capitalism, the ordinary bloke, the ordinary woman, the free enterpriser, and the person who wants to use his initiative.

Though a free marketeer in philosophy, Peters was for the most part a staunch supporter of Muldoon. During the 'colonels coup' late in 1980, however, he performed an interesting double shuffle. Dissatisfaction with Muldoon had been welling up for a number of reasons. There was concern over his political style, and a belief that the electorate was increasingly coming to tire of such a combative politician. There was also concern in some quarters over the direction of economic policy. But it was the embarrassing loss of the East Coast Bays by-election that was the immediate spur for a serious attempt to topple the leader. The plotting began while he was away overseas. MPs who wanted to see Muldoon brought down began lodging their letters with Eric Holland.

One of those MPs was Peters. He still admired Muldoon, but those close to Peters suspect that he believed Muldoon was now doomed, and that he wanted to be on the winning side. It is possible, too, Peters believed Muldoon's electoral appeal was fading. Whatever the reasons, the MP for Hunua lodged his letter with Holland. When Muldoon arrived back in the country the political winds began quickly blowing in the other direction. The Prime Minister began a highly successful populist appeal to the voters over the heads of his caucus. Key figures such as Jim Bolger, who was then Minister of Labour, changed sides. Peters rushed back to Holland and retrieved his letter.

Pugilistic, philosophically free market, politically pragmatic — Peters was all of those. In his first term he also seemed error-prone at times. He had not long been an MP when he was sent from the House for disorderly conduct — a rare occurrence in those days. Then there was the *faux pas* over the 'nourishment centre'. A soup kitchen had recently opened in Otara. In Parliament Peters claimed that it was not a soup kitchen but a 'nourishment centre that serves a full meal'. He rather marred his case by reverting to the words 'soup kitchen' later on in his speech. Various people were to make fun of Peters' euphemism.

In his first term Peters did, however, manage to make two strong populist gestures. One was his criticism, along with Norman Jones, of a performance at the Beehive theatrette by the radical theatre group Mairangi Mai. The performance ended rather shatteringly with a beer bottle being thrown against the wall of the theatrette, apparently by a friend of the group. Opposition to Maori radicalism is one of the few stances Peters has held consistently throughout his career. His comment on this occasion was, 'You do not fight past injustices with a tissue of lies.' Peters' remark earned an anonymous phone call to his wife Louise, threatening to blow up the family home. Peters was forced to take security measures.

The other occasion for a populist gesture occurred late in 1981 when Peters was a New Zealand delegate to an Inter-Parliamentary Union conference. The conference was held in that well-known bastion of Parliamentary democracy, Havana. Fidel Castro produced in his opening address one of his tiresome anti-western tirades. When it was Peters' turn to speak he gave as good as he got — something that was far from appreciated by the Cuban authorities. Though no one back home could cavil with what Peters said, some of his Hunua party workers questioned whether he should be attending the conference at all. Peters had not even told them he was going. An election was looming and Peters was defending a highly marginal seat.

Peters was always facing an uphill battle in Hunua. Most commentators were expecting the General Election to be at least as close this time around as it had been in 1978. Demographic changes were boosting the working class population of the electorate. The Appeal Court judgment on informal voting would help the Labour Party. To make doubly sure, Labour were distributing 'how to vote' pamphlets in Polynesian languages. And though Peters appeared to have been active in the electorate, he had been far from diligent as an electorate MP.

Labour's candidate this time around was Colin Moyle, the man who had resigned from Parliament in a storm of controversy after an exchange with Muldoon one evening in the House. Perhaps the later Peters would have been cunning enough, or ruthless enough, to exploit the cloud which, rightly or wrongly, hung over Moyle. But the 1981 Peters ran a fair campaign. The closest he came to innuendo was his claim that, while the nationwide contest was a test of the credibility of the parties, the contest in Hunua was a test of the credibility of the candidates. In view of the eventual outcome, Peters must have regretted making that statement.

Election day came. By the end of a long night there was a hung Parliament. The official count eventually gave National one extra seat, enabling it to continue in government. But the verdict on the night for Hunua was plain: Labour were ahead by over 700 votes. This was far too much to haul back on specials. Moyle was the new MP for Hunua. In his speech to his supporters Peters blamed the media for not asking the questions of his opponent that he himself had felt unable to ask. Then he and Louise went to Otara to congratulate Moyle in person — a gesture made by too few losing candidates.

The earliest phase of Peters' political career had now ended. He had served his apprenticeship, gaining experience and gaining confidence. Though for the moment his career was over, he was in no doubt that he wanted to return to Parliament. It is customary for defeated National MPs to attend one final caucus meeting. When it was Peters' turn to speak he was aggressive, almost defiant, in telling caucus they had not seen the last of him. The General MacArthur touch was not lost on his colleagues.

Peters went back to law, setting up a practice in Howick. Two years passed, away from political life. Louise had their second child, a daughter, Brittany; their son Joel had been born during Peters' time as an MP. Peters had certainly not forgotten politics. He was not the first former MP to miss the intensity of the experience, the long adrenalin surge of life in Parliament Buildings. As the 1984 election drew nearer Peters explored a number of avenues for re-entering Parliament. He seriously considered trying for the Rangitikei selection, even using his caucus contacts to engineer an invitation from the local party organisation. But Peters asked for an assurance in advance that he would win the selection. The electorate could not give that assurance. In the end Peters decided not to try for Rangitikei.

Then Peters' chance seemed to come. Peter Wilkinson was stepping down from the safe National seat of Kaipara. In those days the Kaipara electorate boundaries stretched right up to encompass Whananaki, Peters' home patch. For Peters it was a golden opportunity. He put his name forward for the nomination. So did Pat Baker, his old adversary from the Hunua selection. So did John Carter, who would later become MP for Bay of Islands. Others put their names forward. One of them was a comparative unknown called Lockwood Smith.

Though it was a keenly sought seat, Peters was confident of winning. He was the home town boy and and the only former MP in the field. But in the course of the meet-the-candidates meetings, Smith noticed something strange. Peters was so anxious to give answers that were pleasing to the audience of the moment that he was giving different answers to the same questions on different occasions. Smith got his supporters to ask questions designed to show up the inconsistencies in Peters' replies. The tactic worked. On the day of the selection meeting Smith won comfortably.

To Peters the loss was devastating. It was a much worse moment than the loss of Hunua two years before. The Hunua loss had been half expected, no matter how unwelcome it may have been. By contrast, missing out on Kaipara was the most serious blow to Peters' confidence in his entire political career. He talked about giving up politics. One friend recalls cheering him up with a book about Abraham Lincoln, another politician who had suffered his share of setbacks.

Then Tauranga MP Keith Allen announced he would be retiring at the next election. A sick man, Allen had stayed in Parliament for as long as he had only because a by-election might have eroded National's slimmest of majorities in the House. Peters was rung by Ed Morgan, a prominent member of the party in Tauranga. Would he make himself available for selection? Friends in the National caucus from the class of '78 also encouraged Peters to stand, and lobbied the electorate on his behalf. Allen's majority in 1981 had been around 1800, with Social Credit gaining the second highest number of votes. The seat looked more than winnable. Peters when MP for Hunua had ridiculed carpetbaggers, once telling Mike Moore in Parliament, 'I am not a carpetbagger. I do not run around New Zealand in order to get a seat because I am so imbued with the wish to get into power.' Circumstances alter cases. Peters sized up the Tauranga electorate, and at the very last moment put his name forward.

Perhaps his late entry reflected the blow his confidence had suffered at Kaipara. He may well have been waiting to see the strength of the field before committing himself. In the event the field did not look formidable. This time Peters would make no mistake. He spent several weeks working on the voting delegates so that when the day of the selection meeting came around the ground had been covered. Ross Meurant, later the MP for Hobson, had made it through pre-selection and was there on the final night. Others still in with a chance were *Hansard* reporter Colleen Singleton, Auckland lawyer Russell Bartlett and Papatoetoe teacher Heather White. On the night Peters gave by far the best of the speeches. He was also astute enough to include a tribute to Allen, the retiring member. None of the other candidates had thought to do that. Peters won on the first ballot.

It was then May 1984. Peters, like all Parliamentary candidates, was expecting the General Election to be called around November. He reckoned without Muldoon. Soon New Zealanders were to watch open-mouthed the sight on their television screens of the Prime Minister, unusually inarticulate and looking for all the world like he was drunk, calling a snap election for 14 July.

The campaign for Tauranga was fast and furious. Peters introduced a touch of the bizarre when he claimed he had evidence Russian submarines were plotting the geography of the sea bed in Cook Strait. The evidence never surfaced. But

Peters was well ahead in Tauranga, even as it looked more and more certain that after eight-and-a-half years National's grip on office was slipping away. On election night a new generation of Labour leaders stood ready to assume office. In Tauranga the third party vote split evenly between the New Zealand Party and Social Credit, pushing Peters' winning margin out to around 4000. Peters was back. And he was back for what would be the most eventful three years in New Zealand politics for at least half a century.

CHAPTER THREE

Ferry Bottoms

July 1984–December 1986

*T*HE fall of the Muldoon administration did not just signal the
death of a government. It marked the passing from political
power of an entire generation. It was the generation that had
grown up while the consensus was being formed that would
shape New Zealand's political life right through the post-war
period. That national consensus was for ANZUS, a heavily
controlled economy, a substantial welfare state, and generally
conservative social policies. Muldoon exemplified that
consensus, was its last major figure, and yet lingered on into an
era where some of its basic tenets were starting to be
questioned. Muldoon was the last of his line. His political
inheritors had new ideas, new priorities and new prejudices.

The first three years of the Fourth Labour Government
were unparalleled by any previous government for at least 50
years. Such was the scope of the changes wrought by Labour,
and such was their dizzying pace, that we are not likely to see a
similar government for at least another 50 years. It was a time
of huge economic and social reform.

For Peters these changes altered enormously the political
landscape he faced. It was in this new landscape that he would
eventually come to his maturity as a populist politician. It would
not be until Labour's second term that Peters was able to master
the new environment. But it was the changes between 1984 and
1987 that largely defined the attitudes he has struck, the
rhetoric he has adopted and the resentments he has played on,
right down to the present day. Without those changes, Peters'
eventual spectacular rise in the opinion polls might never have

occurred. At the very least Peters' rise would have taken a different form.

Peters would be able to make full use of the new political environment for his own purposes. He would be quicker than his colleagues to sense the hardening of public opinion in favour of Labour's anti-nuclear policy and to position himself accordingly. He would take advantage of public anxiety over the Treaty of Waitangi and of a general feeling that too much emphasis was placed on things Maori. He would be the most powerful spokesperson for the sense of grievance and injustice felt by many of the victims of Rogernomics. And he would recognise that public disillusionment with the political process provided receptive ground for arguments for political reform.

Most of those developments were several years away. For the moment, as Peters took his new seat in Parliament, there was more than enough tumult going on inside his own caucus. The next three years would be miserable ones for the National Party. It would be riven by political infighting and philosophical divisions. It would try vainly to exorcize the ghost of Muldoon. It would go through three leaders, none of whom would look like winning an election. It would go through four finance spokespeople and five different front bench line-ups. There would be musical chairs all the way up and down the caucus scale, as National MPs endlessly changed places on the basis of who was hot, who was not and who had just been put down.

As for Peters, he was sniffing the air, trying to decide which way the new political currents were flowing. There were no more speeches from him promoting free market economics. That rhetoric had gone for ever. There were few signs of a new philosophy in its place. His initial attacks on Rogernomics were general, unspecific in what they revealed of his own position. As Maori affairs spokesman he had greeted very cautiously the Treaty of Waitangi Amendment Bill, which opened up Treaty claims back to 1840. National, however, had not opposed the bill's introduction to Parliament. Peters had also floated the idea that parents not caring for their children's health should lose their welfare benefits.

Already there was a change, too, in Peters' attitude to his colleagues. He was less of a team player than in his first term.

He was spending less time in caucus forums, more time in the press gallery and in the bar talking to journalists. He had always been a loner in his working methods, secretive by nature. Now it was even more pronounced. And for the first time Peters' record of attendance at select committees was starting to come under criticism.

An MP's attitude to select committee work is a key indicator of his or her true motivation. Select committees consider legislation that has been referred to them, hear public submissions and recommend what changes they consider appropriate. In many select committees there is a fair degree of bipartisan spirit. Sitting on a select committee is generally an unglamorous job. It is mostly anonymous, allowing few opportunities to score direct political points or promote oneself in the media. Where legislation is technical or highly complex, select committee work can be deathly dull. Yet select committee work is the only time an ordinary MP can play a direct role in the process of government. Those MPs who are serious about understanding and influencing public policy will be diligent about their select committee work. MPs who are lazy, or primarily concerned with promoting themselves, will tend to shirk select committee work.

Slackness in select committee work was one outward sign of the change that shrewd observers of Peters had noticed. Self-promotion was now his main game. Some of Peters' colleagues, such as Ruth Richardson, took an instant dislike to a man they saw as hollow of substance. But Peters was certainly not without friends in caucus. His charm of manner, friendly grin and sense of humour were potent weapons. For all his self-absorption most of his male colleagues found Peters good company. They called him Luigi on account of his dark complexion and Italianate hairstyle. Peters renewed his friendship with Paul East and Don McKinnon, fellow survivors from the class of 78. He also struck up a firm friendship with 1981 MP Philip Burdon. The four of them flatted together and would continue to share the same house for the whole time National was in Opposition.

They were an odd quartet: the laid-back East, deceptively bright; McKinnon, genial and the perfect team man; the rich and aristocratic Burdon; and Peters. They used only one car — Burdon's. Like most MPs' flats, the house was used only as a place to come back to late at night. In Peters' case 'late at night' could mean several hours into the next morning. He was well known as a nocturnal animal, and had a capacity for getting by on very little sleep. Nor was he the earliest of risers.

No matter how late the hours he kept, Peters was fastidious in the care he took over his appearance. Neatness and cleanliness were close to obsessions. Ironing a shirt was a precisely calculated and lengthy affair, while he must have been the only MP in history who bothered to iron his socks. His suits were kept looking spotless. Peters got the idea of wearing double-breasted suits from press gallery journalist Barry Soper. The double-breasted suits would become one of his trademarks. Peters was good-looking, he knew it, and he was keen to make the most of it.

National Party infighting was never far below the surface during 1985. Muldoon, deeply wounded by the loss of the leadership, had set his sights on three people — Jim McLay, party president Sue Wood and general director Barrie Leay. McLay was living death to Muldoon because he had taken the party leadership from him. Wood and Leay were Muldoon's chosen scapegoats in his campaign to blame the election loss on the party organisation. Already Muldoon had called publicly for Wood and Leay to resign. An organisation calling itself The Sunday Club had started up within the party as an outrider for Muldoon. In April Peters weighed into this battle with a public call for Leay to resign. It led to a sharp public exchange between Wood and Peters. Wood said that MPs should concentrate on attacking the government. Peters repeated his statement and said that a majority of caucus wanted Leay's removal.

It is unlikely Peters was acting as an outrider for Muldoon in any direct sense. But it is characteristic of him that he should enter the fray on behalf of his old boss. Peters had a great deal of admiration for Muldoon. He admired his mental agility, his populism, his combative political style. For all that, Muldoon and Peters were never very close in personal terms. They were rarely seen together and there was certainly no laying on of hands from one to the other — no apostolic succession. The relationship between the two men was more indirect. One former colleague has described it as like an affair between two people that was not actually going on, but where both parties were flattered to hear themselves talked about in those terms, and both were enjoying the *frisson*. Peters was flattered when people talked about him as Muldoon's successor. And so was Muldoon.

Peters was absorbing a good deal of Muldoon into his own political style. Whether he did it consciously or unconsciously is not clear. But Muldoon was undoubtedly an important model, and there are too many similarities for it to be otherwise. Even their backgrounds had similarities. Both men were outsiders who made their way in the National Party without connections or inherited wealth. Both instinctively saw politics as a combat. Both men made numerous personal attacks on others, inside and outside Parliament. Both men were populists. Muldoon always had a deep streak of populism, while Peters would become the most undiluted populist in recent political history. Both men appealed directly to ordinary New Zealanders over the top of more conventional institutions and power structures.

Both Muldoon and Peters also became masters of using the media. Both invested a large amount of time in working the media: farming the press gallery, cajoling journalists and, where necessary, intimidating them. From Muldoon, Peters probably learnt the technique of stringing out a story to earn maximum media exposure. From Muldoon, Peters also learnt that most publicity is good publicity. To get publicity you need to be 'good copy' for journalists. Provocative thoughts expressed in short, pungent sentences were good copy. Muldoon supplied these in abundance and was excellent copy.

Muldoon was the first New Zealand politician to master television — and here his influence on Peters was perhaps at its greatest. Television is the crucial medium in modern politics. With a capriciousness that is awesome, political careers are regularly made and destroyed on the basis of how well a politician comes across on the small screen. Muldoon's career was hugely aided by his television skills. Muldoon kept his head still, looked straight into the camera and spoke slowly. He kept his thoughts straightforward and his sentences short; his message came out in easily digestible segments. He was above all entertaining: humorous, combative and provocative. Peters lacked Muldoon's natural wit but he has mastered Muldoon's television techniques. Peters' slowness of speech, stare into the camera and short, punchy sentences are all classic Muldoon.

The attack Peters made in Parliament on Justice Casey in July 1985 was also classic Muldoon. Opponents of an All Black tour to South Africa had applied to the High Court for an interim injunction stopping the tour proceeding. In a surprise judgment, right on the eve of the tour, Justice Casey granted the injunction. The tour was effectively scuppered. Justice Casey's decision seemed to many people to be arbitrary and contrary to sound constitutional principles — a bad case of judicial activism. The judgment could legitimately be questioned on that basis. Peters in Parliament went much further:

> I am most disturbed about some allegations that concern me as a lawyer and a member of the bar. I ask the government and the people who should know the answers to answer now the allegations: that there was a prime ministerial servant constantly at court; that of late the judiciary articulates policy choice rather than constitutional principles; and even worse — and these allegations must be laid to rest — that the judge was a Labour Party choice in 1974; that his wife was a tour protester in 1981; and that he privately and personally has expressed his opposition to the tour. Those allegations must be laid to rest.

Though he did not quite come out and say it, the meaning of Peters' innuendo was plain — that Justice Casey had delivered a politically biased judgement. This illustrates what would become a standard Peters' technique: cooking up a very grave charge from the thinnest of ingredients. Most New Zealanders had a personal opinion, one way or the other, on sporting contacts with South Africa, as had most judges. Hundreds of thousands of New Zealanders were tour protesters in 1981, and Justice Casey was in any case scarcely answerable for his wife. (It later turned out she had not been a tour protester.) Certainly

Justice Casey was appointed by the Labour Party, but then the Chief Justice whose interpretation of the Electoral Act helped send Peters into Parliament was appointed by National. Perhaps the Prime Minister did keep an observer at the case, but so what? The case had clear political implications and the Prime Minister was entitled to be apprised of its progress. Peters' innuendo disintegrates after more than two seconds of analysis.

No wonder the Auckland Law Society received many complaints from its members about the use of Parliamentary privilege to attack the integrity of a judge. The society wrote to both Peters and McLay over Peters' behaviour. Peters was asked by the media to repeat his statement outside the House. He refused to do so.

There were other conspiracy theories that Peters was running around this time. There was an allegation that Lange had gone to Australia to have a secret operation. It proved to be groundless. Later in the year, when there was an unconfirmed report of a submarine near Great Barrier Island, Peters said he had every reason to believe it was a Soviet submarine. No evidence was produced. At this stage of his career Peters was making strong speeches in favour of ANZUS. Talk of Soviet submarines was entirely consistent with that message. Later, when Peters' line on ANZUS changed, submarines remained submerged.

As 1985 moved towards a close, morale in the National caucus was deteriorating. Victory in the Timaru by-election had provided a boost, but only temporarily. National was well behind in the opinion polls and McLay's own poll rating was disappearing off the chart. Muldoon was sniping at McLay. Jim Bolger was deliberately positioning himself in his speeches as distinctly more 'interventionist' than McLay. His strategy was to place himself at the centre of gravity in caucus, to be the man all factions of caucus could live with. October saw a very public tit-for-tat exchange between Muldoon and McLay, in which Muldoon provoked McLay into dispatching him to No. 38 — the lowest rank in caucus. After that Muldoon was openly derisive of McLay. By now there was constant speculation of a leadership challenge by Bolger. In the first week of December there was an attempt to organise a Bolger coup. It proved precipitate. George Gair was away overseas, while Bruce Townsend threw away what chances the plotters had by blabbing to the news media. This allowed the McLay forces to rally.

But only for the moment. Early in the new year McLay made the reshuffle of his line-up that would seal his fate. It was a forward-looking reshuffle and a very bold one. In general McLay promoted the free marketeers and the good performers, and demoted the dead wood. Off the front bench went John Falloon, Gair and Bill Birch. On to the front bench came McLean, Kidd, Richardson and Cox, who picked up the finance job. Those promoted were the ones articulating the policy direction National would eventually follow in the 1990s. Those promoted were also very obviously McLay supporters. McLay's fatal mistake was to demote Birch and Gair. By so doing, he overreached himself. The two old stagers immediately began plotting a coup. This one would be successful.

As for Peters, he must have been thoroughly brassed off at his own treatment in the reshuffle. He had kept his responsibilities as spokesperson but he had gone down two in the rankings. Worse, most of his peers had moved on ahead of him; only the first term MPs and the deadest of dead wood ranked below him. On merit, Peters had not deserved promotion. In neither of his areas — transport nor Maori affairs — had he seriously troubled the government. His attacks had lacked substance. In his latest headline he had strayed into the finance area with a far-fetched claim that New Zealand would lose $500 million from the default by Rakiura Holdings on its tender for government stock. If New Zealand lost anything from that default, it was only a tiny fraction of what Peters claimed.

Peters had made no attempt to publicly destabilise McLay prior to Christmas. But now, with nothing to lose, he set to with a will. The reshuffle had clearly drawn the battle lines: between those who wanted to distance themselves from the previous administration and those who did not. Peters joined that fray. Peters defended Think Big, claiming history would be on the side of Birch. (It was not, and years later Peters would change his line on Think Big.) In a speech to the annual meeting of his electorate, Peters also criticised in coded fashion the direction of the party and advocated pragmatism rather than 'cavalier theoretical experimentation'. The speech marked another step in Peters' move away from the free market principles of his first term. Gradually Peters was adopting the language and rhetoric familiar to us, and with which he would lambast Rogernomics.

There were others making public comments designed to destabilise McLay. They included Muldoon, Tony Friedlander, Norman Jones and Bolger himself. Bolger gave a speech in which he argued for a greater government role in the economy. In the end the Bolger coup was a straightforward affair. McLay was presented with a petition calling for his resignation. It was signed by 25 out of the 38 MPs. McLay chose to put his leadership to the test in a hastily-called caucus. At the meeting there were some impassioned speeches in McLay's defence. Bolger supporters said nothing. They had the numbers, as the ballot shortly demonstrated.

There was a touch of theatre from Peters when it came to the deputy leadership ballot. Before the meeting Peters had put up Neil Austin to nominate him. On the calling of nominations Gair, the heavy favourite, was the first one to be nominated. Then Austin stood up and nominated Peters. Peters thanked Austin but said he would not be putting his name forward. He would defer to the seniority of Gair. It was pure display from Peters; his support for deputy leader would have been negligible. Peters' friends were amused at that attempt to position himself within caucus as a man on the rise.

Peters, Friedlander and Muldoon all received their payoffs for helping to destabilise McLay. Peters went up seven places to No. 15 in the new line-up. His responsibilities were unchanged. If he had been expecting a greater promotion, he did not get it. Muldoon came back on to the front bench and took foreign affairs. McLean, Kidd and Richardson all lost their front bench places. Cox stayed on the front bench but lost the main finance job to Gair. Birch was also back on the front bench, where he has stayed ever since. The sight of Muldoon back in a major role set hearts aflutter in urban New Zealand.

Overall it was a confused, plodding new line-up, and it set the scene for National's election rout the following year.'

Plodding many of his colleagues may have been, but Peters himself was to become positively ballistic in taking the fight to the enemy over the next few months. His problem would not be his energy but his strike rate. One of his campaigns concerned the Russian cruise ship *Mikhail Lermontov*, which had sunk in the Marlborough Sounds. All the evidence pointed to a straightforward case of pilot error. But that was far too prosaic for Peters. He repeatedly called for a full inquiry into the sinking. At one point he reportedly claimed that the sinking was no accident, that the ship may have been carrying sensitive spying equipment, and that there was a cover-up between the New Zealand and Soviet authorities. These astonishing claims were not accompanied by any evidence whatsoever.

The nautical flavour that had been firmly set by Soviet submarines and the *Mikhail Lermontov* was continued in Peters' great Cook Strait ferry crusade. Fairly or unfairly, it was the ferry campaign which came to symbolise the early, 'unguided' Peters. It started on the day of the very first live telecast of Parliament, conducted on an experimental basis. Knowing Peters' penchant for the television cameras, we can be sure he held back his 'scoop' for the week the cameras were there. It was question time:

> Peters: On 29 March did a Cook Strait ferry briefly run aground in the Tory Channel; and if so, what were the circumstances and what was the result of any report of that grounding?
>
> Prebble: The answer to the first part of the question is no; and the answer to the second part is that the Ministry of Transport does not prepare reports on incidents that have not happened.

There were guffaws from the government benches. Vowing that he would wipe the smile off the Minister's face Peters battled on. He got into a tangle on his second supplementary question, though, when he referred to the Picton Harbour Board. A cascade of voices told him there was no Picton Harbour Board. Peters was given the chance to rephrase:

Peters: Has the Minister made any inquiries of the Marlborough Harbour Board about whether or not it received a report of a brief grounding of a Cook Strait ferry?

Prebble: It appears the member for Tauranga is getting his ships confused.

The allusion to the *Mikhail Lermontov* brought redoubled laughter.

As the cameras packed up for the day Peters must have been seething at the way things had turned out. But he was not finished. He told the media he had information that on 29 March there had been a near collision between two ferries at the entrance to Tory Channel; that one ferry took evasive action; and that in doing so it grounded on the bottom of the channel. Peters called for an inquiry. In Parliament the following day Prebble made a statement denying all those charges. He did, however, admit that on the day in question the *Aratika* sailed closer than normal to the starboard side of the channel. As a precaution divers afterwards had inspected the hull but found no evidence of grounding. Prebble tabled a report from the Railways Corporation. Then there was another belligerent exchange between Peters and Prebble at question time.

Clearly there had been more to the incident than Prebble had let on the previous day. Prebble had in fact been deliberately stringing Peters along. The tactic served two purposes. It allowed the government to extract maximum value from the spectacle of Peters chasing a story that no one else seemed to care about. It also meant Peters was taking up some of the limited question time available to the Opposition each day in Parliament. Sure enough there was a third round the following day, but still no evidence of a ferry touching the bottom. Nor would any evidence surface when Peters pursued the matter through the communications and road safety select committee.

There may have been a comic opera side to Peters' various sea stories. But there was nothing funny about Peters' next attacks. In one speech in Parliament he made tasteless attacks against both Housing Minister Phil Goff and Social Welfare

Minister Ann Hercus. He labelled Goff a 'proven property speculator' — a phrase evidently designed to elicit shock and horror:

> I know how he got his first house. It was virtually given to him by his parents when he was a student. He then sold it for about 80 percent profit.

If the house had been 'virtually given to him', selling it for a profit is precisely what you would expect. *Non sequiturs* have rarely worried Peters. A furious Goff had to be restrained by colleagues from marching up to Peters' desk. Goff made a personal explanation in which he told the House he had never been a property speculator. He had only ever owned two properties, including the house he was currently living in. Peters then explained how he had obtained his information: he had searched the title of Goff's property when working as a solicitor. Goff's selling price, said Peters, was 580 per cent higher than his purchase price. Peters failed to mention that there was a nine-year difference between the sale and the purchase — a period over which there was huge price inflation. It was partly through making an allowance for inflation that Peters must have arrived at his 80 per cent profit — though precisely how that number was calculated is not clear. What *is* clear is that calling Goff a 'proven property speculator' on the evidence presented was clearly nonsense.

The Hercus attack was just as fatuous. Peters charged that Hercus was a 'rent racketeer' on the basis that she rented out for $125 a week a one-bedroom flat in an apartment block. At the end of Peters' speech Hercus too made a personal explanation:

> I have been accused by the member for Tauranga of rack-renting a property that I own. The facts are these. When I first became a member of Parliament eight-and-a-half years ago I bought an ownership flat in Hobson Court, Hobson Street. When I was given a ministerial house I let the Hobson Street property at $125 a week, which exactly covered the very large mortgage on the property, the rates relating to it and the service and management fee. The income is declared each year in my income tax return. There is no profit whatsoever to me in the renting, and I despise the member.

44

Both Goff and Hercus challenged Peters to say the words he had used in the House outside Parliament. Peters refused. Goff and Hercus joined Malcolm Douglas, Hugh McCarthy and Judge Casey on the list of those Peters had attacked under the protection of Parliamentary privilege.

As 1986 drew towards a close Peters had made little progress in establishing himself as a figure with political credibility. After five years as an MP he was regarded on both sides of the House as a something of a joke — a lightweight who on occasion provided some sharp entertainment, but who was not to be taken seriously. His image was one of eccentric claims and knee-in-the-groin tactics. He had invested a lot of effort into his attacks on Prebble over transport issues. So keen was Peters to nail his opposite number that he even pursued Prebble over an allegation that he had been driving while reading a newspaper. At one point Peters even claimed he had affidavits to prove it. They were never produced.

In the end nothing thrown by Peters stuck to Prebble. The Minister of Transport was a hard man to pin down and a deft counter-puncher. He was more than Peters' equal when it came to a scrap. Peters had put much less effort into attacking Maori Affairs Minister Koro Wetere. This was a serious strategic mistake, one which Prebble had gone out of his way to encourage: he knew that time spent by Peters in attacking him was time Peters would not spend attacking the more vulnerable Wetere.

Peters, along with others of the National caucus rat pack, had also been ordered out of the House numerous times by the rigid and irascible Speaker, Gerald Wall. This had added to Peters' image as a loose cannon. It looked as if Peters' biggest scoop of the year would be his revelation that Ann Hercus was using excessively expensive stationery. It was hardly in the *j'accuse* category.

All that was now to change. The man who had done everything except worry the government was suddenly to land a very solid blow. For Labour it was as traumatic as it was unexpected. It began with a leak.

CHAPTER FOUR

First Blood

December 1986–September 1987

*I*T started on 16 December with a Peters question in the House to the Minister of Maori Affairs. It was a bland sounding question about Maori unemployment, but Peters had a sting ready in his supplementary question. It was just as well for Wetere that he was not in the House that day; his question was being handled by Peter Tapsell. Wetere was not quick on his feet and might have said anything in response to Peters springing his surprise. Peters' claim was that the Secretary of the Maori Affairs Department, Tamati Reedy, had been in negotiation with an American financier to raise more than NZ$600 million in loan finance. Peters claimed that Reedy had sent a letter of authority to the financier agreeing to a finders fee of NZ$20 million.

Tapsell told the House he knew nothing about it, and the question might have been dismissed as another wild Peters allegation. But this time Peters had a document. It was a draft agreement drawn up by Reedy in which his department agreed to pay one Michael Giscondi, a Hawaiian, a 3.5 per cent finders fee for securing a US$300 million loan for the purpose of assisting the development of the Maori people. At the bottom of the document was Reedy's signature.

Government departments in New Zealand are not allowed to borrow even one cent in their own right, let alone a massive sum like US$300 million. Everything about the loan looked fishy. The finders fee looked excessive, the interest rate on the loan suspiciously low. Peters' document was certainly an embarrassment for the government. It sent Acting Prime

Minister Geoffrey Palmer into an immediate meeting with Wetere, Reedy and other top civil servants. On emerging, Palmer announced that State Services Commissioner Rod Deane would carry out an immediate investigation. He also confirmed that no authority had been given for the loan and that the loan had not in fact taken place. Nothing else was said.

Palmer's colleagues believed he had panicked in ordering an inquiry. Before announcing it Palmer consulted no other ministers — not even Lange, who was overseas. Most ministers thought that ordering an inquiry into a loan that had never actually taken place was something of an over-reaction. Even Lange was of that view when he learnt of the affair. An inquiry certainly gave the affair an added importance in the eyes of the media. It also gave the Opposition more of a platform with which to make trouble for the government.

The Maori loans affair, as it came to be called, would bring forth a rich and entertaining cast of characters. There was the splendidly named Rocky Cribb — Rotorua businessman, discharged bankrupt and member of the National Party — who had been authorised by Wetere to go to Hawaii to explore trading links between Maori and native Hawaiians, and who had become involved in loan negotiations. There was Dennis Hansen of the Maori Affairs Department — another discharged bankrupt — who went to Hawaii for the loan negotiations and didn't come back. And there was German financier Max Raepple for whom Giscondi was acting. Lange claimed in Parliament that Raepple might have been the same man as a Werner Rohrich, who had an international police record. Herr Raepple would come to New Zealand in an attempt to establish his credentials, check into a hotel under an assumed name, be feted by some in Maoridom, have his requests to see Lange refused, be roundly abused by Lange, threaten to sue Lange, and then finally leave the country, all without producing documentation establishing his credentials.

The day after the loan scandal broke there was a rowdy debate in Parliament. Peters claimed that the NZ$20 million finders fee was so excessive it raised grave suspicions about the propriety of the transaction. Palmer stressed that Cabinet had known nothing about the loan and that the loan had not in any case gone ahead. He tabled a Treasury report which had been sceptical on the proposal. Trevor de Cleene injected colour by suggesting that the source of the loan finance might have been Ferdinand Marcos, then living in Hawaii.

Later that day Deane came out with his interim report. It revealed that Reedy had signed the fee agreement despite being told by Treasury Secretary Graham Scott that as a civil servant he had no power to borrow. Reading between the lines of the report, it seemed clear that Wetere had instructed his officials to call the loan negotiations off only after Treasury alerted Roger Douglas, who must then have talked to Wetere. It was also evident that Wetere knew of the loan negotiations for some time before they were abandoned. Exactly how long was unclear. Deane accepted that the parties to the affair acted in good faith. However, he concluded that 'the manner in which the negotiations were conducted, the apparent disregard of the advice given by the Secretary to the Treasury, and the unauthorised signing of certain documents by the Secretary of Maori Affairs raised serious doubts about the management of this project.' Peters was soon calling for the resignations of both Wetere and Douglas.

The next day another thunderous debate in Parliament generated plenty of heat but not a great deal more light. Wetere spoke for the first time, saying that once he had heard of the loan proposal he had put a stop to it. Bolger thumped his desk so hard as he called for Wetere's resignation that his glass of water was shattered as it fell on to the floor of the House.

Though Peters had exposed a staggering degree of amateurishness in Maori Affairs, Reedy was not the Opposition's target. They dearly wanted to pin something on a minister, but as yet they had no smoking gun. The Deane inquiry would be no help to National: Deane was empowered to assess the actions of civil servants, but not of ministers. Peters and Bolger continued to call for a full public inquiry by a judge. Peters even refused to give Deane the documents he claimed he had in his hands, saying the Deane inquiry was a whitewash.

Various colourful facts trickled out on the loans affair. It was revealed that the proposal had involved using Maori land as collateral for the loan. Peters issued another document showing that on top of Gicondi's 3.5 per cent fee, Max Raepple would have received 2.5 per cent, totalling 6 per cent of the loan value merely for fees. On Christmas Eve Deane's final report was released. He was strongly critical of Reedy, saying that he acted unwisely and made a serious error of judgement in signing the document. Reedy was also criticised for failing to keep his minister well enough informed on the proposal. Treasury were criticised for not sooner alerting their own minister as to what was going on.

The arrival of Christmas put a temporary halt to Peters' momentum on the loans affair. Rocky Cribb added a tantalising new angle when he stated Wetere was told of the loan proposal in a meeting as long ago as 21 October 1986. If true, this brought Wetere's knowledge of the proposal much further back in time than had previously been realised. Cribb's claim, however, contradicted what he had told Deane under oath. The Christmas break saw many figures in Maoridom coming out strongly in support of Reedy and the loan proposal. Both Deane and Peters were heavily criticised. Deane had to defend himself against charges that he was harming the interests of Maori. An exasperated Lange talked about a 'cargo cult' mentality amongst some Maori, and he slammed the notion that 'if you are a Maori and well intentioned you have a licence to do anything'.

Peters made excellent use of his January. He spent one week in Hawaii, holding meetings with a number of the players involved in the loan fiasco, including Max Raepple. Peters claimed from abroad that he had new evidence showing Wetere's involvement in the proposal much earlier than publicly admitted. On the very day Peters arrived back in New Zealand the government ruled out a full inquiry into the affair. Peters' claim to have important new information was regarded with scepticism. Given Peters' strike rate prior to the Maori loans affair, Labour had every reason to be confident. Unbeknown to them, Peters *did* have new information and was saving it for Parliament.

Peters' attack in Parliament came in question time. The issue concerned a trip to Hawaii that Wetere had at one stage been planning for December. Though there was a document showing that Reedy had linked that trip in his own mind with the loans proposal, Wetere had told the Deane inquiry that, as far as *he* knew, the trip was solely to attend the inauguration celebrations of the new Hawaiian Governor. Peters' opening question to Wetere received a reply simply reaffirming what Wetere had told Deane. Then came Peters' stinger:

> How does the minister explain that Governor Waihee was not elected until the first week of November, and that the minister did not get an invitation until mid-November, yet his diary note of his discussions with Rocky Cribb on 20 October reads 'Expect deputation in November. Further discussions. Minister to travel to Hawaii'.

'Square that!' Peters added with relish as Wetere rose to reply.

It was indeed a hard circle to square. It looked as if Cribb had been right to say Wetere knew about the proposal as long ago as October. Why else would 'Minister to travel to Hawaii' have been scrawled in the context of a meeting with Cribb? Wetere did not succeed in squaring it, nor did he after Peters came at him a second time. Lange then sprang to Wetere's assistance, asking him to confirm that an invitation to the inauguration could have been anticipated well in advance of the election. But the Labour bench had no answer to the Cribb linkage. Peters had scored a direct hit, and no amount of raucous laughter from the Labour side, and jokes about smoking guns, could disguise that fact.

Wetere was to immediately make it worse for himself. Outside Parliament he changed his story, telling the Press Association that he had considered going to Hawaii to look at funds for Maori development. In a statement the following day he gave out yet another version: he linked the note 'Minister to travel to Hawaii' with the Cribb meeting, saying that the trip was to discuss trade and the export of modular housing; but he said the words 'expect deputation in November' related to a deputation of Hawaiians extending an invitation to the inauguration.

Now Wetere was really in trouble. By changing his story he risked charges that he had misled Parliament. He was not the first politician, nor the last, to find that changing stories in midstream is not the best way to get to the other side. Meanwhile Peters continued to apply pressure by issuing a list of documents that he claimed had not been given to the Deane inquiry.

Of all possible dates on the calendar, the following day was 6 February. Wetere and Lange had a short meeting in Lange's office. History has not recorded what was said, but both came out looking under great strain. Down below, the Waitangi Day celebrations were ready to start. During the ceremony Wetere, the most amiable of men, looked to be almost in tears. He stuck to his speech notes. After Wetere had got through his address a hymn was sung. During the singing Lange was seen moving from his assigned place to stand beside Wetere. It was a telling gesture. The two bulky figures stood shoulder-to-shoulder: one comforting the other, supporting him, sharing his loneliness.

From the government's point of view there seemed to be two feasible options. One was to take the heat out of the affair by sacrificing Wetere. Sacking the Minister of Maori Affairs would cause major unhappiness in Maoridom. The other option was to box on, hoping there would be no more major revelations and that the affair would slowly fade away as a news story. The worst possible option from Labour's point of view would be to give way to the Opposition's calls for a full public inquiry. That would drag the affair out endlessly and could lead almost anywhere.

By the weekend Lange and Palmer had between them come up with a further option. Their plan was for Wetere to resign not only from Cabinet but from Parliament. Wetere would then stand again as Labour candidate for Western Maori in the by-election, win the by-election, and go straight back into his old job in Cabinet. By this manoeuvre, they reasoned, Wetere would be re-endorsed by his own people, most of whom were supportive.

It is hard to see how two such intelligent men as Lange and Palmer could come up with such a strange idea. It was not in the eyes of his own people that Wetere had fallen short. If Wetere had failed it was by the standards of ministerial accountability within the Westminster tradition. A Wetere resignation would be an admittance, tacit or otherwise, that he had been at fault by the standards of that tradition. The fault would not be erased by Wetere's re-election by the voters of one Maori electoral district, most of whom would vote Labour if the candidate were a tailor's dummy. The whole manoeuvre would give further ammunition to the Opposition charge that Wetere was a mere token — a man to whom lower standards applied.

Over the weekend Lange travelled to Napier to talk to leading figures in Maoridom, including the Maori Queen. He put to them the plan for Wetere that he and Palmer had hatched. Other ministers knew nothing of what the two were thinking. Prebble stumbled upon the plan when he saw Wetere in at the Beehive on Sunday. Prebble thought 'something must be *real* serious for Koro to be in here'. Wetere told Prebble that Lange and Palmer had asked him to give his resignation to Cabinet on Monday. Prebble told him not to do that.

At Cabinet Wetere opened up with the line, 'I will resign *if Cabinet wants me to.*' A discussion ensued. Prebble and Douglas argued strongly that Wetere should not resign. Douglas, who sat next to Wetere, put his hand on Wetere's shoulder. 'Nothing personal, Koro, because I like you,' he began. 'I don't know about the rest of you, but having Koro on TV every night for the next six weeks is not my idea of how to start off election year.' That concentrated a few minds. In the end few saw merit in the Lange/Palmer plan. Wetere's resignation offer was turned down. For him the crisis had passed.

After Cabinet Lange needed all his skills to get through the press conference. He stated that Wetere had offered his resignation but that Cabinet had turned it down. Then the questions came. Wetere's statements to Parliament, Lange admitted, represented 'a series of pieces of corroboration tendered that were not themselves sequentially logical.' Yes there were still unanswered questions about the affair, Lange said, but — in the way only he could — 'there are some things where, if it is not critical, it is better to have an air of mystery. You have got to have something like that in life. It is what makes it different from the utterly rational.' It was Zen and the art of damage limitation.

Peters had not given up. He slammed Cabinet's decision not

to accept Wetere's resignation as paternalistic, claiming that it implied a less rigorous standard for a minister who was a Maori. There was undoubtedly some truth in this criticism. Peters also released another document, this one appearing to show that Maori Affairs had taken a long time to call off the loan negotiations after being ordered to by Wetere. Peters also continued his scrap with the government over Cribb's evidence to the Deane inquiry about the 21 October meeting. Peters issued his own, selectively edited version of the transcript of Cribb's evidence. For all Peters' continued activity, however, the Maori loans affair was winding down as a story. When Deane, sick of people playing politics, issued full transcripts of the inquiry, little of central importance emerged. Even when Peters issued two more documents, providing further evidence that Wetere knew about the loan proposal in October, no one seemed especially interested.

Despite Peters predicting more revelations, there would only be minor touches of theatre from then on. Werner Rohrich gave an interview from Germany, weakening the theory that he was the same man as Max Raepple. A Maori crooner living in Hawaii said that Maori Affairs had paid his fare to New Zealand to deliver loan documents. Those who had followed the affair and been richly entertained by a parade of the absurd, were now seeing the last of it.

For Peters the failure to force a ministerial resignation must have been frustrating. Yet the affair was a major boost for his own political standing. Not only did he gain a large amount of television coverage, but the affair rocked the Fourth Labour Government as no other scandal was to do. For most of its term the government had looked comfortably on top of the Opposition. Now it suddenly looked vulnerable. In many ways the affair was a strange one to have dealt the government so much damage. As Palmer kept reminding everyone, it was about a loan that had not happened and could never have happened. Yet it dominated the news for two months.

Peters had pursued the affair with real persistence and aggression, demonstrating that when he actually *had* a story he could run it effectively. His initial tip-off had come from Edwin Perry, then chairman of the Taupo branch of the National Party.

Perry was an associate of Cribb's. Once the story had broken, Peters assiduously did the rounds of those involved in the affair, many of whom were disgruntled at being labelled amateurs and con-men by members of the government. They had every temptation to give Peters embarrassing documents. Peters used this material skilfully, spreading out the release of documents for maximum publicity.

The Maori loans affair was a turning point in Peters' career. Had it not occurred, it is unlikely he would have been promoted to the front bench after the 1987 election. The affair also constitutes one of the few positive contributions he has made to public life in New Zealand. It hardly rates as a major contribution, but it *was* salutary to expose to public view the rank amateurishness that went on in a government department. Peters may even have added impetus to the review of Maori Affairs that was to radically restructure the department.

Just as the Maori loans affair was winding down, the Cook Strait ferry story, which had been submerged for some months, briefly jumped to the surface. Peters flourished a leaked Railways Corporation report from the master of the *Aratika*. The report stated that when the ship went in for dry-docking in July 1986 it showed 'signs of contact with seabed shingle'. This dry-dock inspection had taken place four months after the alleged grounding. The Railways Corporation hastened to play down the report, stating that more senior people than the *Aratika*'s master had concluded there had been no grounding. According to Railways, the paint scratches noted in the report could easily have been caused by logs or gravel-bearing kelp, and the absence of buckled plates was evidence no grounding had taken place. The paint scratches could also have occurred at any time over the period leading up to the dry-docking — not just on the day Peters claimed the grounding occurred. The weight of evidence was against Peters' claim. Still, Peters now had more evidence than he had before — which was none. To this day, when ribbed about the 'ferry touching the bottom' story, Peters insists he had a report 'proving' he was right.

Things soon settled back to normal after the Maori loans affair. Peters was again criticised for not turning up to select committee meetings. He was even criticised by Labour for a poor voting record in the House. Then Peters had the most serious of his stoushes with the imperious Speaker Wall, aptly named on account of his adamantine immovability. Wall had sent Peters out of the House, as he was wont to do. Peters was then found back in the House before Wall thought he had given him permission to return. Peters had rejoined the game before his period in the sin-bin was up. Probably it was simple confusion but it resulted in Peters being 'named' — suspended from the service of the House for 24 hours.

Later in the year Peters indulged himself in two more personal attacks under Parliamentary privilege. The first of these was a largely incoherent attack on Roger Douglas, where Peters appeared to allege some sort of conflict of interest. Just over three years previously, Douglas and three others had bought an option to purchase a property in two years' time. As it turned out, a substantial capital gain was made. It was hard to see what impropriety had taken place. It was even harder when it was explained that Douglas's involvement was purely to help a friend who wanted to buy the building where his business was located.

Pretty thin fare for Peters. But prior to tabling his documents with a flourish he was able to wax eloquent:

> Who is looking after his mates; who is part of the speculator's government; and who has made this country a paradise for moneylenders? It is that man over there, who I believe has breached his trust in a most serious way. He had a vested interest in inflation going up — and by massive amounts. He had no commitment whatsoever to getting inflation down.

Given Peters' own record of opposition to anti-inflationary policies, this was a particularly rich accusation. Given how sharply inflation would soon start to fall, under the tight monetary policy initiated by the very man Peters was accusing, it was even richer. Before long Peters would be slamming the government's objective of eliminating inflation as hopelessly unrealistic. The economic rhetoric that Peters would use to such powerful effect in Labour's second term was gradually falling into place. By the end of the year all the familiar elements of Peters' assaults would be present: Rogernomics, monetarists, the Treasury, the Reserve Bank, big business, the Business Roundtable. These were the heretics who would need to be combated with bell, book and candle.

Peters' second personal attack was one of the most unsavoury attacks under Parliamentary privilege of his career to date. It concerned Rod Deane. After a long period of service with the Reserve Bank Deane had effectively been given leave of absence to head the State Services Commission for a short while. Deane then resigned from the Commission to head Electricorp, thus severing his links with the Reserve Bank. His entitlement from 28 years in the bank's superannuation scheme, totalling $750,000, was transferred to an Electricorp scheme. That is certainly a large amount of money, but Deane was a highly paid official and the Reserve Bank's superannuation scheme was a generous one.

Peters somehow learnt of the $750,000. He erroneously called it a golden handshake, and on it he constructed a conspiracy theory. While he was at the State Services Commission, Deane had undertaken two well-publicised investigations. One was an inquiry into the sending out of Budget documents in advance of the 1986 Budget. Deane had found that to have been a simple administrative error. His other inquiry was into the Maori loans affair. As we saw, Deane was not empowered in that inquiry to investigate the actions of ministers — it was simply beyond his brief.

Armed with those materials, this is what Peters fashioned:

He has received $750,000, which is 30 times the average earnings of a New Zealand family. It is revolting. I wanted to know why it was paid — but I have the answer if I go back into the inquiry into the Budget leaks. Dr Deane found one lonely woman, on secondment to the department, totally guilty of the release of 9976 copies of the Budget: It was a whitewash. That same man interviewed the Minister of Maori Affairs on 16 December 1986 about the Maori loan affair. It is interesting that, with all the witnesses interviewed, there was no transcript of the interview between Dr Deane and the minister. No written notes were taken. What kind of inquiry is that? Dr Deane is the person who said 'I can't investigate the actions of ministers of the crown.' What a whitewash!

In other words, Deane's $750,000 was a pay-off for political services to the government. The suggestion is as outrageous as it is unbacked with the slightest piece of evidence.

Seven years before, the MP for Hunua had said:

> It is always a shame to see members hiding behind the privilege of Parliament when they seek to attack somebody who is not in the House. Such behaviour is characteristic of the lowest of the low.

By now the 1987 election was only weeks away. Late in the piece National released its Maori Affairs policy. The policy was cautiously worded and for the most part bland. There was a qualified bow in the direction of the Treaty. National would:

> work towards eliminating outstanding grievances between Pakeha and Maori, recognising the standing of the Treaty of Waitangi *and the passage of history since its signing in 1840.* (Author's emphasis.)

From these words it is not easy to be sure how National would have handled Treaty issues had it been elected to office in 1987. Also in National's policy was a commitment to review the criminal justice system so as to enable non-violent Maori offenders to be dealt with by their tribes.

It was well for New Zealand that National were roundly defeated in the 1987 election. They were not ready for office. The National campaign had been a shambles. They had never managed to agree on a credible economic policy. National's alternative to GST, the infamous Extax, was soon quite literally an 'ex' tax; it had proved so unpopular with the business community that it was never mentioned during the campaign. Various spokespeople talked of needing to cut $500 million, $1 billion or $1.5 billion off government spending; numbers were thrown around like so much confetti. No one said how the cutting would be done. The old devil from Tamaki chimed in on one of his favourite subjects — the need for direct intervention to bring down the exchange rate. This was contrary to party policy. So was Doug Graham's unscripted lapse into talking about tax increases.

If economic policy was a babble of voices, in few other policy areas did National excite the public imagination. Bolger's reformulation of his party's position on ANZUS into 'we'll expect them not to bring nuclear ships but respect their neither-confirm-nor-deny policy' was such an obvious piece of political sludge that it probably fooled no one. Bolger stomped the campaign trail energetically and with surprising dynamism; but Lange's media skills and an urban economy that was holding up remarkably well were too much for National.

For National it was not a happy locker room after their defeat. There was a short but intense period of infighting. By the end of it, Peters' flatmate McKinnon had emerged as the party's new deputy leader, while Bolger had made wholesale changes to his front bench, including the promotion of Richardson to take on the finance job. Ironically, the new National line-up now had much more of a McLay look than it had previously. But there was one new front bencher who McLay was most unlikely to have promoted. On to the front bench came Winston Peters.

Peters had not been prominent either in the campaign or in the post-election manoeuvrings. But he had made up ground over that time. He had been keeping his head down while all about were losing theirs. He had not dropped the ball during the campaign. Some of the pundits had discussed him as a possibility for the front bench. But he was by no means considered a certainty. His loose cannon image still hung over him. Just as Bolger saw the need to accommodate the forces Richardson represented, he also sought to accommodate the very different forces Peters represented. Peters' style was the aggressive throw-all-things-at-them style of politics. He had struck gold once — in the Maori loans affair. Bolger reasoned that if Peters hit that form again he could be a useful player. More importantly, Bolger reasoned that he could not afford to alienate Peters.

Bolger's portfolio choices for Peters seemed sensible in the circumstances. They recognised that Peters was more effective as an *op*poser than a *pro*poser — that he was better at attacking the government than at building a policy platform. Bolger gave Peters employment in place of transport, and left him with

Maori Affairs. Employment was a major social issue where the government was politically vulnerable. It was good opposition territory. At the same time, employment was not a powerful portfolio in terms of real policy action. The key decisions for economic and social policies — even for employment policies — are made elsewhere. In terms of Peters' strengths and weaknesses employment seemed a natural choice.

Natural, but almost fatal. Within 12 months Bolger would deeply regret his promotion of Peters. He would be wishing for a formula that would get the genie back into the bottle.

CHAPTER FIVE

Rise of a Populist

September 1987–July 1988

*F*OR a time the Fourth Labour Government looked unstoppable. There was a sense that Labour were cleaning out the cluttered debris of an era grown stale. There was a new feeling of freedom. Labour had direction and momentum: they were continually forging a new agenda while their political opponents — like a species failing to adapt to its new environment — were still fighting battles that had already been lost.

Some of it was illusion. In Labour's first term economic forecasters were continually predicting a downturn in the economy. It failed to arrive. Although there was a sharp rural recession, activity in the cities was still expanding. Deregulation of the financial markets, the uneven pace of restructuring and a remarkable boom in the sharemarket all helped to stave off the urban downturn. The economic crunch still lay ahead. On election night 1987 Lange promised that in their second term Labour would move on from economic policy to social policy, garnering the social policy dividend of successful economic reform. Perhaps Labour deserved that outcome. But it was not to happen. 15 August 1987 was the not the beginning of the end of economic adjustment for New Zealanders. It was the end of the beginning.

Early in Labour's second term the economy weakened and moved into serious recession. The October sharemarket crash gave this movement an added impetus. Domestic demand collapsed, business confidence fell, bankruptcies and liquidations soared, and unemployment started climbing strongly. Month by month the pool of unemployed grew larger. The recession was in part the price New Zealanders had to pay for the inadequacies of the Muldoon years. In part it was the price that had to be paid for the imbalances in Labour's reform programme. But whatever its causes the recession had arrived, and it was real enough. There would be no immediate economic dividend available for social policy. And for many New Zealanders there seemed no end in sight to the economic stress. The glamour days of Rogernomics were now over. To those affected, Rogernomics now seemed much less fun, much less fair and much less justified.

In all sorts of ways many New Zealanders — particularly older New Zealanders — began to feel strangers in their own land. Some of these factors were more symbolic than real in the sense of directly impacting on people's lives. But the symbolism conditioned the public mood. Post offices were closing. Foreign investment was increasing. More Asians were settling in New Zealand. The Treaty of Waitangi was being taken increasingly seriously. There was more emphasis on things Maori than ever before. Crime at all levels was rising. New Zealanders felt there had just been too many changes on which they had not been consulted. In good economic times the changes could have been much more easily borne. In bad times the changes seemed threatening, almost subversive, in many minds.

A 1990 Massey University study of New Zealanders' values and attitudes vividly illustrated the public mood of cynicism and mistrust. Of those surveyed 58 per cent believed government officials and political parties were not interested in what the public thought; only 9 per cent believed they *were* interested. It was a remarkable response when one considers the huge role public opinion plays with even the most 'unlistening' government. Not only were the survey respondents mistrustful of the Wellington élite who governed, they were also mistrustful of each other. Only 37 per cent believed most people could be trusted — a low figure by international standards. The same survey showed scepticism over the Treaty of Waitangi and a feeling that too much was spent on Maori.

It was in this climate of deepening gloom and cynicism that Peters was to make his extraordinary impact on the public. He was well placed by his spokesman responsibilities. Unemployment would dominate the headlines for most of Labour's second term. Every two or three weeks there would be a new statistic on jobs, and it was almost always bad. This gave Peters many opportunities for exposure. Race relations was also a very high profile issue. Here Peters had a built-in advantage over every other member of the National caucus — his race. Peters may not have felt very Maori, but he certainly looked Maori. As a Maori he was able to say what many in the electorate — and not just its redneck component — felt instinctively to be true. A European making some of Peters' statements would have been tarred and feathered by left-liberal New Zealand. With Peters it was different. His most natural constituency, paradoxically, was the redneck element. Some of that constituency would have been little inclined by instinct to like *any* Maori politician. Peters appealed to this constituency in two ways. He articulated their views on race relations. And he enabled them to rationalise more comfortably their half-submerged racism by saying 'I like this Peters fellow.' After all, Peters was a Maori himself!

Yes, Peters had natural advantages. But there was much more to his exploitation of the public mood. He became a thoroughgoing populist at a time when the climate was more favourable to a populist message than any time in the last 50 years. To understand Peters it is crucial to appreciate at least something of the populist tradition — a line in which Peters is the purest New Zealand exemplar.

Populists and populism have been a recurring feature of political history at least since the time of the Greek city states. Populism is not easy to define. But all populists place strong emphasis in their rhetoric on the will of the people and the soundness of their basic instincts and reactions, as opposed to other — corrupting — influences that are found either inside or outside society. There have been populist movements throughout English history: the Peasant's Revolt in the 14th century, the Levellers of the 17th century and the Chartists two centuries later all had elements of populism. The American populist movement in the late 19th century had its roots in the economic hardship suffered by farmers in a rural downturn.

The enemies of the American populists were big business, bankers and the city élite. Russia at a similar time in its history also had a strong populist movement.

Populism has been an element of most fascist movements. Hitler was a populist, though there was also much else to his political make-up. The Social Credit party in Alberta was populist. In the 20th century populism has spread out to all continents. Peron in Argentina, Gandhi in India and Nyerere in Tanzania were all in their different ways populists.

Populism is not an ideology. It is more a collection of attitudes and images that are easily borrowed and easily discarded. Populism arises when a large enough body of people feel alienated from the centres of power, whether that power be economic or political. Populism thrives in economic depressions or when societies undergo adjustments that are traumatic for large numbers of people. Populism rarely manifests itself as a structured political party. It produces movements and charismatic leaders but rarely a coherent political programme. Populism is often a transitional phenomenon: born of protest against a certain state of affairs, it melts away as conditions improve or is transformed into a greater movement. Most populist movements fail.

More than most other political movements, populist movements define themselves by what they are against. Populism is against capitalism — or at least its big business component. Populism is against bankers. Populism is against urban élites — both bureaucratic élites and political élites. Populism is fundamentally anti-establishment. Populism is against foreigners, and sometimes against distinct racial groups. Prejudice is a strong motivating force in most populist movements. Conspiracy theories also play a leading role. Malign forces are alleged to be at work. These forces conspire against the aspirations of the common people. It could be outside forces, such as foreigners or multinationals, or inside forces such as bankers, big business or the political élite.

Populism is anti-intellectual. Instead it stresses the reasonableness and decency of the common citizen. In New Zealand Muldoon's talk of the 'ordinary bloke' was a calculated element of populism. The key to Mike Moore's political appeal is the buoyant way in which he identifies himself, through images, with the ordinary man or woman.

Populism is romantic rather than rational, moral in its appeal rather than programmatic, communal in its rhetoric rather than individualistic. Its language is emotional rather than logical, more about how people feel than what they think. Populism is rarely revolutionary; it is more often reactionary. It is fundamentally nostalgic: populism looks back to a mythical golden past of stable communities and traditional values. It wants to restore that past, and sees politics as that restorative act.

Currency reform has been a favourite topic of populism. Populists almost everywhere advocate a more expansionary monetary policy. Populism is often distrustful of Parliamentary politics, which it sees as elitist and out of touch with the concerns of ordinary people. Populism often advocates more direct participation by citizens in government. In foreign policy populism is almost always isolationist: it distrusts military spending and entangling alliances.

During the Labour Party's second term in office Peters was to adopt the politics of populism almost as if he were giving a textbook example. The conditions for a populist message in New Zealand could scarcely have been more propitious. There was the worst recession for 50 years. There was sharply rising unemployment. There were large numbers of people who had been pushed to the margins of society by economic restructuring. There was the stress of social change, and nostalgia for the more stable world that had existed up until 1984. There was cynicism and disillusionment, a sense that ordinary New Zealanders had been betrayed. And to top it off, there was a group of people doing conspicuously well: the new rich, often in the financial sector, who were benefiting from the freer economic environment.

Peters the populist was to articulate, far more powerfully than any other Opposition politician, the sense of betrayal felt by the casualties of Rogernomics. He was the ultimate nostalgia politician — nostalgia for the past of full employment and a more stable, less individualistic society. Peters was the 'anti' politician: anti-Treasury, anti-Reserve Bank, anti-Business

Roundtable, anti-Rogernomics. Peters offered a simple, attractive message to the dispossessed. Their plight was the result of a conspiracy to hijack economic policy. A mad experiment was being run by spotty-faced Treasury officers scarcely out of school, who had never experienced life outside Treasury. The Business Roundtable was supporting the experiment because it meant their members could line their pockets at the expense of ordinary New Zealanders. Foreigners were also supporting the experiment because it meant they could rip off New Zealanders.

To call the Peters world-view a caricature of the facts would be too charitable. It was totally at variance with the facts. But it struck a chord with many New Zealanders. In the best populist tradition, Peters spent little time on rational argument. It had never been his strength. His pitch was an almost entirely emotive one. He was the 'feeling' politician *par excellence*.

There was also an element of anti-intellectualism in Peters the populist. He often denounced Treasury and the Reserve Bank for being too 'theory driven', for being infatuated with a theory which did not fit the facts. This was a common criticism from the private sector at the time, but Peters himself plugged it relentlessly. More originally, Peters coined the term 'sickly white liberal' for a certain type of European who, Peters charged, patronised Maori by dwelling on the past wrongs of Europeans rather than on the need for self-improvement in Maori. In adopting the label Peters clearly had in mind the pontificating classes of academics, writers and journalists.

When it came to advocating specific policies, the stances taken by Peters were textbook populism. He would slam the government's 0-2 per cent inflation target and urge its abandonment; he wanted a more expansionary monetary policy. This was fully in line with the old populist illusion that you could grow richer by some sleight-of-hand involving the quantity of money. Peters was suspicious about reducing border protection. He tended to view the rest of the world as a threat rather than as a set of opportunities by which, through trade, New Zealanders could become better off. Peters would advocate a referendum on ANZUS and switch his support to the growing anti-nuclear sentiment in New Zealand. He would oppose the ANZAC frigate project. He would be conservative on immigration and foreign investment. All of these stances would be entirely consistent with the long isolationist tradition of populism. Peters would advocate electoral reform and greater use of referenda. This was consistent with another populist theme — the call for more direct democracy.

At first Peters rarely advocated populist policies that were directly contrary to National party policy. For a time he stuck to the broad rhetoric of populism — thundering against the forces of darkness but advocating little concrete outside his own responsibilities of employment and Maori Affairs. Once he had risen in the opinion polls he grew bolder and began directly articulating stances that went against party policy.

Many elements went into Peters' remarkable rise to nationwide popularity. There were his spokesman responsibilities. There was the fact that he was a Maori. There was his mastery of television. And there was the full-blooded rhetoric of populism. But there was another element just as important as any of these. His name was Michael Laws.

Laws had joined the National Party research unit some years before. He was intelligent, vain and eager to make his mark. To Laws politics was marketing. He would talk explicitly about National MPs in terms of whether they could be 'packaged'. According to Laws, Peters was someone who could be packaged. Peters was Maori, he had the looks and he had the voice. Laws contested the Hawke's Bay electorate for National in the 1987 election. He lost. He returned to the research unit and, at his request, teamed up with Peters. Few marriages of minds in politics have at first seen such spectacular results. Few marriages of minds have ultimately proved so disastrous.

Without doubt Laws was an ace at bringing Peters publicity. He was assiduous at uncovering stories Peters could run. He made very effective use of the Official Information Act. Once he had a story, he was very helpful to Peters in packaging it. Laws wrote most of Peters' speeches and press releases.

Laws never provided Peters with a really big scandal, but he supplied a steady stream of middle-sized news stories. Sometimes in his enthusiasm Laws went too far, such as when he put out a press statement saying Peters would be meeting

President Ronald Reagan while in the United States. On arriving back in the country Peters had to put up with many a gleeful enquiry as to whether he had *really* met the President. But in general Laws played an invaluable role in anchoring Peters and in toning down his previous eccentricities. Gone were the bizarre allegations that could not be supported by evidence. Gone too were the sleazy personal attacks. Under Laws' influence, Peters quickly began to shed his 'unguided missile' image which, despite the Maori loans affair, he still held. The bovver boy image also receded. There was a new focus to Peters' attack on the government.

Laws undoubtedly speeded up Peters' rise in the opinion polls. But in the long run Laws did Peters more harm than good. As it turned out, the two men were too alike to be a safe combination. Laws, like Peters, was a populist. Laws, like Peters, lacked a sense of danger. As a team their strategic grasp was very weak. They had the wrong strategy, or perhaps no strategy at all. They ignored the need for Peters to build up support within caucus. Once Peters had risen in the opinion polls their fatal error was to believe Peters could then articulate policies directly contrary to party policy. That would prove to be a calamitous misjudgement. It would rob Peters of the leadership of his party and the Prime Ministership. It would rob Laws of the chance to play a significant role in the next National government.

But that was all in the future. At the beginning Laws was solid gold to Peters. And while Laws was fashioning the weapons for Peters to fire, Peters' own delivery skills were still improving. We have seen what he had learnt from Muldoon. The key medium was television. Peters looked very good on television. Not only was he good-looking, he came across as a well-integrated person. To use perhaps old fashioned language, Peters had a face which comprised both the 'masculine' qualities of strength and rationality and the 'feminine' qualities of sympathy and intuition. His voice was authoritative and sincere. And at lighter moments he could break into the boyish grin that was not the least of his attributes.

Television transforms most politicians either for the better or the worse. Peters is one of the lucky ones — the camera treats him extremely kindly. A former Labour MP recounts how he was once debating with Peters on television. The Labour MP thought he was doing rather well. He then had the unnerving experience of glancing up at the television monitor, while Peters was talking, to see how it was coming across to viewers. He was amazed at how utterly different the man on the screen was to the man sitting opposite him in the studio. Not only was the Labour MP amazed, he was envious.

Select committees were to provide Peters with plenty of opportunity to pursue the government. His general attendance at committees was still poor, but when there was a chance to score political points he made sure the media were there as well. In the labour select committee there were sharp words from Peters over not receiving enough time to examine the Labour Department's budget. Soon he was also complaining to Bruce Gregory, chairman of the Maori Affairs select committee, about the delay in examining the Maori Affairs estimates. Gregory's response was that if Peters actually turned up to one of the meetings, he might learn more about the committee's timetable.

Peters also used the select committee to press an accusation that Maori Access trainees were used as cheap labour on a Hastings strawberry farm run by Wi Huata and his wife Donna Awatere. Peters further claimed that Huata had physically threatened those on the course who had crossed him. Awatere dismissed the accusations as 'unmitigated humbug'. She said the trainees were not just picking strawberries but learning welding and bricklaying skills. Peters failed in his attempt to get an inquiry through the select committee, but the Audit Office was sufficiently interested to start its own investigation. In the end the Audit Office pronounced itself satisfied with the project.

The next 'scam' was one, strangely enough, where the government made most of the running. Lange claimed in Parliament one day that there was evidence of another Maori loans affair in the offing, and that he had ordered an Audit Office inquiry. Peters' first reaction was to claim that the affair involved another $500 million loan and to demand Wetere's resignation. It quickly became apparent that the target of the

Audit Office inquiry was the Te Arawa Maori Trust Board in Rotorua. The board had made a Mana Enterprises loan of $390,000 to one Whakaari Developments. Acting as consultant for Whakaari Developments was — you guessed it! — Rocky Cribb. Since the Maori loans affair Cribb had had his nomination as National Party candidate for Eastern Maori vetoed by party headquarters — a relatively rare occurrence.

Like most sequels, Rocky II was to be a pale imitation of the original which had screened so memorably the previous summer. Whakaari was involved in a venture to export kitset houses to Hawaii. One of the directors, Alec Wilson, who was also on the Trust Board, protested that Wetere had personally approved the venture. Early in the New Year, Wilson was ordered by Reedy to leave his job as overseer of Rotorua's Maori Access schemes and take up duties in the department's Rotorua office. In March the Audit Office finally completed its report. It was critical of the $390,000 loan, saying it had been undertaken without proper evaluation. It did, however, accept that all were acting in good faith. It found no evidence of an overseas loan.

Peters now turned around and used the Audit Office report to ridicule the government's claims of a second Maori loans affair. Undaunted, Lange claimed in Parliament that Cribb and Waaka Vercoe, the Trust Board secretary, had visited Japan in an attempt to obtain a NZ$500 million loan from a Japanese bank. Vercoe promptly denied that the two had been seeking a loan. With Lange's claim and Vercoe's denial the public slanging ended.

If the last few months of 1987 had been good ones for Peters, the opening months of 1988 were even better. He was constantly in the media. Right at the start of the year Peters made headlines by using Labour Department figures to claim that only 28 per cent of Access trainees went on to obtain jobs. His use of the statistics was selective to say the least, but it constituted more bad publicity for the Access scheme.

Peters also produced an unsigned paper from Wetere to Cabinet asking for $148 million extra in funding for employment and training for Maori. Confusion ensued over whether the paper had actually gone to Cabinet or not: Lange claimed it had not, while Maori Affairs officials said it had gone to an *ad hoc* Cabinet committee. Peters claimed that the paper showed Wetere was unable to get resources from Cabinet for Maoridom. According to Peters, Lange was now the de facto Minister of Maori Affairs. Peters also at this time attacked the devolution policy by which the government was seeking to devolve many of the functions of Maori Affairs to tribal authorities.

Peters next treated us to the sight of a Maori Access committee whose members had never been told of their appointments, who had never met, and yet — according to information supplied by Maori Affairs — had apparently spent $600,000. Once again Maori Affairs had managed to inject a dose of surrealism into the dull business of government administration. The 'committee' was the Manawatu-Rangitikei Maori Access committee. Wetere responded that the committee had never actually been appointed and that a different authority had spent the money. Peters — or presumably Laws — continued to dig into the matter. Wetere consistently refused to name who was actually spending the money.

Soon Peters had information suggesting the total spent was over $2 million and he asked the Audit Office to carry out an investigation. Peters also unearthed a letter from the accounting firm Arthur Young denying they had received $900,000 in Maori Access funding, contrary to what Wetere had told Parliament. Eventually an Audit Office report on the affair detailed a story of woeful confusion and incompetence. As a result, a new tribal-based Maori Access committee was set up in the area.

Peters was becoming more forceful in his denunciation of the extreme elements of Maoridom. In one speech he warned of a white backlash, saying there could be violence in the streets within ten years. The speech brought a critical reply from race relations conciliator Wally Hirsch, who labelled it a self-fulfilling prophecy. An unrepentant Peters responded that Hirsch was not living in the real world. The publicity from this speech was so good that Peters was soon giving another speech in which he claimed a Maori minority wanted half the power to govern New Zealand.

Peters continued to track the devolution process going on in Maori Affairs, claiming from various pieces of evidence that the process was on hold. He also gave out School Certificate pass rates showing the huge disparity in achievement between Maori and European students. Peters said Maori parents had to understand that education was not an anti-Maori institution. He has long articulated the view that education is the key to a better future for Maori. It is one of the few stances he has held consistently through his career.

Eventually the government issued a detailed paper describing its devolution proposals. Maori Affairs was to be phased out and replaced with a small policy ministry. The remaining functions of the department were to be transferred to other departments, or devolved to tribal authorities. The stance Peters took on devolution contained more than a touch of irony. The restructuring of Maori Affairs was taking place partly in response to the shoddy practices he himself had exposed. He had consistently attacked the performance of Maori Affairs. Devolution, however, was not a popular policy with Maoridom. In a politically astute move, Peters now attacked devolution and argued for the department's retention.

As employment spokesman Peters repeatedly called for large-scale work schemes of the type conducted by the previous government. All logic and evidence, however, was against them. Not only were they extremely expensive to administer, they had done little to prepare the unemployed for genuine work in the private sector. It is quite possible that the net effect of those schemes on total employment had been negative under Muldoon. For that reason the Labour government had largely phased out make-work schemes, concentrating instead on training and skill-building. Peters, however, performing a complete U-turn on the view he had expressed as a first term MP, pledged that National would put all the unemployed on work schemes.

It was now May, and Peters was given another chance to cross swords with Wally Hirsch. The occasion was the 'kill a white' remark made by Hana Te Hemara at the Auckland University marae. Hirsch said that he could not take action over the comment because it had not been made in public. He may well have been technically right, but every talkback caller and taxi driver in the land thought otherwise. Peters leapt into the fray, claiming that Hirsch's ruling betrayed a 'liberal guilt conscience'.

Fair or unfair, that sort of rhetoric was winning Peters a real following. The next Heylen poll was to contain a real sting in it. Two months previously, Peters had made his first appearance in the 'preferred Prime Minister' stakes, collecting just 2 per cent. He had maintained that ranking the following month. But now Peters had leapt to 9 per cent. For an MP who was not, and had never been, leader or deputy leader of his party, that was a very impressive rating. Bolger, who for a period straight after the election had been ranking rather well (for him), fell further to just 12 per cent.

It was not panic stations for Bolger. Though his own performance as leader had been less than inspiring, Labour's second term troubles were already well under way. The economy had soured; Lange had publicly reversed the Douglas flat tax rate and the period of infighting had begun. Labour were well behind in the opinion polls. Bolger knew that his caucus was essentially conservative: as long as National remained well ahead of the government he would be safe.

Despite that, Peters' rise was thoroughly unnerving. Bolger is quickly jealous when someone else in the team begins to shine too brightly. As leader he has placed most of his trust in uncharismatic plodders like Wyatt Creech and friend Bill Birch — men who could not possibly replace him. Peters' comet-like appearance in the political firmament was not what Bolger wanted, nor what he had bargained for. At the next of the regular front-bench meetings, which Peters hardly ever attended, there was a very explicit discussion about Peters and Laws. 'This man Laws is undermining me,' said Bolger. It was agreed Bolger would commandeer Laws for himself. There was even a press statement released saying Laws would now work on 'special projects' for the Opposition leader.

Laws never completely stopped working for Peters. For a time Laws did do some work for Bolger, especially on commercial law issues which were then prominent. Laws made no secret of the frustrations of working for Bolger. He considered Bolger was too slow in making up his mind, and too cautious in what he was eventually prepared to say. Bolger was certainly a very different political animal from Peters. Before long Laws had drifted back to Peters. Why Bolger let him go is not clear. Perhaps he just hated dealing with him.

Peters was highly annoyed when Bolger made his grab for Laws. But Peters continued with the lines of attack on the government that had proved so successful. He came up with a second case of a seemingly legitimate Maori authority being bypassed for the dispersal of Maori Access funds: this time it was Taranaki. Peters sent his information to the Audit Office. Peters floated the idea of creating enterprise zones, similar to those in Britain, as a means of creating employment. He had a flick at an Access training course that was teaching karate. And he queried the granting of a concessionary mortgage by Maori Affairs to the daughter of Reedy. The State Services Commission cleared Reedy of any improper involvement.

Far bigger than any of these stories was the finding of the Waitangi Tribunal upholding a claim by Northland Maori for fishing rights in their waters. The tribunal found that the existing fisheries management system was in conflict with the Treaty, and it recommended substantial relief to Maori. A long and difficult process of negotiation lay ahead of the government. Peters' reaction was to again question the relevance of the Treaty to today's society. In a snap debate in Parliament later that week, Bolger called on the government to halt temporarily the work of the tribunal so that New Zealanders could gain a breathing space.

Significantly it was Bolger who led off the debate, not Peters. With Peters rating so well in the polls, his leader was not going to give him the top spot on such an important occasion. Peters saw it as another attempt by Bolger to cut him down to size. His anger was plain. He was conspicuously absent during Bolger's speech, as well as from the speeches of most of his colleagues.

Bolger's efforts were to no avail. The next Heylen poll in July showed Peters surging from 9 per cent to 17 per cent as preferred Prime Minister, just five points behind Lange. Bolger was unchanged on 12 per cent. To add insult to injury, 38 per cent of National Party voters thought Peters should lead the party, compared to 32 per cent for Bolger.

It was a remarkable result. From now on Peters would be asked repeatedly about his leadership ambitions. His standard reply — that he was happy just being the member for Tauranga — would for a time become the most widely quoted words in public life. As for Bolger, when he was asked at his press conference whether Peters' popularity was putting other MPs' noses out of joint, Bolger's own nose grew perceptively longer as he said, 'I think caucus has got a very relaxed and accommodating style towards Win.' He went on to say, managing his straightest face, 'There is no caucus tension over Win.'

CHAPTER SIX

Riding High

July 1988–August 1989

*T*HERE was plenty of caucus tension over Win. He was far
from popular. Some of it was old-fashioned jealousy, more
of it was frustration at a prima donna who was increasingly
treating his colleagues with contempt.

Peters had not been a team player since his re-entry into
politics in 1984, but he was growing worse. Despite being a
member of the front bench he rarely deigned to attend front
bench meetings. He always turned up late to caucus meetings
— if he bothered to turn up at all. His attendance at caucus
committees was patchy at best. He was highly secretive in his
working methods. He worked alone or with Laws. Hardly
anyone knew what Peters was thinking or what he was planning.
His colleagues found out after the event. To discover what
Peters was thinking you generally had to read the newspaper.

In almost every way Peters' colleagues were getting the
message that he was far more interested in promoting himself
than in contributing to the building of a shared policy platform.
His attitude to select committees was a case in point, and was a
source of real resentment by his colleagues. The Maori fishing
issue was a good example. This issue spent many months in
front of a select committee. Fishing spokesman Doug Kidd
attended all the meetings, followed all the ins and outs of a
highly complex piece of legislation, wrote a long paper for his
colleagues summarising the issues, and generally did most of
the work for the Opposition. Peters popped up from time to
time to provide sound bites for television.

Though Peters was not popular in caucus, at the time of his

initial rise in the opinion polls the situation was still retrievable. If Peters wanted to displace Bolger his strategy was obvious. He needed to work harder at being a team player. He should take part in caucus forums, communicate more with his colleagues, pretend to be interested in their views. At the same time he should carry on with the thundering populist rhetoric and the stories Laws was feeding him. By so doing he would have positioned himself as the natural — indeed the only feasible — alternative, if and when Bolger stumbled.

If Peters had followed that strategy — and there was absolutely no reason why he could not — he would almost certainly have been Prime Minister by November 1990. A point was going to be reached when the National caucus would be actively wanting a change in leader. National MPs are nothing if not pragmatic. A previous National caucus had dumped Jack Marshall for Muldoon. Sad to say, a majority of caucus 15 years later would not have had moral scruples in dumping Bolger for Peters. The leadership was there for Peters' taking.

Instead of following the simple and obvious strategy, Peters took precisely the opposite course. From the moment of his opinion poll success he began venturing out into public pronouncements in areas other than employment and Maori Affairs. From then on he had no hesitation in deviating from the party line on a host of issues. No subject was too big, too small or too sensitive for Peters to have a view on it, even if it put him at odds with the official party spokesperson or the leader. In the two most important areas of policy at the time — economic policy and the relationship with New Zealand's former ANZUS partners — Peters would clash repeatedly with more senior people.

The stances Peters took were all 'populist' in terms of the populist tradition discussed earlier. They were also in a literal sense 'popular', in that they were stances enjoying public support in opinion polls. In so acting, Peters took the last step towards becoming an entirely poll-driven politician. If a majority of New Zealanders was in favour of a policy, so was Peters. If a majority of New Zealanders was against, so was Peters.

Peters was now a politician entirely adrift from any moorings except those of public opinion. Some might ask: What is wrong with such a strategy? Are not the people sovereign? And is it not the role of the politician to reflect, as nearly as possible, the wishes of the electorate? It is a superficially attractive line of reasoning but not a tenable one. Taken to its logical conclusion it would replace MPs with sophisticated opinion pollsters.

The elected representative is not in Parliament simply to bow to public opinion on every issue. The role of the elected representative is to provide leadership. Public opinion is sometimes informed, sometimes ill-informed. It is perfectly consistent with the sovereignty of the people to admit as much. Many influences go into informing public opinion. One crucial influence is the articulated views of elected representatives. That is what being a leader — as opposed to a mere follower — is all about. A leader takes a stand and explains the reasons for that stand, confident public opinion will coalesce around their view. Sometimes leaders takes a stand even when they are uncertain whether public opinion will ever catch up with them.

For a man who has said that being a populist is the essence of democracy, Peters has strange heroes. His greatest is his namesake, Winston Churchill. Sometimes a photograph of Churchill, strategically placed, appears on camera when Peters is interviewed at his desk. Yet Churchill, at least in the English-speaking world, is the most dramatic example this century of a man who refused to betray his people by sacrificing his judgement to their opinion. The 1930s policy of appeasement had public opinion firmly behind it. Churchill was then in the political wilderness, from which it seemed unlikely he would ever emerge. That did not stop him from repeatedly urging rearmament and a firmer line against Nazi Germany.

The popular stances taken by Peters guaranteed that he would be a continuing success with the public. But in terms of his leadership aspirations his tactics were a disastrous misjudgement. Instead of becoming more of a team player he was becoming less. Every time he expressed a view that was contrary to party policy he made an enemy of the spokesperson whose area he had just trampled over.

The constitutional role of an Opposition is to be an alternative government. To be a credible alternative government an Opposition has to develop and articulate a policy platform — if only in broad outline. That would have been quite impossible if everyone in the National caucus had behaved as Peters did. Having a babble of voices promoting different policies is simply not a feasible way for an Opposition to operate. It was one of the reasons National had failed in 1987.

It is a real mystery why Peters and Laws chose the strategy they did. Perhaps they did not in fact have a strategy at all. Or perhaps they thought that so long as Peters was riding high in the opinion polls his colleagues would be bound to turn to him. Peters may have been misled by the example of Muldoon. Few in the National caucus had liked Muldoon; but they turned to him because of his undoubted electoral appeal. But there was a crucial difference between Muldoon and Peters. Muldoon had proved himself able to be part of a team — Peters could not.

Perhaps Peters was impatient at the thought of having to sit back and wait for Bolger to stumble, and decided to force the pace. Whatever his conscious plan, the sheer intoxication of his opinion poll ratings probably clouded his judgement. For a long time after his opinion poll rise he would repeatedly allude to his high poll standing when speaking in Parliament. He must have known that it hardly sounded modest; but he was so full of his success that he could not help himself. With the drug of public adulation pumping through him, all real sense of strategy evaporated.

Peters' first major tilt at another spokesperson's area saw him crossing swords with Richardson. Peters gave a speech in which he advocated loosening monetary policy. He claimed New Zealand should follow the example of countries that had increased liquidity in the wake of the sharemarket crash. According to Peters, those countries had been successful at avoiding recession. He also attacked the floating exchange rate. Though the comparison with the rest of the world may have struck a chord at the time, history would not be kind to Peters: many countries — most notably Britain — would find that they had loosened monetary policy too much after the crash, and subsequently had to tighten, bringing recession further down the track.

From that speech onwards Peters would make periodic calls to loosen monetary policy. He is still making those calls today. It is a line Peters has plugged more fiercely, and more often, than any other. During the long Labour recession it was doubtless an attractive line with many in his audiences. It is tempting to think we could all be better off, or that we could be spared the pains of economic adjustment, if those in the Reserve Bank simply injected more money into the system. How printing more money would make us better off is never explained by Peters. It is never explained because any attempt to do so would immediately expose the absurdity of the suggestion. No country can inflate its way to wealth. Events have not borne out Peters' dire warnings about the folly of aiming monetary policy at controlling inflation. New Zealand has now experienced four years of economic growth combined with stable prices. Peters said it could not happen. It has.

When Peters made his first 'loosen monetary policy' speech, the National caucus had no agreed position on monetary policy. Richardson had been consistently opposed to loosening monetary policy. She had argued that the problem was not monetary policy: what was needed was a reduction in the budget deficit and liberalisation of the labour market to take the pressure off monetary policy. In response to Peters' speech she reaffirmed her commitment to a tight monetary policy. Bolger, who was himself unsure on this issue, called the two of them in to see him. As was usual on those occasions, nothing was sorted out.

By this time Peters and Richardson were the two dominant personalities in the National Opposition, yet whenever they were in the same room the air crackled with the animus they had for each other. Both were proud, fearless and pugilistic characters, but there the resemblance ended. Richardson loathed Peters because she saw him as a poser whose populist ambitions were a real threat to her policy agenda. Peters loathed Richardson because she sought to cut him down to size, and because her style of conviction politics was totally alien to him.

The two of them were locked in combat over economic policy. From Richardson's point of view it was mortal combat.

She did not have the instant public appeal of Peters; she was going to survive by winning arguments, if she was going to survive at all. She almost didn't survive. When she took on the finance job she was the fifth National spokesperson in less than three years. Her support from Bolger was intermittent. Every key element in National's economic strategy had to be fought for, in the face of a sceptical Bolger and Birch. Bolger and Birch, like Peters, were opposed to the Reserve Bank Act. Labour market reform had to be won in the face of antiquated attitudes from the two men, as did a credible fiscal strategy.

Richardson won these battles by doggedness and luck. Peters supplied the luck. Had Peters unseated Bolger, Richardson's political career would have been over. Even if Peters had just been present at a crucial caucus meeting, late in 1989, his rival would have been history. Typically enough Peters had not turned up. That incident could be an epitaph for Peters' career.

Soon after their first public sparring on monetary policy, Peters followed up with a call for New Zealand to follow the more 'flexible' economic policies of Britain. Later, as the British economy ran into trouble, the Peters line on Britain was to change and he would criticise Thatcher's economic policies. But while the British economy was going through a good patch he used it as a stick with which to beat Rogernomics.

Peters and Richardson were both given top speaking slots at National's 1988 annual conference. Peters was to speak on race relations, Richardson on the economy. It was not a good conference for Peters. First he had to suffer the sight of Richardson receiving a standing ovation for her speech. Then Bolger in his leader's address ad libbed a none-too-subtle jab at Peters. Talking of National's prospective election victory, Bolger added, 'I don't want anyone with a personal ego or personal agenda getting in the way of that victory.'

Peters must have fumed at that put-down. In his own speech the next day he cutely added the Maori proverb, 'When the old net is shot full of holes, the new net goes fishing.' Peters' speech was a strong call for the Treaty to be reassessed. Only a few days previously a poll had shown that a sizeable majority of New Zealanders were in favour of either abandoning or renegotiating the Treaty. That may have emboldened Peters. He said, 'As a constitutional device the Treaty may well have served its time. In some ways, it is a talisman of the past. Our aim must be to the present and the future.' Peters also said, 'A review of the Treaty's relevance to the New Zealand of today is long overdue.'

Peters did not get a standing ovation. Worse, his speech raised the ire of Maori delegates such as Maori vice-president Sir Graham Latimer and Eden candidate Hiwi Tauroa. Not surprisingly they took Peters to be urging the abandonment of the Treaty. There was an impromptu meeting. Peters told Latimer and the others that his speech had been misinterpreted. This was the first major occasion where Peters used his 'read my speech' defence to party colleagues. It was to become one of his trademarks over the next four years. Typically he would make a speech that heavily implied a certain policy position without actually coming out and saying it in words of one syllable. Rounded upon by his colleagues he would then infuriate them by saying, 'I didn't say x [or y or z]. Read my speech.'

The result of the meeting with Latimer was the drafting of a remit asking that the party resolve all Maori land and fisheries issues within ten years. The remit was seconded by Bolger and carried unanimously. Though the remit did not mention the Treaty, Peters was widely seen as having been 'rolled'. Bolger had come down on the side of the Maori delegates. The whole undignified shambles, in full view of the media, must have pleased Bolger not a bit. It further strained relations between Bolger and Peters and it also deepened the mistrust and animosity between Latimer and Peters. Already they disliked each other. Latimer would often say to people that Peters 'has stardust in his eyes'. He would be a permanent and powerful foe to Peters.

After the conference Peters went back to the business of staying in the headlines. Hirsch provided him with another free hit when he censured the *Sunday Star* for reporting the 'kill a white' comment. Peters this time called for Hirsch to resign. There was also a Peters accusation that Wetere had shown a confidential paper to Massey University Professor Ngatata Love. And there was a claim from Peters that the government had loaned $154,000 to an angora rabbit farm that had bred only 25 rabbits in three years.

Even when Peters took off for a five-week tour in America the press releases kept coming, thanks to Laws. Peters opined that Dukakis would lose the coming presidential election — a safe enough bet by that stage. And the reason?

> My own impression is that he is an intelligent and perceptive candidate but his campaign lacks the vital spark of charisma. He is rarely, if ever, seen as exuberant or angry. To win . . . requires a larger than life personality.

Digs at his leadership were the least of Bolger's worries. In another statement from America Peters came out firmly against the ANZAC frigates project. While public opinion was clearly against the frigates, National's policy was that New Zealand needed a blue water navy capacity. Bolger was forced to reiterate the Opposition's position. In yet another statement from America, Peters hinted there may be a way out of the ANZUS impasse that satisfied all sides. He did not elaborate.

During Peters' absence it was Bolger who was fronting for the Opposition on Maori issues. Ever the lone wolf, Peters had not appointed anyone to deputise for him. On Peters' return to New Zealand Labour devoted the whole of their weekly general debate in Parliament to attacking him — a sure sign they feared a leadership challenge to Bolger. Labour knew only too well that Peters the populist, the man with charisma, would be a formidable leader of the Opposition. He was capable of cutting deeply into Labour's blue collar support. But if Labour had known Peters' standing in his own caucus, they would not have wasted their time. For all their talk about 'already the numbers are being done', there were no numbers being done in the National caucus. The reason was simple: if a leadership ballot had been held at that time, Peters would have been lucky to get six votes, including his own.

Peters' reputation as a team man was scarcely enhanced when he and Ross Meurant were absent without leave from Parliament, costing the Opposition the chance to embarrass the government on a controversial tax bill. The incident happened on a Saturday when Parliament was sitting under urgency. Had the two National MPs been present the Speaker would have been forced to use his casting vote. Meurant said that he had been at a Santa parade. Typically enough, Peters would not even say where he had been. Perhaps he was playing Santa.

The year 1988 drew to a close with the Opposition still well ahead of the government in public support, and with Peters still riding high. Labour were reeling from a year's bitter infighting, culminating in the resignation of Douglas right at year's end. The new year started in familiar enough fashion for Peters: he yet again caught Maori Affairs with its trousers down. This time the embarrassing document was an internal audit of the department's Auckland housing and building section. Peters had obtained a copy under the Official Information Act, with sections of the report withheld. He had also had leaked to him a copy of the uncensored version. The officially censored parts of the report had contained scathing criticisms of the Auckland housing programme. On Peters' appeal, the Ombudsman would rule that some parts of the report had been unreasonably withheld. In the meantime Peters made his umpteenth call for Wetere's resignation. Perhaps Laws had a special stamp with those words on it to go into the press release.

In February the man who said he was happy to be the member for Tauranga gave an address to the Taradale Rotary Club entitled 'State of the Nation Speech'. Only leaders or gnarled old ex-leaders did that sort of thing — until Peters. It was guaranteed to rile Bolger, as was Peters' announcement that he intended making it an annual event. In the speech itself Peters concentrated on a familiar theme — the white paternalism that saw Wetere stay in his job only because he was a Maori.

Later that month there was an entire speech on the environment. What effect it had on environment spokesman Roger McClay, one of Peters' closer associates, can only be imagined. Peters also created a stir by producing a Treasury report predicting a 'third wave' of joblessness. Though Peters in his rhetoric was virulently anti-Treasury, he never blushed at using Treasury as an authority when it suited him.

Early in the year National held a three-day caucus meeting at Waipuna Lodge in Auckland. At the meeting Richardson made her second attempt to have something agreed by caucus on economic policy. She emerged with a thin, bland document. The Waipuna document, as it came to be called, was an advance for National in some respects. But it was vague on monetary policy — still a fierce battleground in caucus. For a time economic debates within caucus would take as their point of reference the Waipuna document.

Richardson's pleasure at finally having something down on paper was shortlived. First Bolger wandered around the press gallery, late one night, saying he was considering splitting the job of Minister of Finance into two portfolios. Then Peters was to further muddy the waters. The event triggering the scrap was the 21 March statement by new Finance Minister David Caygill. The statement included a 2.5 per cent hike in GST and some moderate measures to contain government spending. Richardson criticised Labour for putting up taxes and for not reducing government spending enough. Peters took completely the opposite line on government spending: he said Labour's moves to contain spending would adversely affect the economy. Peters also called again for a loosening in monetary policy. Peters' opposition to spending reductions was plainly contrary to the Waipuna document, which had promised to 'diminish the demands of the state on the economic resources of the nation'.

Peters' comments had highlighted divisions within the Opposition just when they had the chance to attack the government over an unpopular economic package. Letting her frustration get the better of her, Richardson put out a tart press release:

> Maybe this is the opening round in the formation of the Win Peters Party. But with the policies he is espousing it will be the 'Lose Peters' Party.

This led to a Peters rejoinder and a fair old stoush.

Bolger's behaviour over the next few days stood out as a model of inconsistency. First he got the two pugilists together for the ritual private chat, ticking off both of them. Then he broke his public silence and lashed out at Peters, saying he didn't know what Peters wanted. Then, after a messy and intensive caucus debate, Bolger changed his tune. Now he said that Peters' comments were within party policy. Chased around mercilessly by journalists at his post-caucus press conference, Bolger cut a far from convincing figure. When asked if a policy that advocated both loosening and tightening of monetary policy was not too general, he said, 'You can interpret the Bible a thousand ways — and the Ten Commandments which are pretty tightly worded.' Peters had come out of the caucus meeting claiming 'total vindication'. More eloquent was the look of daggers on Richardson's face as *she* came out of caucus.

Bolger's performance at his press conference was greeted with such rage by Richardson's supporters that the next day he changed his mind again. He swung back towards Richardson by rejecting Peters' call to loosen monetary policy. He even talked for the first time about sacking Peters if he continued to go against party policy. Now it was Peters' turn to furiously confront Bolger and complain about his treatment.

Nothing in essence had changed. No one had won and policy was still a muddle. By his own lights Peters had probably won: the next Heylen poll showed him as the most popular politician in the country. Peters was on 19 per cent, overtaking Lange for the first time. From now on, when Peters' colleagues complained to him about something he had said or done, he had a new weapon: he was 'the most popular politician in the country'. His lack of tact in pointing it out did nothing to help his popularity in caucus.

Peters' charisma as champion of those who felt dispossessed under Labour was now at its height. He drew big and enthusiastic audiences in his public meetings. His speeches were powerfully delivered, with real force and apparent sincerity. A typical Peters speech had a maximum of emotion, a minimum of argument. Time and again he would talk about how his audience *felt*, as he excoriated the familiar set of devils who had done so much harm to ordinary New Zealanders. There is no denying that Peters had an aura. For many in his audience hearing him was a cathartic experience, even if it left them none the wiser. Increasingly Peters was being greeted with a fervour that was almost religious in its intensity.

Indeed no New Zealand politician for many years had

rivalled Peters for the intensity of their emotional response. At times a Peters meeting was more like a revivalist meeting than a political forum. It might even be that this 'Scotsman with a suntan' had more Maori in him than either he or his critics realised. Peters could be seen as the latest exemplar of a long Maori tradition — that of the political leader who is also a spiritual or religious leader. It is a tradition that has encompassed all manner of cranks and visionaries, saints and sinners. Te Kooti, the famous guerrilla leader of the New Zealand wars, was in this tradition of the mystic-leader. So was his contemporary Titokowaru, less famous but at least as formidable as a warrior. The pacifist and mystic Te Whiti o Rongomai was of the tradition. So in our own century was Ratana — founder of a church and of a political alliance. It is possible — just possible — that the Peters phenomenon is an echo of this rich and ancient line.

The revivalist atmosphere of a Peters meeting was intensified by his habitual late arrival on stage. It was a tactic that heightened the tension and the sense of expectation among the audience. Already in 1989 Peters' late entrances were becoming famous or notorious, depending on one's taste. On one occasion Peters would adamantly deny a media report that he had spent 20 minutes waiting in a carpark outside his meeting hall. The suspicious side of Peters was well aroused by the incident: he spoke darkly of a plot within the party to discredit him. He even threatened to name those responsible but, like many a Peters threat, he never followed through.

Given Bolger's attitude to Peters it is not surprising that the glamour boy was not getting many chances to ask questions of the day in the House. The man who had once hogged question time for a whole week chasing a Cook Strait ferry, had by the end of April not asked a single question of the day for the whole of 1989. Nor did Peters' stocks with his leader improve when he gave a speech in Papatoetoe that had something in it to annoy just about every member of caucus. Peters again opposed Richardson's economic line. He again opposed the ANZAC frigates. And he argued that the anti-nuclear debate should be solved by a referendum.

After a two-week trip to Britain, Ireland and the US, Peters was back in the country little altered and ready to keep sniping at Bolger. During Peters' absence the Australian Liberal Party, then as now in Opposition, had dumped the uncharismatic John Howard for the more charismatic Andrew Peacock. Peters was undiplomatic enough to say there were parallels with New Zealand though, in his typically Cheshire Cat fashion, he refused to elaborate. This was at least the third time in 1989 alone that Peters had taken an oblique swipe at Bolger. The first occasion was when a rather facile television current affairs programme had likened the selling of politicians to the selling of soap powder; it had suggested that Peters as leader would be a new improved formula for National. Understandably the National leadership rubbished the programme. Peters disagreed, saying he thought the programme had a serious message.

Then there was the memorable occasion Peters was asked by Paul Holmes on radio what Bolger's strengths were. The complete paralysis this question caused in Peters was richly comic, and it sounded genuine rather than feigned; probably Peters simply could not think of anything to say. It was an exchange that sounded even funnier than the transcript suggests, replete as it was with stupified pauses:

Holmes: Mr Bolger's strengths; what are they Mr Peters?

Peters: Well you've got a number of strengths in him. Um! One of them is that he has a good solid New Zealand background. He has spent a lot of time in the city. He has got a — one of his marvellous strengths is that he has got an amazing woman for a wife, and you name them. That is the situation.

Holmes: His strengths Mr Peters? All I can see there is that Mrs Bolger is a lovely woman and he's got a New Zealand background.

Peters: Well, I mean, how do you mean what are his strengths?

Something had evidently changed from the time, two years earlier, when Peters had told Parliament:

Government members are seeking to turn the election campaign into a character assassination of the leader of the

> Opposition . . . They are wasting their time, because our man
> has got three qualities that they do not have — he is honest; he
> is reliable; and he is a person that New Zealanders can
> associate and identify with.

Stoushes with Peters' colleagues continued unabated. John Falloon chose a party conference to lash out at 'selfish prima donnas'; there were no prizes for guessing to whom he was referring. At the following caucus there was a good deal of heat over whether Falloon, like Richardson with her 'Lose Peters' jibe, should have saved his criticism for inside caucus. Then on the Treaty of Waitangi a clear public gap opened up between Peters and constitutional spokesman Doug Graham. Graham argued that the Waitangi Tribunal, now that it had been set up, needed to be continued. Three days later Peters hit back with a proposal that the tribunal be downgraded to something approaching a research unit.

Then came the speech on labour market reform — one of the key issues National would have to confront as an Opposition. Peters' speech was a strong attack on those — both in the caucus and in business — who advocated labour market 'deregulation':

> For them individual freedom means maximum latitude for
> commercial rip-offs, and the right to suppress the ambitions
> and aspirations of not just others, but whole groupings of
> society. The calls from a certain business élite in New Zealand
> for the deregulation of the labour market . . . means creating an
> industrial law of the jungle . . . I have met members of that
> business élite who argue for no industrial law. They truly desire
> a return to the law of the jungle where the strong prosper and
> the weak perish.

The stark Darwinian picture of the market as a place where 'the strong prosper and the weak perish' is another long populist tradition at which Peters was adept. His speech was a world away from calls for a free labour market made by the young MP for Hunua. The speech especially puzzled Roger Kerr of the Business Roundtable. No one at the Roundtable had ever argued for no industrial law. Moreover, only three months previously, Peters had stated to Kerr in a letter that he (Peters) had been 'a supporter of a deregulated labour market for 20 years'. Kerr now wrote back to Peters asking what he meant by his latest speech in light of what he had written before. Peters airily dismissed Kerr's letter as 'a mere impertinence'. Obviously Peters was both for *and* against labour market deregulation.

The gutsy Maurice Williamson, the only National MP other than Richardson to fully appreciate how far National would need to go on labour market reform, was incensed at Peters' bucking of what was admittedly a fairly indistinct party line. He decided to have a go at Peters in the next caucus. He was a first-term backbencher and he was attacking the most popular politician in the country. His hand shook as he held up the Waipuna document and accused Peters of undoing the work of other members in selling labour market deregulation. A general wrangle ensued. Peters took his usual line of 'read my speech'. It was fetched; so was one of Birch's speeches. There was a howl of laughter as it became apparent that Laws had written them both.

Peters was asked to pull his head in. But the occasion ended, as usual, with compromise. It was agreed National would not talk about labour market 'deregulation', which smacked too much of the nasty medicine of Rogernomics. Instead National would 'reform' the labour market. The debate had been so heated that Peters almost got into a punch-up with Ian McLean as caucus broke up. 'You're a liar Peters,' said McLean. 'No one calls me a liar,' said Peters, coming shoulder to shoulder and grabbing him. They were close to blows.

Around this time Peters took advantage of Richardson's absence through illness to get his employment position paper through caucus. The paper called for work schemes for all those who had been unemployed for over six months. It was a position paper, not final policy. In the next year Richardson would have the last word on employment policy.

Race relations still provided a happy hunting ground for Peters. The appointment of Chris Laidlaw to replace Hirsch as race relations conciliator provided an opportunity to rubbish Laidlaw as a 'sickly white liberal'. Then, on an Australian television programme, Peters made by far his most provocative statement to date on race relations. He claimed Maori gangs were involved in the Maori land rights struggle and that they would play a more direct role in future. 'Clearly they have been involved for some time as para shock troops to militant demands by certain radicals,' he said. As a description of reality this was off the planet. There must be something about appearing on Australian television that makes Peters throw caution to the wind. Three years later he would again go on Australian television, creating a sensation back home.

It was no surprise to most in the caucus when Peters was not chosen to address National's annual conference. After his prolonged undermining of the leadership and disregard for party discipline, no other decision could reasonably be taken. If any other member of caucus had stepped out of line as often as Peters had done, they would have been demoted long ago. Peters was different. Because of his immense popularity Bolger was scared to act against him. But though he may have been windy of sacking Peters, Bolger was certainly not going to give him a platform at the conference.

To Peters, the news that he had missed out almost certainly came as a surprise. He had come to think of himself as indispensable to the party. Bolger's move was a signal that Peters was not regarded as indispensable. Instead of heeding the warning Peters put himself further offside. On the eve of the conference he said in a speech that National had been lulled into a false sense of security by its opinion poll lead and was not attacking the government vigorously enough. Once the conference was over Peters called it a public relations flop.

Peters seemed quite oblivious to the fact that tactics such as these were further isolating him in caucus. Soon events would move very quickly. A tumble was coming for him, and he was the last person in the world to suspect it.

CHAPTER SEVEN

Derailed

August 1989–November 1990

*T*WO factors served to change the temperature in the
National caucus. First, there was a brief and lonely period
of good economic news. The 1989 Budget had seen interest
rates fall temporarily in response to the government's decision
to repay domestic rather than foreign debt. Retail spending had
risen just before GST went up, as consumers brought forward
their purchases to beat the price rises. Other indicators also
looked more positive. This unsustainable 'recovery' would soon
be dashed. But for the moment it disconcerted the National
Opposition.

Then, quite suddenly, Lange resigned after five years as
Prime Minister. The immediate spur to his resignation was the
re-election to Cabinet of Douglas — the man who had become
'living death' to the Prime Minister. Though Lange may have
seen his resignation as inevitable once Douglas was back in
Cabinet, few pundits at the time predicted the announcement.
It was an announcement packed with drama: Lange had
presided over five extraordinarily colourful years in New
Zealand politics. Even those who had long ceased to support
him felt the sense of occasion. The transition was particularly
well handled. Ever the old stager, Lange wrung every ounce of
emotion out of his resignation press conference and his address
to the House. In the ballot to choose the new leader Palmer
emerged victorious over Mike Moore, while Helen Clark
became the new deputy.

When the news of Palmer's success over the more
charismatic Moore was handed into the National caucus

meeting there was a spontaneous burst of applause. National MPs were convinced Moore would have been a more dangerous opponent in the 1990 election. National were in confident mood at that moment, but they were less happy when the first public opinion polls came out. The polls showed a sharply reduced National lead over Labour. One poll even showed Labour ahead. Palmer as new leader was enjoying a honeymoon with the voters, while the better economic news was also buoying Labour's popularity.

All of a sudden the National caucus snapped out of its mood of easy complacency — 'sleepwalking to victory' it had been dubbed by the press. Suddenly life was real and earnest. There was widespread dissatisfaction with the indecision and drift of Bolger's leadership. Indecision and drift were all very well when National were 20 per cent ahead in the polls; it was quite a different matter when the lead had narrowed sharply. Bolger had compounded his sins with the address he gave to Parliament in response to Lange's resignation speech. Completely missing the valedictory mood of the occasion, Bolger put in a graceless performance that hit almost every possible wrong note.

This was the moment that had been made for Peters. Had he played his cards right over the previous 12 months, he would now have ousted Bolger. Caucus were dissatisfied with their leader, were wanting a change and were actively discussing it. Bolger survived only because there was no one else. Peters had put himself offside with almost everyone. He was so disliked by the majority of his colleagues that his supporters for the leadership consisted only of a tiny group of cranks and malcontents. If Peters was sitting there waiting for a delegation to knock on his door, it never came.

Richardson's support was a good deal higher than Peters' — despite a flinty-faced image that seriously detracted from her potential appeal as leader. It was the Richardson camp who provided whatever internal challenge there was to the Bolger/McKinnon leadership. Richardson's first plan was an attempt to unseat McKinnon. Murray McCully was her numbers man. He reported 21–19 in Richardson's favour: too close for comfort. On McCully's advice Richardson decided to hold off going for McKinnon and see if she could topple Bolger directly a few weeks down the track. Bolger and McKinnon knew something was up. For three or four weeks McKinnon would visibly tense up before each caucus meeting, and then emerge relaxed after having made it safely through again.

Richardson probably did not have anything like the numbers to topple Bolger. But Bolger still had a problem. By design or by inertia he had for some time been straddling the two high energy points of Peters and Richardson. So long as he continued to sit balancing Peters against Richardson, he would continue to give off an impression of blur and indecisiveness. That was inevitable because Peters and Richardson were opposites in so many respects, and above all on economic policy. Bolger did not want to get rid of Richardson. She had sizeable caucus support that he did not want to alienate, and she was a major plus with the business sector. Nor did Bolger want to get rid of Peters, and for an equally obvious reason: Peters was hugely popular with the public and with many of the party rank and file. Faced with these choices Bolger preferred to sit tight and drift. By allowing Peters to continue taking pot-shots at everything, Bolger looked weak. But he preferred that to the unknown terror of disciplining Peters.

While the National caucus sat pondering its leadership problem, Peters was energetically hammering away at his latest scandal. It was a story of which Peters had high hopes — so high that he was even going round telling people it would bring down the government. Unfortunately for Peters no one else found the story half as interesting as he did. The allegations concerned a $638,000 contract the Health Department had let to public relations firm Needham Consulting Group, two members of which — Ross Vintiner and Caroline Rennie — had been on Lange's personal staff. It was a hook on which to hang one of Peters' conspiracy theories.

Peters produced a briefing paper sent out to prospective bidders for the contract. The paper said that the Health Department had a policy of 'not establishing relationships with agencies which promote products or services which may be seen as being injurious to public health, particularly tobacco and alcohol'. According to Peters, Needham Consulting

Group's parent company, known as DDB Needham, promoted tobacco products. Peters' charge was that the group was afforded preferential treatment because of its links with Labour. 'Those linkages reek of corruption, cronyism and the very worst political preference,' he declared in Parliament.

Unfortunately for Peters the information he was relying upon regarding DDB Needham appeared to be out of date. Needham Consulting Group had provided a written assurance to the Health Department that it was setting up as a legally separate company. Interestingly Clark stated that the briefing paper to potential bidders had gone too far in implying the department had a hard-and-fast rule on alcohol or tobacco advertising; there was merely a preference not to award contracts to firms with such links. Though the department had been at fault in that respect, there was no evidence to suggest ethical impropriety.

The story did not bring down the government, or even cause it much difficulty. Peters was disappointed that few of the media took his scoop very seriously, and it was probably this disappointment which led him shortly afterwards to make a speech criticising the media. According to Peters, the media showed insufficient initiative in probing behind the news and were 'attracted by the baubles of immediacy'. Peters' accusation had a large element of the pot calling the kettle black, since 'baubles of immediacy' was rather a good description of his own political style. Many a lazy journalist has filed a Peters story, with little examination of its inherent worth, simply because the story was good copy. Journalists liked Peters because he did and said colourful things that provided entertaining reading, listening or watching. Peters liked journalists — and spent a huge amount of time with them — because they were the people who gave him what he craved — publicity. Peters and the media built each other up. Neither party had any incentive to point out that often enough the other was empty of content, attracted by the baubles of immediacy. Given their mutual independence, journalists were a strange target for Peters.

By now Bolger's rating as preferred Prime Minister had dropped in the latest Heylen poll to just six per cent. Peters was at 19 per cent. Bolger was uncomfortably close to that symbolic four per cent level, regarded as dire when it hung around the neck of Jim McLay. There was media speculation about Bolger's future. It may well have been that latest development which tempted Peters to make his fatal speech of 18 October. It was the most direct attack he had so far made on Bolger and his colleagues. Peters talked of a 'chronic lack of political leadership' in New Zealand:

New Zealanders are searching for effective political leadership. The polls suggest that has not been found . . . Where is the vision? Where are the policies designed to achieve that vision?. . . I must confess that distrust of politicians is not the exclusive phenomenon of the Labour Party.

Peters repeated his criticism that National could not 'sleepwalk to victory'. He said that if National wanted to win the next election it had to get 'hungrier, leaner, more innovative, more daring and strong enough to say to the public what our working alternatives are'. If it failed to do that the spectre of a third-term Labour government loomed large.

The speech was strong stuff. Understandably it enraged large sections of the caucus. It also enraged Bolger. A good many MPs made representations to him, saying he now had to act against Peters. A crisis atmosphere had developed among the small circle of Bolger's close advisers. At just six per cent in the opinion polls he could not afford to make a mistake. If he disciplined Peters and it turned out badly, Bolger could be history. If Peters stayed put and kept making those sorts of speeches, Bolger might well be history anyway.

Bolger was in a huddle with his closest advisers late into the night. Birch advised caution. Bolger's own staff urged action. By morning Bolger had made his decision. First, however, the ritual had to take place at caucus. As expected, Peters' colleagues laid into him over his speech. Peters defended himself badly: 'Read my speech and show me where it says . . . ' They had heard that line many times before; they were fed up with it. Trial over, Bolger delivered the verdict: Peters had lost his employment responsibility and was demoted from eight to 13 in the line-up. He was no longer on the front bench.

Peters was shaken. Some were to speculate that he had

deliberately provoked his leader into demoting him as part of a strategy of undermining Bolger. They did not know Peters. Being demoted was no part of his strategy, nor did he in the least imagine it would happen. Peters was a stunned man as he walked out of the caucus room. Close friend and flatmate Burdon, who was moving on to Peters' vacant front bench place, was also visibly upset. Further evidence that Peters was caught off guard was provided by his spur-of-the-moment reaction over the Maori Affairs responsibility. Bolger said that he had wanted Peters to keep Maori Affairs since he was the only Maori in caucus. Peters immediately labelled it tokenism and rejected Maori Affairs as well. He then regretted his decision and told Bolger he would keep Maori Affairs.

At his press conference Bolger said it was Peters' attack on his colleagues which had finally led to his demotion. As for Peters, he was apologising for nothing. It would be business as usual:

> There is not a person in this room who believes I'm going to change. I'm going on with what I believe is a proven record of performance. I will work harder than I have ever worked before and I hope in due course all of my caucus colleagues will see it that way.

It was to be a vain hope. Peters also made the amazing statement that nothing he had ever said was contrary to party policy. Despite being repeatedly questioned on his leadership ambitions by journalists, Peters refused to be drawn. He was still happy to be the member for Tauranga. And he was 'not going to desert those hundreds of thousands of forgotten New Zealanders' — another favourite Peters phrase.

Having manoeuvred his hero into the cactus, Laws soon afterwards abruptly left the national research unit. Officially he was leaving to chase the National Party nomination for Hawke's Bay, which he soon secured. However, there were unconfirmed reports that Laws had been sacked by Bolger. The speech that precipitated Peters' demotion certainly had a Laws sound to it, and it would have been more than understandable if Bolger had moved against Laws. Despite leaving the research unit, Laws would continue to do some work for Peters. But Peters would miss having Laws' full-time services. Over the next year Peters would come to rely more heavily for research and advice on his secretary, Canadian-born Sarah Neems.

The aftermath of the Peters sacking was fraught with tension and confusion. There was immediately intense media speculation about a possible challenge to Bolger's leadership from either the Peters or Richardson camps. Peters no more had the numbers for a challenge than he had ever had. The Richardson camp were looking to their numbers. Bolger became so worried about who might be talking to whom in which smoke-filled room that he began to wander the corridors late at night. At one point he even burst into a room of startled plotters, who then had to pretend they were talking about something else.

To add to the complications for Bolger, there was pressure from the lower-ranking MPs for a major reshuffle of his line-up. They wanted more responsibility for the less experienced caucus members and pruning of some of the dead wood. Implicit in this pressure was a threat by some of the lower-ranking MPs to withdraw support from Bolger if he did not come up with a satisfactory reshuffle. By this stage almost everyone in caucus was talking to the media about the internal ructions, either on or off the record. The general impression was one of chaos. Chief whip Robin Gray faxed an instruction out to all MPs not to talk to the media any more: all it succeeded in doing was to spur Peters and McCully to head down to the press gallery again.

Peters was true to his word about not changing his style. He stole a march on Bolger by meeting the new American ambassador, Della Newman, before Bolger had done so himself. Peters explained that it was not a big deal and that both he and Newman had been invited weeks ago to the same function at Weddell Crown. But Peters' appearance on the Paul Holmes television show afterwards was a strange way of playing the incident down. There he hinted at his reservations over National's policy on nuclear ships. A rattled Bolger lashed out at Peters again. Peters had also enigmatically cancelled a planned speech on foreign policy 'for the good of the party'. Possibly Peters had been talked out of giving the speech by one of his

97

close friends like Burdon. Many others, however, saw the cancelled speech as a publicity stunt. The cancellation was certainly consistent with the standard Peters technique of using suspense to build up an air of expectation on an issue.

In his first public speech since his demotion Peters was patronising enough to say that Bolger and the National caucus had the 'potential' to provide the vision, management and leadership New Zealand needed. Peters again called for greater use of referenda as a means of giving the public more say in decision making. He said, 'We must begin exploring a new political partnership; one that sees the public in the driving seat and not the politicians.' This would become an increasingly common public theme with Peters.

Suddenly one Heylen poll caused all the ructions in the National caucus to melt away. The poll showed National shooting back up to a very healthy lead over Labour. And — wonder of wonders! — Bolger had doubled his rating to 12 per cent while Peters had fallen back from 19 per cent to 16 per cent. The poll also showed less public support for a potential Richardson leadership than for a Bolger leadership. The poll was good news in every possible way for Bolger. He had moved against Peters and been rewarded by strengthening public support. He was through his sticky patch, and there would be no further real doubt over his leadership.

Peters must have been livid at the latest turn of events. The man who had just demoted him — the man for whom he had so little respect — had gained popularity at Peters' expense. Just as the Heylen poll was coming out Peters was leaving for a three-week trip to Britain. He had a lot to think about during that trip. He had lost his employment job and his place on the front bench. His strategy, if he ever had a strategy, had gone seriously awry. A re-think was needed. But there was little sign on Peters' return that he had done any strategic thinking. Instead, he was immediately back into the same old tactics that had failed to bring him the leadership. In a speech to bankers Peters continued his sniping at the Richardson economic line and advocated incentives for export development.

Increasingly for Peters it was now becoming sniping from the sidelines. Bolger's successful demotion of Peters had altered the whole balance of forces within caucus in favour of the Richardson camp. There was a new fiscal discipline; there were fewer extravagant promises. Burdon unhitched himself from Peters' wagon and made an attempt to look like a free marketeer. Caucus barometers like East began to drift in Richardson's direction. Peters' own employment policy was rewritten by Richardson and the new employment spokesman John Banks to give it a new focus. The commitment to put all long term unemployed on work schemes was removed from the policy. Early in the new year Richardson produced a document, National's Economic Vision, which was a clear statement of the economic strategy she advocated: price stability, reduced government spending and labour market reform. Bolger and most of caucus bought the document. The Richardson era was beginning.

But first Richardson had to get through a moment of real danger. The Reserve Bank Bill was about to go through its final stages in the House. The bill enshrined price stability as the principal objective of the bank. Supporting the bill was a confidence issue for Richardson. Bolger was opposed to the bill, as was Birch. At a critical caucus meeting there was a bare one vote majority in support of it. Muldoon was absent from that caucus, seriously ill in hospital. As for Peters, he had not turned up. Perhaps he thought he would lose the issue. As it turned out, Peters' absence was the difference between winning and losing. Bolger does not vote in caucus unless the votes are tied. Had Peters turned up, Bolger would have used his casting vote against the Reserve Bank Bill. Richardson would have resigned as finance spokeswoman and history would have been different.

The episode was a classic example of what was becoming a repeated phenomenon with Peters. He would put many hours into publicly promoting a policy stance — often in conflict with the party line. Yet usually he would not put ten minutes into actively engaging on an issue where it really made a difference — within caucus. Peters had made many speeches berating the 'mad monetarists' who wanted monetary policy to be aimed solely at price stability, but when there was a debate in caucus over a bill designed by those very same 'mad monetarists',

Peters showed no interest whatsoever. He took no part in any of the caucus forums in which the bill was discussed, even before his decision to stay away from the final caucus meeting.

So ended 1989. The new year saw some media discussion about a possible Bolger-Peters reconciliation in the context of Bolger's long-awaited reshuffle. Some senior caucus members were lobbying Bolger hard to promote Peters, feeling that he had served his period in exile. Peters had done nothing to earn promotion. However, there were unconfirmed reports that Bolger had weakened to the extent of offering Peters No. 11 — just two higher than his current rank. If Bolger did make that offer, Peters told him what to do with it. There was no reconciliation. In his state-of-the-nation speech at the Taradale Rotary Club, for which he had to miss part of National's three-day caucus meeting, Peters made plain his displeasure about how life in the National caucus was treating him:

> I have always been appalled by the two maxims given new political interns once they are elected to Parliament. The first is 'to breathe through your nose' — in other words quash your feelings till you have learned how to play the political game. The other . . . 'that an ounce of loyalty is worth more than a ton of cleverness'. In other words toe the party line, bury your integrity and you will find promotion an easier route, with all the financial rewards it brings.

The Taradale speech also signalled an important shift by Peters into mainly new territory. He had noted the deep mood of cynicism and mistrust in which the public now viewed its politicians. He sensed that reform of our political institutions was increasingly coming on to the political agenda, and he wanted to be out there in public on the right side. He put forward five suggestions for political reform:

- a move to petition-driven referenda
- the abolition of the conscience vote in the House, with 'moral' issues settled by referendum
- a bill of rights
- an upper house
- some form of proportional representation

Bolger, who alternated between trying to ignore Peters and snapping back at him, was, after the Taradale speech, in snapping back mood. He made a scarcely-veiled invitation to Peters to leave the caucus if he wished. 'He has symbolically left the caucus,' Bolger told journalists. 'He has to decide what his political future is. . . I'm going to run a political party to run the country. Winston has the choice whether to be in or out of it.' Two days later Bolger announced his reshuffle of responsibilities. Peters was unchanged in ranking at No. 13 and retained Maori Affairs. The rest of the reshuffle had a pronounced Richardson look, especially in the big promotion of Jenny Shipley to take on the social welfare job.

National was now moving quickly to make final decisions in key areas of its policy. Early in March the Economic Vision document was released, setting National's direction in monetary, fiscal and labour market policy. A few days afterwards came the dramatic U-turn on ANZUS, with National swinging in behind Labour's anti-nuclear policy.

In the following month Bolger announced the setting up of a new caucus committee to look at options for electoral reform. He stated publicly that he expected the committee would recommend holding a binding referendum on proportional representation. Bolger's sudden move to embrace electoral reform was the latest turn in what had been a long and meandering road towards proportional representation.

Peters turned up to few, if any, meetings of National's caucus committee. His contribution to the debate on electoral reform within the party was negligible, if not zero. One current National minister who has been closely involved with electoral reform cannot personally remember Peters ever, at any stage or in any year, making a single contribution on the issue in any caucus or Cabinet forum. Despite Peters' busy schedule precluding him from such involvement, he did find the time in the early months of 1990 to prepare and deliver a large number of speeches on electoral reform, repeating the calls he had made in his Taradale speech. In one of those speeches he described Parliament as 'a cringing vassal of the executive wearing the cloak of democratic artifice'.

Soon afterwards Peters brought into double figures the

number of people he had attacked under Parliamentary privilege. This time the target was Colin Carruthers, who had just been appointed a Queen's Counsel. Carruthers had acted for the Labour Party in the Wairarapa electoral petition. Peters claimed Carruthers was not paid by the Labour Party but instead had struck a deal with Labour that he would be made a QC. Peters' accusation appeared to be based on no perceptible evidence whatsoever. The next day Attorney-General David Lange made a statement in Parliament setting the record straight:

> The member for Tauranga also ventured the observation today that the Labour Party was broke at the time. Can I assure him that the Labour Party was not broke before it paid Mr Carruthers; after that it was slightly fractured. The Labour Party paid Mr Carruthers. In the past 24 hours the member for Tauranga has made an allegation that was specific in two respects: first that Mr Carruthers had not been paid; and, second, that the deal in relation to non-payment was that he would be appointed a Queen's Counsel. Both of those are totally incorrect. In my view it is a matter for the member's leader to judge whether the National Party would embrace that kind of abuse of Parliamentary privilege.

> The House had been the subject of comment from the member for Tauranga recently. He has referred to it as a place in which those people who fall short of normal practices and principles are given a licence to do as they will to the detriment of all their colleagues. In the past 24 hours the member for Tauranga has demeaned Parliament. I do not say he has demeaned himself: I think he has kept himself on a pretty constant plane. The House has suffered, although I do not think Mr Carruthers has. His integrity is unchallenged.

Whether or not Carruthers suffered, he joined Malcolm Douglas, Hugh McCarthy, Judge Casey, Phil Goff, Ann Hercus, Roger Douglas, Rod Deane, Ross Vintiner and Caroline Rennie in the Peters' Parliamentary privilege club.

Race relations issues were less prominent in 1990 than in earlier years. But in May there were further public ructions within National over the Treaty. Peters told the media he believed he had caucus support for wiping the Treaty from all existing legislation and settling grievances through direct negotiation between the government and Maori. He repeated his call for the Waitangi Tribunal to be downgraded to research unit status: its job would be to establish the historical facts. Naturally Peters' comments caused an eruption from the Maori members of the party. Bolger made a heroic attempt to reinterpret Peters' comments by saying they were in line with an earlier speech of his own. However, all Bolger had said was that 'our goal, *over time*, must be to eliminate all legislation based on race' — a statement quite different from Peters' call to immediately downgrade the Treaty. Behind the scenes Peters was being kicked into line, because the following day he claimed he had been misquoted. 'Misquotation' has been an endless feature of Peters' career.

Peters continued with his speeches questioning National's economic line, adding a topical new theme — corporatisation and privatisation. He questioned the wisdom of privatisation — especially of monopolies. At that time Labour were engaged in the deeply unpopular sale of Telecom New Zealand. By then Labour's deep unpopularity had extended to virtually everything. The economic gloom had intensified in the course of the year, and unemployment had continued to rise. Palmer's own personal popularity was sinking rapidly. National's lead in the opinion polls had widened from large to truly frightening.

Probably it was the supreme confidence in National's ranks that led to Peters gaining a speaking role in that year's national conference. The conference was the scene for the launch of National's Maori Affairs policy. Peters had not wanted the policy launch at the conference, and he was far from happy at having to share the presentation with Bolger. As it turned out, the launch went well, with no repeat of the farcical scenes of two years before. Both men received standing ovations for their speeches.

The Maori Affairs policy had certainly taken its time coming together. National's policy committee had waited for an age before they even received a piece of paper from Peters. The paper ended up being largely rewritten by Doug Graham, after heated tussles. Though the policy bore the marks of compromise, Peters largely lost his fight to eliminate the Treaty from legislation. The policy recognised the Treaty as the founding document of New Zealand, and aimed to settle all outstanding Maori claims by the turn of the century through direct negotiation between the Crown and Maori. Peters' main victory was the commitment to review the tribunal's power to make mandatory recommendations under the Treaty of Waitangi (State Owned Enterprises) Act, with a view to their abolition. In government, however, National would not alter the tribunal's mandatory powers.

In September National released its policy on electoral reform. The policy contained a commitment to a binding referendum on proportional representation. There was also a commitment to bring in non-binding citizens-initiated referenda. Peters had made little or no contribution to the formation of the policy within the party. That did not stop him from claiming credit for it, or making the highly arguable claim that he had been the first politician to put the issues in front of the public.

By this stage the election was only a few weeks away. Palmer had stepped down as Prime Minister in favour of the more telegenic Moore. From now until the election there would be a constant crossing of swords on economic policy between Peters on the one hand and Bolger and Richardson on the other. Bolger was never more solidly in line with Richardson than he was during those weeks. Peters' efforts, if they were aimed at anything other than his own self-promotion, were counter-productive, underscoring just how badly he had played his hand on economic policy. Every time Peters made an attack, Bolger felt bound to stand even more squarely in line with Richardson.

When Moore announced Labour's new growth agreement between the government and the unions, Peters claimed it would not work because the 0–2 per cent inflation goal remained. Since that target was also National policy, Peters was criticising his own party. The only difference between the parties was that Labour's price stability target was for 1992 while National's was for 1993. Since the Gulf War had broken out, prospects for higher imported inflation had raised the whole issue of inflation targets to special prominence. Soon afterwards Peters criticised National's price stability goal more directly, even going on the *Holmes* show on television to say that the goal was stupid, unrealistic and growth stifling. Bolger made no attempt to hide his displeasure. When asked by journalists how Peters' behaviour was affecting his Cabinet chances Bolger said, 'Oh, I'm sure we could find something that's not too demanding . . . because he's shown that tough targets are not for him.'

Peters' stance also earned him a long hammering from his colleagues in the next caucus meeting. By now he was well used to taking caucus punishment. Afterwards, no doubt enjoying the *frisson*, he still refused to commit himself to supporting his party's inflation target. He said that if he was asked for his views on monetary policy and inflation he would say they are well known, adding, 'There is nobody in New Zealand who expects Winston Peters to keep quiet.'

That last remark was at least true, if also typically Peters in self-dramatisation. Nor did he keep quiet. The very next day he was at it again, though this time he confined himself to slating the government's inflation target. And he kept it going day after day. He frequently attacked the 'clowns' in government who had set the target, even saying 'I do not know of one credible or reputable economist, business person or trader who believes that two per cent inflation is possible.' Anyone who believed in the target was obviously not 'credible or reputable' in Peters' eyes. Yet how credible or reputable did Peters' own prediction turn out to be? As it happens, 1992 was the year that would see sustainable, non-inflationary growth take hold in New Zealand. By the end of 1992 inflation was well under two per cent, and was one of the lowest rates in the OECD. Economic growth, at around two per cent, was above the OECD average. The following year, in 1993, inflation remained well under two per cent while growth was between four and five per cent — almost the highest rate in the OECD. It made nonsense of Peters' claims that the inflation target was impossible, and that it would kill economic growth. For all his condemnation of the 'spotty-faced economic theorists' in government, Peters' own predictions had a woeful record of failing to measure up against the facts.

Other issues reared their heads during the campaign. The

seriously deteriorating fiscal position led Bolger and Richardson to state that not all of National's spending commitments would be implemented immediately, but would be phased in over the next three years. It was an entirely responsible position for National to take in the circumstances. But it provided Peters with a chance to wax indignant. Showing a new-found conversion to sound caucus processes, Peters complained that Bolger and Richardson would be acting unilaterally if they postponed the commitments. 'When [Bolger] stood up and said, "The pain stops on October 27" what did he mean if we're not going to do anything — if we're not going to do the things we promised?'

Peters' own programme in the run-up to election day was a campaign in itself, and in some ways more interesting than the predictable result being played out between the party leaders. Peters swept through 22 electorates in 30 days. He drew big and enthusiastic crowds. In putting together his timetable he even showed more co-operation with National's head office than he had done at the 1987 election. He insisted, however, on visiting only electorates where the hall would be large enough and where a big media contingent would be present — including television cameras. But Peters' hopes of substantial coverage from the television news editors were dashed: he more than once complained that the six o'clock news showed only the party leaders.

Perhaps it was this lack of recognition — a feeling that he was not enough in the limelight — that caused Peters to make attention-grabbing statements all through the campaign. There was a public difference with Bolger over Bastion Point. Soon afterwards Peters stated that National should be worried by the latest opinion poll, which had shown a narrowed difference between the two main parties. After Richardson had said National was looking at ways of encouraging solo parents into employment, Peters pointedly defended solo mothers, calling them 'the real heroines'. Peters also kept up his attack on the inflation target.

In his visit to the Laws territory of Taradale Peters was tempted to make the most direct swipes at those who had crossed him. He again complained about television focus on the leaders, saying that Bolger's 'best-remembered performance was with a foul-mouthed sickness beneficiary who fought off four policemen'. It was a phrase with a real Laws ring to it. Quite likely this remark riled Bolger personally more than all of Peters' statements on the inflation target, and it showed just how dangerous an influence Laws could be on Peters. Peters also made a catty reference to John Banks, the man who had taken on the employment job after Peters was demoted. Peters described Banks as 'a minor National Party MP'. Two days before the election Peters summed up the campaign as 'deathly dull'.

Much of Peters' behaviour during the campaign defies rational analysis. Constant sniping, just days before Bolger would be drawing up his Cabinet, was hardly designed to better his prospects. It is possible Peters was so blind to anything other than his own huge popularity that he thought he could walk into Cabinet no matter what he said. Deep down, one part of Peters may never really have wanted to be in Cabinet at all. The political style that had brought Peters his popularity was based almost wholly on being *against* things. If he made it into Cabinet he would suddenly have to be part of a government that was forced to take responsibility and make hard decisions in an extremely difficult economic environment. Subconsciously Peters may have been recoiling from that prospect. But however one looks at it, Peters' behaviour during the campaign remains a puzzle.

Peters may have been unpopular with his colleagues, but he did not want for popularity in the Tauranga electorate. On election night he boosted his winning margin to around 8600 — the highest majority of any National MP. National captured 68 out of the 99 seats in Parliament. It was the biggest landslide in New Zealand's history.

The major talking point was now Peters' chances of making Cabinet. On any normal criteria he would have been left out, but he remained one of the most popular politicians in the country. Bolger had to weigh up the costs of Peters roaming freely in Cabinet against the costs of his roaming even more freely on the back benches. It was a horrible choice. The huge size of National's new caucus suggested, if anything, that there were added dangers of Peters becoming a focus of discontent among backbenchers if he were left out of Cabinet. On the other hand, Peters' total inability so far to plan a strategic campaign against Bolger within caucus suggested that danger could easily be overrated. On balance the arguments for leaving Peters out of Cabinet were strongest. Including him would give him an unwarranted legitimacy and status. It would most likely set the scene for a messy falling out, with added difficulties further down the track. And it would expose him to information he could later use against the government.

Many people gave Bolger advice — solicited and unsolicited — over his decision. Latimer wanted Bolger to leave Peters out of Cabinet and take on the Maori Affairs portfolio himself. Many others in Maoridom wanted Peters there as Minister of Maori Affairs simply because of his race: he was the only Maori in caucus with a prospect of making Cabinet. Richardson was adamant Peters should be left out. Birch and others urged a more cautious line. In the end Bolger's cautious nature prevailed — Peters was included in Cabinet, but at the low ranking of 17. It was his second demotion. His sole portfolio was Maori Affairs.

It was Barry Soper who broke the news to Peters. On being told he had made Cabinet, Peters' first question to Soper was not, 'What portfolio do I have?' but 'What ranking am I?' When he heard it was No. 17 Peters was not a happy man. He looked gloomy during the swearing-in ceremony. By then he had already made it clear to the media that he would not be backing away from the public stances he had taken in Opposition. Collective Cabinet responsibility would not be for Winston Peters. After he had been sworn in Birch turned to his old friend Bolger and whispered a sentiment that most in the room must have been feeling: 'Too late now.'

CHAPTER EIGHT

Ministerial Days

November 1990–May 1991

*T*here were two distinct phases to the first three years of the Bolger administration. In the period up to the 1991 Budget, major progress was made on an agenda for reform. A range of social welfare benefits were cut, abolished or more tightly targeted. The government formulated in broad outline its reforms to health provision, and to housing. A new discipline was exerted on departmental expenditure. The Employment Contracts Act was enacted and price stability was largely cemented into place. In that period, the government may not have fully completed the economic reform programme first begun by Douglas. But it did enough to put in place the conditions for sustained economic recovery.

Richardson's 1991 'Mother of all Budgets' was the last of its reforming line. After that, unnerved by the sharply contracting economy in the first half of the year, and alarmed by the hostile public reaction to its social policy changes, the government battened down the hatches — even reversing some of the Budget measures. The second phase of the Bolger administration had begun. It was a phase dominated by a continually improving economy. The economic upturn had begun around the time of the 1991 Budget. As time went on the recovery grew increasingly stronger, aided by lower interest rates and the huge success of the Employment Contracts Act. Even unemployment, which had risen steeply in the government's early months, began by 1993 to trend in the right direction.

The improving economy was a major political boost for the

government. But it did not in the end prove quite enough to rescue its fortunes. It never succeeded in persuading enough New Zealanders that the tough fiscal measures of its first year in office had been fair or justified. Two albatrosses in particular hung around the government's neck — superannuation and the new health charging regime.

National in Opposition had repeatedly promised to repeal the superannuation surtax. It was a promise that should never have been made, and it was opposed by some from the outset. But National were keen to buy the votes of wealthy superannuatants. Bolger was particularly identified with this promise: he talked about repealing the surtax — 'no ifs, no buts and no maybes'. Bolger had also talked repeatedly in Opposition about honesty and credibility. In his final television debate with Moore, when the cue came for his most important message to New Zealanders, Bolger looked straight into the camera, gave his most sincere look, and talked about honesty and the importance of politicians keeping to their promises.

Life for Bolger became more complicated after the election. There were two major problems with keeping to the promise. It would cost big money at a time when the government was already fully stretched trying to contain an expenditure blowout. And when the government was cutting the incomes of many of the poorest in society, giving money away to well-off superannuatants scarcely sounded like good public relations.

National were in a bind of their own making. Breaking a promise was bad enough, but they made things even worse for themselves in the way in which it was done. The 1991 Budget not only failed to repeal the surcharge, it stiffened substantially the income-testing component of national superannuation. Amazingly, some superannuatants now faced an effective marginal tax rate on their earnings of 90 per cent.

It is hard to imagine just how a Cabinet of 20, few of whom were complete idiots, could have come up with something so extreme. How on earth did it happen? It certainly was not for lack of time spent studying the options: officials crunched through a vast number different scenarios. Yet after wandering all round the garden, ministers ended up right in the compost heap. Dislocation had occurred between officials and ministers on a grand scale and, bizarre as it may sound, few if any ministers had any idea they were looking at options involving such crippling effective marginal tax rates. The final option chosen had the stiffest rate of them all, 90 per cent, and had been flung on the Cabinet table at the very last moment by Wyatt Creech. The reasoning went as follows: an option involving a relatively large income threshold before the surcharge applied, combined with a relatively steep rate of abatement for superannuation, would affect the smallest number of people. Cabinet accepted Creech's argument that punishing a small number of superannuatants severely was less bad than punishing a large number of superannuatants moderately: it added up to fewer votes lost in the crude political calculus of winners and losers.

It may have seemed plausible at the time, but the howls of outrage that greeted the 90 per cent abatement rate told ministers something rather different. Before long, strong pressure from the back bench had forced a backdown on the abatement rate, though even then the option finally settled upon by the government, after a renewed bout of angst, still had a tougher income test than the regime they had inherited. Bolger was permanently maimed by his broken promise on superannuation and further damaged by the shambles over the abatement rate. To add insult to very considerable injury, the fiscal position eventually improved so much that by 1993 Bolger must have bitterly regretted breaking his promise, just as he must have bitterly regretted making it in the first place. National's whole sorry performance over the surtax did nothing at all to improve the respect in which politicians were held, and was eventually to provide Peters with an important new political constituency — the well-off elderly.

Scarcely less damaging to the government was the deep unpopularity of the new health-charging regime. For good reasons and bad, it was hated by the public. Health Minister Simon Upton's job of selling the wider health reforms was always going to be a battle and it was made still more difficult by the added controversy of the new part charges. To make matters worse for the government, Helen Clark was bruisingly effective in the role of Opposition health spokeswoman. Even when, late in the piece, Birch-the-kneecapper was brought in as Health Minister to replace Upton-the-rational-persuader, it made no difference. From beginning to end health was fraught with political trouble for the government.

What role did Peters play in these great events as a member of the National Cabinet? The short answer is very little. Bolger had placed Peters on none of the really powerful Cabinet committees, which meant that the Monday Cabinet meeting was the crucial time for Peters' input into government decision making. But his participation was erratic to say the least. Despite having all weekend to read his Cabinet papers, he often arrived with them still in their sealed envelopes. Sometimes they were still there at the end of the meeting. Peters also slept a good deal of the time.

In Peters' defence, Cabinet meetings *were* boring. Bolger's style of chairmanship would have driven a saint to distraction. Everyone had their own way of coping with the slow patches. McKinnon and Richardson passed each other humorous notes like naughty schoolchildren. Upton scribbled away at his *Dominion* article. Graham's witty cartoons and caricatures of his colleagues entertained those in his immediate vicinity. But Peters was the only one who actually slept. Nor did he even give himself time to get bored. A minister who sat near him recalls that in most meetings he 'fell asleep the moment he got there and woke up in time for morning tea'. It brings a new perspective to one of Peters' favourite sayings: 'Wake up and smell the coffee.'

Even when he was awake Peters rarely said much at Cabinet, nor was his input regarded by his colleagues as being of very high quality. Every so often he would give his colleagues a general lecture. But on an issue-by-issue basis Peters scarcely participated. It is also significant that he passed up the opportunity to attend the two-day weekend Cabinet meeting at Vogel House held to discuss the social policy reforms in the 1991 budget.

By failing to take part, Peters was repeating the strategic error he had made in Opposition. Indeed as minister he was to repeat almost *every* strategic error he had made in Opposition. He would blithely contradict the party line, proceed without reference to Cabinet, and communicate with his colleagues as much through the news media as through any other channel. Certainly his actions on becoming a minister showed little sign of his having thought seriously about a new strategy in the light of past events. Either he saw no need to change, or — more probably — he was constitutionally unable to change.

Peters' period in Cabinet can be divided into two phases. In the early phase his main initiative was the policy document Ka Awatea. Its highly unorthodox launch constituted his principal attempt at self-promotion over this period. Then, with his poll rating falling, he reverted to the more familiar territory of taking direct public tilts at his colleagues. It was the old familiar story in a different setting.

Peters' performance in Cabinet may have done nothing to improve his standing among his colleagues, but it was to substantially improve his standing among Maori. When in Opposition, he had been regarded with considerable suspicion by Maori. His attacks on Wetere and his department had been widely viewed as negative and Peters was seen as using race issues to promote himself with the European electorate, at the expense of Maori. Nor was Peters much regarded by Maori as 'one of us'. He did not speak Maori and when asked if he spoke it, he often replied that he was learning it. Whatever attempts to learn Maori he may have made, they obviously did not rank high among his priorities. He never did become a fluent speaker, something which Wetere more than once showed up in the House at question time by launching into an answer in Maori — to Peters' embarrassment. Nor was Peters much at ease with other aspects of Maori culture. He was unsure of marae protocol, and lived in dread of making a mistake.

Becoming Minister of Maori Affairs completely changed the political dynamics of his relationship with Maori. No longer was he an Opposition politician whose basic role was to make trouble for the government. Now he was a minister with a constituency — Maori. Like most ministers, he tended to regard his prestige as bound up with the size of his department and the resources he could acquire for his constituency. Because of the new set of incentives he faced, Peters would see his reputation among Maori growing rapidly.

Peters now had an office in the Beehive. He had lost the services of Laws, who had become the new MP for Hawke's Bay, but he had a much larger personal staff than he had enjoyed in Opposition. His secretary in Opposition, Sarah Neems, came into the Beehive as his personal private secretary. She ran the office and controlled access to Peters and was also his main source of political advice among his personal staff. The work of the office quickly became heavily geared towards media strategy as opposed to policy. Preparing speeches became a key task. Unfortunately the office was often disorganised — Peters would sometimes miss meetings of the Cabinet committee on Treaty of Waitangi issues, a committee he chaired.

Peters' status-consciousness was reflected in the formal manner he adopted as minister. He always called people by their title. All Peters' correspondence was couched in very formal terms. Personal staff were not permitted to call him by his first name. These habits were unusual for a Cabinet minister of his generation. He also had a graciousness of manner in dealing with visitors. Seating arrangements were important to him and were planned with care. Naturally he took just as much care over his own appearance as he had always done, continuing to wash and iron his own shirts and spending considerable time over the treatment of his suits. Under the new demands of life as a minister he also made a serious attempt to improve his physical fitness. He knocked off smoking for a while, and even gave up his favourite drink, scotch. He installed a rowing machine in his office and worked out on it twice a day.

Life as a minister certainly had its attractions. His salary doubled and, as he has never been a rich man, he must have enjoyed the extra spending power. The old gang of Burdon, East, McKinnon and Peters moved out of the house they were sharing, each going into a ministerial residence. Peters' residence was the Plaza International Hotel. For a few weeks Louise and the two children joined him there, but the experiment did not work out and they soon returned to Tauranga.

Sometimes old insecurities showed through. Although there was a debugging service available free from within the government, Peters paid a private firm to search his office for bugs. None were found. At other times, despite now having the status of a minister of the Crown, he would feel intimidated by certain audiences where the territory was alien to him. He would feel shy in the presence of highly qualified people or those with high status occupations such as doctors or diplomats.

Peters would try some status subversion in his first and only one-on-one meeting with Richardson as a Cabinet minister. It was called very early on by Richardson to discuss possible fiscal savings in the Maori Affairs portfolio. Beehive protocol has it that when two ministers have a meeting it takes place in the office of the highest ranked minister. Richardson was ranked four, Peters 17. She naturally expected the meeting to be held in her office. After Peters had failed to turn up, she discovered that he and his officials was sitting immovable downstairs in his office, waiting for her to come down. *She* was the one who wanted the meeting to take place, so Mohammed ended up going to the mountain. It did not help the atmosphere at the meeting, which got nowhere.

Peters' first few weeks as a minister were not especially eventful. On taking office he immediately stated that it was National's policy to abolish the mandatory powers of the Waitangi Tribunal with regard to claims over state-owned enterprises. This was not strictly accurate, since National had said only that it would *review* the powers of the tribunal. He also floated again his old idea of reducing the tribunal to a research body, but Latimer threatened to take the Crown to court again if the mandatory powers of the tribunal were removed, and that seemed to put an end to the matter.

Peters confined himself to just one flick at National's economic policy in the weeks before Christmas. It came in the context of the news that British MP Michael Heseltine was challenging Margaret Thatcher as Conservative Party leader and Prime Minister. Peters had earlier praised Britain as a country achieving good results with policies that were more pragmatic than in New Zealand. Now, with the British economy in recession and Thatcher under siege from the Tory 'wet' Heseltine, Peters changed his story: he was critical of Thatcher's 'strict monetarist line', saying it had failed to work.

A more serious attack from Peters came early in the new

year in his state-of-the-nation speech at Taradale. This time he again turned his guns on the Reserve Bank, which had just pushed up short-term interest rates. He slammed the bank's policies as destroying economic development. 'Unless Dr Brash and his staff can be convinced to change,' he said, 'then they must be changed themselves, otherwise there will be no escape from the straitjacket.' For good measure Peters claimed National's December initiative had been no more effective than Labour's packages in boosting business confidence.

By now Peters was seriously worried about his standing in the opinion polls. Simply by becoming a Cabinet minister he had dropped several percentage points as preferred Prime Minister. The role of Opposition politician, in which he had thrived, was denied him, while the prosaic business of government was inevitably not matching up as a vehicle for self-promotion. From Peters' point of view a lot now hung on the major policy initiative he was planning. In his Waitangi Day speech he spoke of a blueprint for Maori development to be released later that month. He said nothing to his colleagues about it. February drew to an end with no release having taken place.

At the beginning of March, however, Peters' colleagues were surprised to read in the media of an imminent launch of a major plan for Maori development. The plan represented 'dramatic changes in direction and policy'. Peters' colleagues knew nothing of this launch. Cabinet had certainly not approved any 'dramatic' changes in policy — or any changes at all. Peters was acting totally without reference to Cabinet.

The document to be launched was Ka Awatea. It had been written at Peters' request by a committee of three people: Auckland lawyer Denese Henare, Mary Anne Thompson of the Ministry of Maori Affairs and Leith Comer of the Iwi Transition Agency. The report had not been written to Peters' instructions; it was the genuine collective view of the three authors. Peters saw the group only once while the report was coming together. Typically, he was not easily persuaded that the report should contain a section on the Treaty. But the rest of the report pleased him, and he seized upon it eagerly.

Ka Awatea contained both problem identification and

recommendations for action. It brought together a wide range of social and economic data showing the relative under-performance of Maori, and it was also critical of many existing programmes for them. It was particularly critical of the Maori Access training scheme and the Mana Enterprises business development scheme, describing them as poorly focused and lacking in accountability.

Ka Awatea recommended that a new specialist Maori agency be set up, drawing on resources from the existing ministry and the Iwi Transition Agency. The new agency would have both policy and operational functions, the latter to include a training unit and an economic resource development unit, whose activities would supersede Maori Access and Mana Enterprises. Also included in the agency would be an education commission and a health promotion unit. The report recommended that the Minister of Maori Affairs 'assume the role of providing the co-ordination and focus for collective political commitment and take overall responsibility for ensuring the achievement of government's outcome for Maori'.

Even with a more effective Maori Affairs Minister than Peters, selling to Cabinet the idea of a Maori superministry would not have been easy. Parts of the report were inconsistent with National's manifesto, which, for instance, had stated that Maori training would be integrated within National's post-school education and training structure. That seemed to rule out a training unit in the Maori agency. The superministry proposal also ran counter to the general trend in the government sector of separating out policy advice from operational functions. The biggest problem Ka Awatea faced, however, was the minister who would be its advocate. Because of the suspicion with which Peters was regarded by his colleagues, they immediately saw Ka Awatea as a grab for power and resources on his part. It did not help either that Peters had in the past criticised 'separatist' policies for Maori. This made his use of Ka Awatea even less sincere in the eyes of his colleagues.

Despite these difficulties Peters chose precisely the wrong strategy for getting Ka Awatea implemented. By launching it as if it were policy before having taken it through Cabinet, Peters put himself even more offside with his colleagues. Understandably they saw the premature launch as another Peters tactic for gaining maximum publicity at the expense of a sound policy process. Perhaps the generation of publicity *was* Peters' main motivation. Perhaps he reasoned that putting himself out on a limb was the best way to bring his colleagues along with him. If so, he reasoned wrong — there were eager hands waiting to saw the limb off.

As soon as the launch was announced Bolger was stressing to the media that Ka Awatea was not government policy. The day before the launch, on demand from his colleagues, Peters supplied Cabinet with just the report's executive summary. Those MPs not in the Cabinet were even less well informed: they had seen nothing whatsoever of the document and Peters had declined to brief them.

For the launch itself no expense was spared. Peters had hired a public relations firm and an advertising firm had also been involved. He was breaking new ground. In the past, spending on public relations and advertising had occurred to promote government policy. Now it was being undertaken to promote a report that might hypothetically become government policy. Half of Maoridom seemed to be at the launch. There was a media lock-up, a luncheon and a press conference.

When quizzed at the press conference about the unusual process he was following, Peters gave the classic populist response:

> The future I seek to outline involves a bit of straightforward consultation and consensus, first with the people who I'm meant to be serving, the 450,000 Maori out there. The report is for their own consideration as well, and then, of course, because the country is involved in the report's implementation, I would hope I would get a response from the country. And then it's for caucus and for Cabinet to decide, because then they will be better able to judge the merit of the report. I've told the country today. Now am I to be condemned for my openhanded democracy?

Not only did Peters say he was confident of getting the report accepted. He went further:

I will stake my political career. I am staking my political career
on it because it is what this country needs.

The response from Maori was as Peters had hoped. Not only
did they like the substance of Ka Awatea, they were delighted
at having the report presented to them before it was presented
to Cabinet. Peters' standing in Maoridom rose immediately.
The price tag for the whole exercise was more problematical. At
first Peters refused even to give a budgeted figure, saying the
cost would come in well under budget. 'I regard this report as a
legitimate use of public funds,' he said; adding, in one of his
unintended self-parodies, 'at no point is there one photograph
of me.'

At the time Peters made that comment the production costs
of Ka Awatea were already running well over the initial budget
of $170,000. Papers released to the author under the Official
Information Act show that costs were overrunning because
Peters had directed work on Ka Awatea to continue past the
initial planned completion date right up to the launch date. On
top of production costs there were advertising and public
relations costs, and other costs surrounding the launch, which
no one appeared to have budgeted for. Though as yet there was
no written advice to Peters from his officials that costs were
overrunning, Peters' statement that they were coming in under
budget is remarkable.

In the end Peters' office gave out the price of the
preparation and launch of Ka Awatea at $289,000. Bolger
confirmed this cost to Parliament. There were accusations from
the Opposition that the true cost of the launch was much
higher. Prebble disputed Peters' statement that two-thirds of
the 150 Maori at the launch had paid their own air fares,
claiming that Iwi Transition Agency officials had been at the
airport handing out first-class tickets. He also claimed that the
James Cook and other hotels on the night of the launch had
been 'awash with Maori' and that none had paid their own bills.
Despite these claims, the Opposition could not themselves
come up with up with firm evidence to support a higher figure.

Yet the Opposition were right in their suspicion that the
costs of Ka Awatea were understated. The figure of $289,000

cannot be traced to written advice to Peters from his ministry or the Iwi Transition Agency. According to papers obtained under the Official Information Act, the total cost of Ka Awatea was over $500,000. The Ministry of Maori Affairs spent around $280,000, mostly on the production side. On top of that came a payment of $106,000 to the public relations firm Logos Consultants, and a payment of $116,000 to Ayer Advertising. There were also payments for travel and other expenses for some of those who attended the launch. On Peters' instruction all of these costs were picked up by the Iwi Transition Agency.

In relying on Peters' advice Bolger unwittingly failed to give the House the full cost of Ka Awatea. Peters' own statement to the House that the cost of employing public relations consultants for the launch was $122,000 is also a puzzle; Peters may have been attributing only part of the total cost of advertising and public relations to the launch itself. One thing is certain: if Peters the Opposition politician had come across such a contradictory set of numbers he would have been thunderously demanding heads to roll and a full public inquiry.

Once Ka Awatea had been launched, Bolger insisted that its recommendations should go through a normal Cabinet process. An officials committee was appointed to examine the implications of the report. A few weeks after the launch Peters was telling the House that progress on the government's consideration of Ka Awatea was 'nothing short of spectacular'. By that stage the Cabinet strategy committee had not even considered the officials report, which in any case was asking for further guidance from ministers. When the strategy committee did meet, Peters had an ally in Birch, but Bolger and other ministers were sceptical about the superministry proposal. Officials were asked to do further work on options for delivering services to Maori. One week later Peters was hinting publicly that his colleagues were being obstructive, and stating that Maori patience was being stretched by the long wait. He repeated his call to resign if Ka Awatea did not go through. Colleagues saw his comments as an attempt to use the media to put pressure on the Cabinet process.

The following week the second officials report was up before the strategy committee. It contained three options. Option A was close to the recommendations in Ka Awatea. Option B did not give the Maori agency an operational role in the long run. Instead, the operational functions would be carried out through other government departments, or 'mainstreamed'. However, option B also envisaged the Maori agency carrying out some short-term programmes in the transition to mainstreaming. Option C went further in confining the role of the Maori agency, restricting it to policy advice from the very start.

The strategy committee chose option B — substantially a rejection of the Maori superministry. After the meeting both Peters and his opponents got their slant on the meeting out into the media. Peters followed that up with an on-the-record statement that Ka Awatea had gone through the strategy committee in its entirety. This assertion was clearly misleading. Luckily for Peters, his talk of resignation had left him with a number of 'outs'. As *The Dominion*'s Richard Long was to astutely note — at one time or another in his career Peters had expressed a preference for all three options in the officials paper. That meant he could always claim his views had prevailed.

Over the weekend there was public slanging between Peters and Bolger as the media continued to highlight the differences between the two sides. Bolger gave a clear 'mainstreaming' message in his address to a National Party divisional conference. In his own speech Peters hit out at 'political tyre-kickers'. As well as making the familiar invocation of Winston Churchill, he reached further back in time to no less a personage than Jesus Christ, pointing out that both men had been disbelieved by their peers. He quoted Churchill as saying the problem with winning the war was that so many of his colleagues tried to stop him.

The next day Cabinet duly confirmed option B. Announcing the decision, Bolger made it clear that the Cabinet had chosen mainstreaming: the current programmes of the Maori Affairs Ministry and the Iwi Transition Agency would soon be disestablished and transferred to other departments. The Maori agency itself would run just pilot programmes. Bolger's announcement was in line with the Cabinet decision. Peters put out quite a different slant. He claimed he had been given two years in which to transfer the programmes, and that he did not need to hand them over to other departments if he thought they would not run them properly. Neither of these elements was in the Cabinet minute. Bolger and Peters were even at odds over funding: Bolger made no commitment whereas Peters said total funding would not be cut in dollar terms.

Despite Peters' attempts to put a brave face on it, his superministry proposal had clearly been rejected. It had not been a good month for him in other respects either. He had been the minister most associated with the government's decision to write-off $100 million in Maori loans, mainly to failed kiwifruit ventures. The loans had been made under the Muldoon administration. Peters was dealing with someone else's mess, and the decision taken was probably the right one. But there was caucus discontent over perceived favourable treatment for Maori.

Since the launch of Ka Awatea there had been precious little good news. Peters had gained in popularity with Maori, but they are only a small fraction of the total population. Peters was well aware of the electoral arithmetic. Already his poll rating as preferred Prime Minister was slipping again. The following month it would fall to just six per cent — his lowest rating for three years. Peters' Cabinet colleagues were thoroughly enjoying his discomforture. Boxed in by a limited constituency and the conventions of collective Cabinet responsibility, Peters almost looked a spent force.

He decided on a change in tactics. So far he had only intermittently crossed the Cabinet line. Now he took out his heavy guns and started polishing them. He would be aiming them at his colleagues.

CHAPTER NINE

Sacked

May 1991–June 1992

*I*T WAS late in May. Peters started off with two tilts at Justice Minister Doug Graham. First, he complained publicly that responsibility for the negotiation of Treaty settlements had been taken off him and given to Graham. It came as news to everybody that Peters had ever been given that responsibility. The previous government had set up a unit within the Justice Department to deal with precisely that issue, and it had given ministerial responsibility for Treaty negotiations to the Justice Minister. That was to avoid the conflict of interest inherent in having the ministerial advocate for Maori also the negotiating minister for the Crown on the Treaty. A week later Peters was publicly protesting that electoral reform needed to be enacted by 1993 in order to fulfil National's manifesto commitment. No one else in the government believed National was committed to such a timetable, and it was logistically impossible to move to some form of proportional representation by 1993.

Three weeks before the 1991 Budget Peters made a direct attack on government economic policy. He attacked the 'slash and cut' mentality, argued against reducing the deficit in the middle of a recession, and complained that policy had been captured by free-market ideologues. The term 'mad monetarist' was dragged out again. Peters even took advantage of a misreporting of a Richardson speech to take a gratuitous swipe at her. The next day he was at it again, attacking the concept of user pays.

Bolger, though angry, said nothing. For the first time there was serious media discussion about how long Peters could expect to stay in Cabinet making that type of speech. Naturally the Opposition was thoroughly enjoying the spectacle: Moore suggested Peters' behaviour was part of a plan to get himself ejected from Cabinet. The 'provocation' theory might have seemed the only rational explanation for such behaviour, but in fact Peters had no such plan. When he downplayed to the media suggestions Bolger might sack him, he was perfectly sincere. He would be the last person to see what was coming his way.

There was even a warning from the man who had once picked Peters to be New Zealand's first Maori Prime Minister — Sir Robert himself. Muldoon had cooled more than somewhat towards his young admirer ever since Peters had taken up the cause of electoral reform — for Muldoon one of the worst forms of heresy. Picking up on Peters' comment that if he were sacked from Cabinet he would still be the member for Tauranga, Muldoon told *Dominion* journalist Mike Munro, 'Maybe that's what he'll get.' Munro asked him what he would have done with someone like Peters in his Cabinet:

> Muldoon: 'Frankly I don't know . . . he might of been some value in a hangi.'
>
> Munro: 'How far in?'
>
> Muldoon: 'Right in.'

Whatever people might have been saying, Bolger was unlikely to sack Peters just before the Budget. Meanwhile there were more Peters provocations for Bolger to put up with. In a number of forums Peters publicly associated with backbench dissenters such as Gilbert Myles, Hamish MacIntyre and Laws. Already there was talk of some MPs leaving the National caucus. Peters said that the threat of defections was real, and warned National to allow more open debate in its ranks. Myles and MacIntyre would shortly leave the caucus and form their own party, condemning themselves to an entirely predictable political oblivion. Laws, though not the most prudent of political operators, at least had the survival skills to avoid that fate.

There may not have been as much open debate in the party as Peters would like. But there was plenty of open debate about Peters' own future, if nothing else. His old enemy Latimer called for Bolger to assume the Maori Affairs portfolio, stating that Maori were losing out while Bolger and Peters were at odds. But Latimer appeared to be in a minority of one in Maoridom: other Maori leaders came out solidly in support of Peters. Bolger for the first time hinted that Peters should consider leaving the Cabinet if he could not support government policy. Peters made it plain he would not be resigning, even making the astonishing statement that 'My speeches stand on all fours with the party policy.' He blamed the news media for misinterpreting him.

Journalists were misinterpreting his next speech as well. Peters had said: 'Unless we want our domestic economy to continue to contract with all the negative social and economic spin-offs which inevitably result, there is a need for policymakers to begin to loosen the choking monetary reins which govern this economy.' Journalists recklessly imagined he was criticising government policy, and they had to be put right by another Peters denial.

Peters' Cabinet colleagues were as bad as journalists in constantly misinterpreting his speeches. Already there had been a number of attacks on him in Cabinet, and there would be several more. The two Dougs — Kidd and Graham — said their piece. Neither had been able to stomach Peters for a long time. Richardson was not shy either at getting stuck into him. Peters' standard defence was the same one they had tired of long ago: 'Read my speech . . .' On those occasions Peters' old flatmates tended to be the most conciliatory towards him, if anyone was. But the general tone of the messages Peters was receiving from his Cabinet colleagues was loud and clear.

Kicking Peters on a Monday may well have had therapeutic value to the ministers concerned, but there was little evidence those attacks had any effect on the man himself. One of his most striking characteristics was his all but total imperviousness to the verbal batterings he received from colleagues. The value of the Cabinet attacks could only be as a demonstration to Bolger of how unhappy his ministers were over Peters' behaviour. Bolger was the only person with the power to sack Peters, but, for the moment, he was not committing himself.

The Budget came and went, with Peters less than wholehearted in his public support for its contents. Then in a few days came a whole series of speeches and statements criticising economic policy. He attacked the government's fiscal policy and the 'fanciful theorists' who wanted to reduce the burden of the welfare state. Picking up on calls from manufacturers for greater government involvement in the economy, he urged a more 'hands-on' approach and castigated 'laissez-faire' economics. When worsening statistics for Maori unemployment came out Peters rightly refused to take personal responsibility, but made it his cue for another swipe at government policy. Perhaps for the first time, he accused National of not following the economic policies in its manifesto. This would eventually become a constant Peters criticism, and it doubtless gained some credit simply because it was repeated so often. Yet Peters' claim had no basis to it: National's economic policy was almost wholly in line with its manifesto. The price stability target that Peters opposed was clearly spelt out. So was the policy — also opposed by Peters — of balancing the budget by reducing government spending. Time and again it was Peters who was out of line with the manifesto, not his Cabinet colleagues.

Peters' latest statements earned him the strongest attack he had yet received in Cabinet. Richardson did her lecture about how he was detracting from the government's strategy and from its overall public positioning. Falloon did his pep talk about how everyone had to be part of the team. Peters did his 'read my speech' and 'I'm in line with the manifesto' defences. Graham did his lawyerly cross-examination of Peters on the minutiae of his speeches: what had he meant by *this* statement?; how could he reconcile it with *that* statement? Peters floundered. But those who wanted him sacked immediately were disappointed.

For reasons known only to him, Bolger passed up the opportunity to deal to Peters. The time may have seemed right, especially as Bolger had already signalled that he would soon be having a minor Cabinet reshuffle. But Bolger was far from being in the most settled frame of mind. The tough fiscal measures in the Mother of all Budgets had been highly unpopular with the public, and there seemed to be no sign of the economy moving out of its deep recession. National's popularity was sliding rapidly. It was the blackest period for Bolger and his Cabinet. It is possible Bolger feared sacking Peters at a time of such fragile public confidence.

Bolger's relationship with Peters had long since deteriorated into one of almost total non-communication — except through the media. This was well illustrated by the next bout of turbulence between the two men — the Quality Inns affair. To be fair to Peters, on that occasion he appeared to be more in the right than Bolger on the substance of the issues, even if his style in pressing his case was typically unorthodox.

The affair broke as a news story when it was revealed that Iwi Transition Agency general manager Wira Gardiner had abruptly sacked Maori Trustee Neville Baker over his role in the purchase by Maori interests of the Quality Inns hotel chain. There were in fact four companies involved in the Quality Inns purchase — two Maori and two American. The New Zealand companies were Maori International Ltd (a private company) and Te Maori Lodges Ltd, a subsidiary of Maori International which had been purchased by the Maori Trustee as a vehicle to facilitate his involvement in the deal. On the board of Te Maori Lodges was Peters' old enemy, Latimer. In order to settle the deal to purchase Quality Inns, Te Maori Lodges needed to borrow $10 million from the National Bank. The bank required a guarantee on the loan. To provide the guarantee the Maori Trustee pledged around $12 million worth of assets from his common fund, which he managed on behalf of Maori. If the guarantee given by the Trustee were called up, this would expose the taxpayer. It was this pledging of common fund assets which led to the sacking of the Trustee, just a fortnight before his contract was due to expire.

From the outset Peters and Bolger were publicly at odds over the affair. It did not help that much of the controversy took place while Bolger was overseas. Peters supported Gardiner's decision to sack Baker, claiming Baker had not sought approval from his minister as he was required to do. Peters said he did not like the look of the deal. There was also doubt over whether the Trustee's pledge would stand up in a court of law. Bolger took an almost opposite stance to Peters: he questioned the sacking of Baker and was much less dismissive of the deal than Peters. It was revealed that there had earlier been a meeting of Bolger, Latimer and others, in which those involved in the venture had sought government funding. Bolger had agreed to take a paper to Cabinet. Both he and Cabinet came to the view that no funding was warranted.

Given the personalities involved, it was no surprise that Bolger and Peters had different public stances on the deal. Bolger and Latimer were on extremely close terms, whereas Peters and Latimer had long loathed each other. There was also mutual dislike between Gardiner and Latimer. As the details emerged, however, it was Peters who seemed wiser than Bolger in his caution over the deal. Though the Maori interests were contributing two-thirds of the funding, the American interests would gain a big majority of both the dividend shares and voting shares, as well as a majority of directors on the board. It did not look the type of deal over which the Trustee should have put taxpayers' money at risk.

After a threatened legal battle, Baker and Gardiner eventually reached a settlement in which Baker was reinstated but took early retirement when his contract expired. Bolger, speaking from overseas, seemed to take this as a cue to have a further niggle at Peters and Gardiner. In a report to Peters on the dismissal of the Maori Trustee, Gardiner would make plain his exasperation:

> The regrettable feature of this matter has been the media speculation and lies. I was disappointed to see government ministers suggest impropriety on my part. It is difficult enough when one must maintain silence on these matters. This silence is more difficult to maintain when senior ministers intrude in the business of a chief executive and his staff and come close to breaching State Sector legislation.

The day after Bolger's latest comments Peters extracted revenge of a sort in a snap debate in Parliament on the affair. The Opposition used the debate to press their call for an inquiry. Peters said he was not yet in possession of all the facts. Then the following exchange took place:

Prebble: Why not have an inquiry?

Peters: I tell the member for Auckland Central that when the acquisition of all the details is completed if he is not satisfied an inquiry *will be considered*. (Author's emphasis.)

This not-quite-offer would undoubtedly have riled Bolger. He certainly did not want an inquiry and must have regarded Peters' remark as distinctly unhelpful.

For Bolger the final straw in his relationship with Peters came when Peters returned to an attack on economic policy. He slated the 'obsession' with bringing down inflation, and talked of 'essentially wrong' policies that had ignored the social, economic and cultural costs of unemployment. For those who enjoy unintentional irony the title of Peters' speech — 'Low flying with an Erebus economy' — could scarcely be bettered. It was Peters himself who was on a flight path to Erebus, and he seemed oblivious of the need to pull up.

Bolger arrived back in the country over the weekend. At his Monday press conference he refused to be drawn on Peters' future, but he could not resist another kick at him on the Quality Inns affair, saying somewhat improbably that Peters had damaged the faith of foreign investors in New Zealand by his comments on the deal. On the Tuesday Peters promised to release material the following day proving his contention that the deal was a bad one. That evening the more trusted ministers began one-by-one to receive summonses to go up and see their leader. The next day, 2 October, was the day planned for Peters' disclosures. Not long after nine in the morning Peters was called up to see Bolger, who wasted little time coming to the point. 'I've reorganised my Cabinet,' he said. 'You're not in it. Sorry it didn't work out.'

To Peters the news was a shock he had neither expected nor prepared for. The press had speculated for months that he might be sacked. The Opposition had predicted it. Most of the Cabinet had made it plain they wanted Peters gone. Bolger himself had long been hedging in public about Peters' future.

The Prime Minister's staff had told the media off the record that Peters' days may be numbered. There was even a solid precedent for a successful sacking — Peters' demotion from the front bench back in Opposition. Even Muldoon had suggested that soon Peters might be just the member for Tauranga. Yet Peters had convinced himself it could not happen. Now it *had* happened. All Peters could say was, 'Jim, you've made your bed, you lie on it.' Then he walked out.

It might not have been the most original piece of dialogue, but few of us in the circumstances would be up to anything better. Back in his office, an ashen-faced Peters was besieged by media, friends and political allies. His strain showed as he uncharacteristically snapped at a press photographer. Eastern Maori MP Peter Tapsell paid Peters a visit, simply as one Maori MP to another. He told his Labour colleagues he had found Peters a shattered man.

By the time of his press conference in the afternoon Peters had recovered much of his poise. He once again made the claim that his speeches had been in line with National's manifesto. He said that he would remain with the party and that from the back benches he would lead the fight to overturn the Richardson economic policies. He denied this could ever lead to him being expelled from caucus. There were typical Peters rhetorical flourishes. He spoke of the 'tyranny of the few', and of 'the most bitter winter of discontent this country has seen since I was alive'. He talked about Maori unemployment, saying, 'On this I am a driven man. We just cannot go on ignoring the social and economic costs facing our country today.' He had a dig at Bolger's low poll rating and reminded everyone that in Tauranga he had 'The biggest majority in the history of this country.'

It was one of Peters' more Churchillian performances. He even slipped into the royal 'we':

This is one of those temporary circumstances. It is but a temporary aberration. And tomorrow, we'll be back.

There was no denying Peters was a fighter. But the unpalatable truth was that he was no longer a minister and that he would be moving out of his Beehive office. His new office would be with the other non-executive MPs in Bowen House. Sarah Neems was going back with Peters to work as his secretary once again. Peters' salary was halved overnight, but he had obviously grown attached to the Plaza International Hotel: he would stay on for some time at a specially negotiated room rate.

Peters' sacking was the crowning act of his rehabilitation with Maori. In Maori eyes he was now enthroned as a martyr. They had seen him go from exploiter of race relations differences to advocate for Maoridom. They had seen him oppose economic policies that seemed disproportionately to be hurting Maori. Maoridom had embraced Ka Awatea. Though to Muldoon, Peters may have only been a Scotsman with a suntan, to Maori he was *their* Minister of Maori Affairs. Now Peters had lost out in a white man's world. There was a strong surge of public support for Peters from within Maoridom.

Even Whina Cooper, then aged 97, dropped in on Bolger to ask him to reinstate Peters. Shortly afterwards the venerable lady herself led a 300-strong delegation of Maoridom to Parliament to protest at the sacking. Visibly moved by his reception from the delegates, Peters gave of his ringing best. He spoke of 'the dream that must never die' — the dream that by the 21st century Maori would be a first-world people independent of the state:

> We never sold this office out. There have been arguments within Cabinet and caucus but how could one occupy this office and see 30 per cent of our people unemployed and say nothing? We've been here for 1000 years. We are this country's true patriots, not the Roundtable, not those fiscal fruits of the far right who believe in a 28-year-old doctrine from the Chicago School of Economics.

It was not just Maoridom who opposed Peters' sacking. Two polls taken in the wake of the event showed a majority of New Zealanders also opposed. Just as significantly, in the *Dominion* TV3 Gallup poll 49 per cent thought the sacking would have a negative effect on the Cabinet's ability to make the right decisions for New Zealanders. Only 5 per cent thought it would have a positive effect. Perhaps at no other moment in this century had the public shown less confidence in key figures in the Cabinet: in the same poll Shipley's performance was ranked 'very poor' by 52 per cent, Richardson's by 50 per cent and Bolger's by 41 per cent. Just two years later a dramatically improving economy would win the government re-election by the narrowest of margins. But at the time of Peters' sacking National was suffering the fallout from being the only government for many years to have dared cut social spending. Meanwhile, Peters basked in public adulation. The next *One Network News* Heylen poll showed him more than doubling his support as preferred Prime Minister from 8 per cent to 17 per cent.

The slanging between Peters and Bolger over Quality Inns did not stop with the Peters sacking. There were claims and counter claims between Peters on the one hand and Bolger and new Maori Affairs Minister Kidd on the other. The day after his sacking Peters went ahead with his promised release of material to the media. In 24 hours he had already made the full transition back to 'Opposition' politician, a role he had never completely left, but which now he was once again able to revel in. Looking considerably more buoyant, he handed out a huge pile of documentation on Quality Inns. He denounced the government, saying New Zealand was 'in mourning for leadership'. That afternoon at question time Peters happily joined in the grilling Labour were giving the government over Quality Inns.

From then on Bolger and Peters each had an accusation they would periodically press against the other. Bolger would claim Peters had not acted strongly enough to discourage the Maori Trustee from pledging the assets in the common fund. Peters would claim that Bolger gave too much encouragement to Latimer over the deal. The claim of each man infuriated the other, though neither had much evidence with which to sheet home their accusation.

Peters was true to his word about leading an attack on the government's policies. In the following weeks he gave speeches even stronger in tone than those he had given as a minister. He took the backdown on the superannuation abatement rate as an opportunity to slam the government's decision-making process as rushed and undemocratic; he claimed that 'The manner by which policy is blitzed in this country underlies the arrogance which must not continue.' He again called the government's economic policy 'flawed and fundamentally wrong'. According to Peters:

> There is no turnaround in sight, nor does the potential for one exist. In fact the danger is that the base which has been laid is one which will further decline. . .What is doubly serious is that the full impact of our economic mismanagement will only be apparent by early 1992.

This prediction would be proved wrong. Even as Peters was speaking the economy had started to pick up, and by early 1992 it would become widely apparent that sustainable economic growth was under way.

In other speeches Peters again attacked the government's economic policies and the 'small group of ideologues' who had captured the policy process. He slammed the broken promises on superannuation, which he claimed were 'reducing substantial portions of the election manifesto to nothing more than a series of convenient lies'. He called for more protectionist policies. He accused the government of neglecting the concerns of business. He even said the government should listen more to business leaders, though presumably that injunction did not extend to listening to the Business Roundtable. Peters claimed that if National did not switch to a more pragmatic economic line it would face political oblivion in 1993.

Naturally Peters was opposed to the interim targeting regime of the health reforms. But he also attacked their provider side. He claimed that 1500 health administrators were being paid between $80,000 and $140,000; Upton later gave the correct number as 57. Few in Peters' audience of Tauranga superannuatants would have known that he was around 2500 per cent out in his claim. It may be a complete myth that the government would have much more money to spend in other areas if it only cut down on 'wasteful' health administrators, but it is also a potent populist line which met an extremely receptive audience. Peters has been astute enough to use it ever since.

A tempestuous year came to an end for Peters. Thanks to the blaze of favourable publicity surrounding his sacking, he was now ranking as high in the opinion polls as he had ever done, sometimes even topping Moore as preferred Prime Minister. The freedom of the back benches appeared to have given him a new lease of life, and he was again revelling in his unconstrained environment. He was far from being a spent force. Yet few guessed that 1992 would be even more tumultuous for him than 1991, or that it would be the most significant year of his career to date. It was a year in which he was to throw off much of his remaining civilised restraint; a year in which self-promotion and self-destruction would reach new heights; a year in which he would feel the chill and loneliness of the outcast while ever-louder applause was ringing in his ears.

Yet for Peters 1992 started badly. A rash of good economic news over the summer markedly changed the atmosphere in Parliament Buildings. There was a feeling that the economy really was starting its long haul out of recession. Many of the economic 'fundamentals' were now looking good, extremely good. In the Beehive there was a new sense of confidence. Slowly, over time, much greater economic confidence would also be spreading through New Zealand.

Peters opened up the year with an uncharacteristic offering — an attempt at a policy prescription of his own. We had heard a great deal in the past about what Peters was *against*, much less in detail about what he was for. Now he published his five-point strategy for economic recovery, a confusing document written in torturous prose. Under the heading 'stopping cuts to spending power' Peters put forward the dubious argument that the fiscal deficit was purely 'cyclical', i.e., just a result of the economy being in recession. That enabled him to criticise the government's spending cuts as mere 'ideological dogma'. In a muddled discussion, he managed to argue simultaneously that the government's cuts were not saving any money, and yet were reducing spending power in the economy.

Under 'getting business growing', Peters argued for more public investment and took his mandatory swipe at the Reserve Bank Act. Under 'investing in our strengths' Peters claimed we should return to 'picking winners', and that our winners were without question our land-based products. Under 'aiming for a bonus for all' Peters appeared to recommend some kind of tax incentive for investment, though his argument was impossible to follow. Under 'targeting a sustainable economy', there were a few muddled platitudes about the environment and social services. The whole document totally lacked any framework, demonstrating — if demonstration be needed — that Peters was no analytical thinker.

A document with a very similar tone and content to Peters' effort was prepared at the same time by Revenue Minister Wyatt Creech. The two had once been friends and associates. It is just possible that Peters and Creech were acting in cahoots, in a co-ordinated attempt to oust Richardson and shift the focus of economic policy. If so they were unsuccessful. Bolger was wise enough to keep the Creech document off the Cabinet table, and only a limited number of ministers ever saw it.

In February, Peters used his Taradale state-of-the-nation speech as a platform for lambasting the government. In one of his strongest attacks yet he criticised monetary policy, fiscal policy, the government's employment schemes, Bolger's maladroit comments denying a link between unemployment and crime, and the pressure which Peters alleged was put on Tamaki by-election candidate Clem Simich to distance himself from Muldoon. Peters also ridiculed journalists and business people for claiming there was an economic recovery under way.

Given how widely Peters had sprayed his fire, it was no surprise that his reception at National's three-day caucus meeting was distinctly hostile. It was not the first time the government caucus had seen attacks launched on Peters, but now there was a different mood, and a new impatience with those creating trouble for the government. Most MPs were seeing tangible signs of economic recovery in their electorates and many who had wavered in the past over the government's economic strategy were now much more firmly behind the direction set by Cabinet. Some in marginal seats, who in 1991 had almost given up hope of re-election in 1993, now saw Peters much more clearly as a danger to their own chances. In a stormy caucus session a large number of MPs attacked him. Laws, not the most popular man in caucus, also came under strong criticism. Both men were reportedly invited by a number of speakers to leave the party.

Bolger himself said nothing, but the tone of the session was plain: Peters was on notice. At other times during the caucus retreat Peters had a torrid time when he tried to speak. At the end of the third day Bolger disclosed to the media that Peters had been given a firm message by his colleagues. Bolger also hinted that Peters could face expulsion from the party, pointing out that this was an action only the party's national executive could take. As for Peters, he was his usual defiant self. He talked about his 'constitutional right' to promote the party's election manifesto. He was adamant that he could not be sacked:

> The only people who can sack me are the people of Tauranga. I'm not boasting and I would not want this to sound immodest, but you know the latest poll and the level of support I have. If you think this is a simple game of politics you are wrong.

It was a revealing statement. It showed he was still trapped in the delusion that had let him down so badly in the past. Back in 1989 he had thought his poll rating made him invulnerable to demotion from the front bench. He was wrong. In Cabinet he thought his popularity made him invulnerable to sacking. He was wrong. But still he was clinging to the idea that his public popularity would guard him against danger. He would be wrong again.

In March Peters made several more attacks on the government, on one occasion even bringing in a reference to Nazi Germany. He talked of the 'patriotic expediency' with which the government had allegedly justified its refusal to consult, presenting people later with 'subversive illegality made palatable by public relations sugar'. He compared this with the rise of the Nazis. Demonstrating a new-found conversion to the Treaty, he also attacked the slow pace of Treaty settlements.

Then he went ominously quiet for a long period. Hardly anything was heard from him in the course of April and May. He had not spoken in the House all year, and he seemed to be doing precious little else either. It was uncanny. His poll rating, though still high, was drifting down again. People in the

Beehive noted his lack of activity. Many wondered — more from hope than from experience — whether he might be fading away as a source of instability to the government.

We now know what Peters must have been doing in that time. He was hard at work. He was preparing a new attack, a new onslaught on the citadels of government and big business. It was to be a campaign using Parliamentary privilege to a degree unparalleled even in Peters' own past. It was to be an onslaught that would rock New Zealand.

CHAPTER TEN

The Campaign Begins

June 1992

*T*HE first sign that Peters might be re-emerging was his appearance on the Australian current affairs programme, *Four Corners*. The programme examined the events surrounding the two government bailouts of the Bank of New Zealand in 1989 and 1990. The producer, Murray McLaughlin, was the same man who had produced the notorious TVNZ *Frontline* programme *For the Public Good*, the fallout from which had included a rocket from the Broadcasting Standards Authority, a welter of law suits and McLaughlin's departure from TVNZ.

Now safely on the other side of the Tasman, McLaughlin was continuing his fearlessly objective quest for the truth. It was Peters' contribution to the programme which would cause a storm.

Presenter: Big business is hoping to have him [i.e. Peters] out of the game, but not before the Business Roundtable tried to get him on side.

Peters: For some time I had been asked to come and see a certain group in the Roundtable. In fact it was put to me that it was churlish not to, that it could be bad manners not to talk to them. So, in the interests of public propriety, I did. But I was pretty certain as to what the conversation was about, and it was about that; about my swinging behind a certain economic philosophy, and so it went. It was fine wine and the meal was lovely but there was going to be no business between us on that matter over and above the interests of what I perceived was the good of New Zealand.

Presenter: The meeting took place in Fay Richwhite's opulent offices. A fortnight later a Roundtable member not at the meeting phoned Peters with an offer of help.

Peters: I just as a matter of curiosity said, 'What do you mean by help? Do you mean money?' He said, 'Yes.' I said, 'How much?' I nominated a few figures. Each figure was agreed to and I said, 'Well, look, I'm not prepared to sell out the people that I represent in either my constituency or nationwide.'

Presenter : What sort of money was he talking about?

Peters: It seemed to me that there was no limit to support my campaign, whatever they perceived my campaign to be.

Presenter: What did he want in return?

Peters: *That wasn't made clear*, but I had suspicions that once I was on the ticket, then I was clearly, in my mind, and publicly I would have been bought . . . (Author's emphasis.)

It is hard to be sure precisely what Peters was saying in this interview. The first incident described by Peters — the dinner with businessmen — was entirely unremarkable. The businessmen simply lobbied Peters — an activity that goes on with politicians every day of the week. The second incident, as Peters tells it, did involve an offer of money. But even here Peters admits it was not clear whether the businessman wanted anything in return. Most of the impact of the interview came from the innuendo, the dark overtones, and the linking of two entirely separate incidents in guilt-by-association.

Pressed for clarification by the New Zealand media, Peters firmed up on his charge. On television he stated:

I'm saying I was offered money to change my political stance prior to the last election.

Peters also suggested that the political programmes of other MPs had been 'advantaged by business assistance'. But he still refused to name names.

The Business Roundtable denied it had ever tried to buy Peters. There was discussion in the House over whether his allegations were a matter for Parliament's privileges committee.

Above all there were demands for Peters to produce his evidence, if he had any. A genuine allegation of bribery was an extremely serious matter. Peters may well have been regretting making his comments on *Four Corners*. As he was repeatedly to point out, his main target was the BNZ. It was the BNZ which had been the main subject of the *Four Corners* programme, and Peters repeated the criticisms he had made then.

The people's bank had certainly had a troubled recent history. For decades the BNZ had been wholly owned by the government, but in 1987 thousands of small investors participated in the public float of a small fraction of BNZ shares. Unfortunately, poor management in the mid-eighties led to huge losses on the BNZ's lending portfolio in the aftermath of the sharemarket crash. Twice the taxpayer had been called on for large injections of money in reconstruction packages needed just to keep the bank afloat. The first occasion was in 1989, when Fay, Richwhite had gained a shareholding in the bank as a means of providing more capital. Fay, Richwhite, like the small shareholders, was to bitterly regret their BNZ experience. The second BNZ bailout took place just as National took office in 1990: in a complicated transaction both the government and Fay, Richwhite again injected money, while isolating the bad loans of the BNZ's portfolio into a separate 'bad bank'.

There was only one minister in the National government who had opposed the BNZ rescue package brought to Cabinet by Richardson. That minister was Peters. He argued the government should let the BNZ fall over. It was a suggestion of astonishing recklessness.

In government National had a very good record as guardian of the taxpayers' interest in the BNZ. The November 1990 rescue package would be the last occasion it was forced to inject money. Key changes to the board and management of the bank had already been made under the previous government. Richardson as the new Finance Minister demanded and received better performance from the board. The bank's operations returned to profit, and the government even received back much of the money it had spent in the rescue package. Eventually, when the BNZ was in good enough condition to sell, the government sold it to National Australia Bank.

Now, 18 months after the final bailout, Peters had suddenly discovered a keen interest in the BNZ and he launched the opening shots in a long campaign against it. At a press conference, he called for an inquiry into the circumstances of the 1990 bailout, claiming it represented 'an inordinate undue influence of business people in this country's political affairs'. Peters asserted that Fay, Richwhite had been softly treated in the bailout, ignoring the fact that if any party received markedly favoured treatment it was the small shareholders. They had not been called on to contribute anything; all new capital had been provided by the two major shareholders. Peters also raised the question of insider trading over the restructuring of Fay, Richwhite in 1990. However, the authority charged with investigating insider trading — the Securities Commission — did not believe an inquiry was warranted. Other wrong claims were made by Peters at his press conference: the government had put $1 billion into the 1990 bailout (it had not), and that Fay, Richwhite had received a $190 million commission from the government (it had not). Peters even asserted the government had secretly sold its share of the BNZ. A secret sale would have been impossible under stock exchange rules.

Despite his attempts to deflect the debate on to the BNZ, Peters still faced demands to front up with evidence on his bribery allegations. In a torrid caucus session he was repeatedly asked by his colleagues to produce his information, so that all MPs need not feel they were under a cloud. Even Bolger asked Peters directly to come forward with his evidence. Peters refused to do so. Peters' offer to read out his *Four Corners* transcript was met with rage; it was the most galling version yet of the 'read my speech' defence. Later that day in the House, Bolger invited Peters to 'put up or shut up'. Peters promised a 'full disclosure' in Parliament the following week.

There were various claims and counterclaims as the nation waited until the next Parliamentary sitting day. Bolger publicly invited Peters to leave the National caucus. Peters said that he was staying where he was. Tuesday came and with it no explanation by Peters; he was playing his waiting game. Finally on Wednesday he rose to make his personal explanation. It was a long, rambling speech, often difficult to follow and punctuated by interruptions. First he selectively quoted from the *Four Corners* programme in such a way as to telescope his Roundtable dinner and the alleged offer of money into one event. Then, after about quarter of an hour, he finally seemed to be getting down to business:

> Peters: On 26 October 1989 my diary discloses that I attended a 6.30pm dinner at the office of Fay, Richwhite in Auckland with the member for Fendalton, the Hon Philip Burdon. At that meeting the following Roundtable members were present: Messrs Gibbs, Masfen, Richwhite, Myers and Bidwill. All are, as you know, members of the Roundtable. The meeting was not at my request and, in fact, there is a senior journalist in the gallery who witnessed my reluctance to attend such a meeting.
>
> Bolger: Well, why did he go?
>
> Peters: Simply because I was told that it would be damaging to the party's interests if I did not go. That is a fact, sir. As I told *Four Corners*, I suspected what the meeting would be about, and I was right. What I did not tell *Four Corners* was that at the Auckland meeting I put to Mr Gibbs the question of why this group wanted to see me, given that they were already funding the member of Parliament for Selwyn, having shifted their allegiance from the then government. Neither he nor anyone there demurred, or refuted my claim. I put it to them that, that being the case, why would they want to talk to me? In reply one member said that I should be using my skills and public support to swing in behind what the member for Selwyn was saying on economic matters, in which event it was clear in my mind that they would swing in behind me. To those who say: 'Why would those members of the Roundtable be bothered?', let me remind them of what was happening in September–October '89. It was the end of a long political process.

Peters may have been referring here to his dumping from National's front bench in October 1989. But like much else in the speech, the reference is obscure. After an exchange with the Speaker over whether he was straying from the point, Peters resumed:

Now what is relevant about that is that members of this Parliament have, in this House, challenged me to put up and say why would the Roundtable have bothered. Yes they have, and I am happy to give my explanation as to my personal perception on this matter. But if they do not want to hear it we will get on to the real, hard-core evidence. Let me go back to what was said on ABC *Four Corners*: 'To support my campaign, whatever they perceived my campaign to be'; and 'what did he want in return?'; 'That wasn't made clear.' And the remainder of my answer is my perception, having at that time been involved in party politics for 22 years. That is why I used the phrase 'in my mind'. That means that had I taken the money for my campaign I would have felt no longer free — that there would have been a new element in my mind when considering important economic matters. I would personally have felt bought. It is my personal explanation as to my perception at the time that that happened.

Remember, sir, that the offer of financial assistance was direct: it was a departure from the conventional method of funding for political parties. The man belonged to a company associated with the Roundtable — in fact, a major shareholder, if not the major shareholder. And the man, even if his offer was genuine — and I leave that open, and believe it is possible — even if the offer was genuine, was a significant shareholder in a company associated with the Roundtable, and the political tactics of some members of that group had caused me grave disquiet. It was at the man's home that I recalled his business connection. I did not say at any time that this man may not have been genuine, because what was important to me then, as it is now, is how I would have felt about it.

The three sums of money that go with the answers to the transcript are $20,000, $30,000, and $50,000 — not in addition, but alternatively. My diary for that day, rental car, and the man's business profile and business card are attached to this report. He is, sir, Mr Selwyn J. Cushing of Brierley Investments Ltd.

Peters later tabled a diary note of the Cushing meeting, giving the date as 9 February 1990.

All in all it was a singularly unconvincing performance by Peters. For a start, there were major differences with the *Four*

Corners programme. In *Four Corners* the offer of money had come from a telephone call. In the House speech the offer had apparently come at a face-to-face meeting; in *Four Corners* the offer had come a fortnight after the Roundtable dinner; in the House the date of the dinner was given as 26 October 1989 and the date of the money offer as 9 February 1990. That is a gap of over three months. Peters would later admit that even the 9 February date was wrong, and that the meeting with Cushing had actually taken place on 15 July 1990, nine months after the Roundtable dinner. With an interval that long, it is hard to see how one meeting could be a follow-up to the other.

Nor was Cushing at all a likely person to be offering Peters money on behalf of the Business Roundtable. Cushing was not even a member of the Roundtable. He had shown no great enthusiasm for Rogernomics, even criticising government policy from time to time. Peters was thus proffering three different dates for a meeting with a man who turned out not to be a member of the Roundtable at all, and Peters' firmest evidence of funny business was that Cushing had once given him his business card.

There were other puzzles. Though the general tone of Peters' House speech would certainly have made it actionable had it not been protected by privilege, Peters himself admits in the speech that Cushing's alleged offer of money might have been genuine. If Peters had real doubt in his mind, it was surely a contemptible use of Parliamentary privilege to slur a man who even Peters claimed may have done nothing wrong. For most of his Parliamentary career Peters had talked about 'British justice' and the assumption of innocence; it had been one of his standard debating lines:

> In this country's legal history, there have been twin concepts, both of equal importance. The first is that the fellow citizen is entitled to a fair trial, and the second is that the assumption of innocence remains until it is proven otherwise. That is our understanding of British justice.

On this occasion Peters seemed rather dramatically to have suspended British justice.

Finally, if Cushing had improperly offered Peters money in

November 1989, or February 1990, or July 1990, why had it taken Peters two years or more to say anything about it? Why did Peters only come forward when, after some unspecific comments on an Australian television programme, he was challenged by Bolger to put up or shut up?

When it came to his meeting with the five Roundtable members, Peters did at least get the date right in his House speech. In October 1989 Peters actually had two meetings with different members of the Roundtable. Both meetings had been set up by Philip Burdon. The intention of the meetings was to give Peters exposure to the business community. It is not clear whether Burdon thought the meetings might 'educate' his friend a little more on economic policy by exposing him to business, or whether he was hoping the Roundtable members would gain a higher opinion of Peters after having talked to him. Many of those involved assumed the underlying motivation for the meetings was to help prepare Peters for the leadership.

Burdon was one of the last people to realise Peters would not be a suitable man to lead the National Party. As recently as the very day before Peters made his Cushing allegations, Burdon was quoted as saying: 'Winston has enormous talents. His future is entirely in his hands. I would never write him off.' Asked whether Peters would one day lead the party, Burdon replied: 'It depends entirely whether that becomes one of his ambitions.' Back in 1989 Burdon had every reason to believe that a Peters leadership would be positive for Burdon's own career prospects. It would have meant the end of that tiresome little woman from Selwyn who held the finance job, for whom Burdon had long had a reciprocated dislike. Many believed that Burdon fancied himself as Peters' Finance Minister.

The nation was spared that combination. Nor was it brought any closer by the two Roundtable meetings. Neither meeting was a success: Peters was ill at ease and failed to engage seriously with the businessmen. Almost certainly Peters would have felt intimidated in this alien environment. He came across as defensive and arrogant. The first of the meetings took place on the fateful day of 19 October 1989 — the day Peters was sacked from the front bench. The meeting was held at lunchtime in the Wellington offices of CS First Boston; those present included Burdon, CS First Boston chairman Brian Johnson, Roundtable chairman Ron Trotter and Roundtable chief executive Roger Kerr. Peters arrived late. The demotion he had suffered that morning can hardly have helped his equilibrium. He was not forthcoming when asked about his views; he preferred to talk about himself, his background, and the opinion polls. Admittedly Peters had other matters on his mind: he would be holding his post-sacking press conference at CS First Boston straight after the meeting.

The second meeting with Roundtable members was held in Auckland a week later at Fay, Richwhite's headquarters. The cast was as described by Peters: David Richwhite, Charles Bidwill, Alan Gibbs, Peter Masfen and Doug Myers, all members of the Roundtable. Peters again talked a good deal about himself, and about how he had risen from a poor background. When the businessmen pressed him for his economic views Peters was dismissive: his message was that they should not need to ask him. They should read his speeches. He had been a free marketeer long before they had. Peters' response was hardly designed to persuade top businessmen they were dealing with a politician of substance. Nor was Peters' reaction that of a man on a moral crusade who was confident of his ground, and who was now confronted with the evil forces he had so often denounced in his speeches. Perhaps in the defensiveness of his response Peters' mind was going back to the memory of the young MP for Hunua who, just like the Roundtable, had wanted lower government spending, less regulation, more private enterprise, smaller government and a free market for labour.

There had been no discussion of funding at the meeting, and certainly no offer of money. In his House speech Peters did not actually say there was an offer of money. What he said was pure innuendo:

> In reply one member said that I should be using my skills and public support to swing in behind what the member for Selwyn was saying on economic matters, in which event *it was clear in my mind that they would swing in behind me.* (Author's emphasis.)

In short, the only link between the Roundtable dinner and the Cushing meeting was what was going on inside Peters' mind.

There was a good deal more to Peters' House speech. Having completed his attempt to substantiate his allegations of an improper offer of money to himself, Peters now started on the second part of his charge — that other MPs had been improperly influenced. That part of his speech was far less interesting and no more convincing than the first part. One of Peters' 'scoops' was a published book by Alan Hawkins of Equiticorp notoriety. Another piece of evidence was the news that somebody had told Peters that somebody had told *them* that 'money was being donated to the National Party by members of the Business Roundtable on the understanding that it would be spent at the direction of the member of Parliament for Selwyn'. It was not even a new story. The final scoop was an existing media report saying that National Party president John Collinge had said that 'had a candidate been chosen in Tamaki, between $500,000 and $1 million would have gone to the party, but that business withdrew when that candidate was unsuccessful'. None of Peters' allegations, even if true, necessarily implied improper financial influence.

To most of Peters' colleagues, his speech was a long, tiring and often tedious charade. Just as Joseph McCarthy, challenged to put up evidence on his alleged 205 communists in the United States State Department, had bored and frustrated his senate colleagues with a marathon speech full of pseudo-evidence and non-connections, so Peters, challenged to substantiate his allegations, had produced a woeful effort full of tangled verbiage but without evidence.

The MP with most reason to be upset at Peters' Cushing allegation was none other than Laws. Cushing lived in Laws' electorate, had been a long-standing member of the National Party, and was a respected community figure. He had long given National financial support, and quite possibly had provided money to Laws' own Hawke's Bay electorate. The last thing Laws wanted was Cushing vilified under Parliamentary privilege by a close associate of Cushing's local MP. Even more deliciously, it transpired that Laws himself had been at the meeting between Peters and Cushing. According to Brierleys' chairman Bruce Hancox, and later Cushing himself, it was Laws who had set the meeting up — something Laws was to deny vigorously. Rapidly pedalling for shore, Laws described Peters' allegation as 'the most dreadful of misunderstandings'. In caucus the following day a distraught Laws rejected the suggestion that he had arranged the meeting — and there were not a few MPs enjoying the sight of Laws' discomforture. It was clear Peters had not consulted Laws before making his allegation. For some time afterwards the relationship between Peters and Laws was under strain.

Immediately after Peters' House speech the first serious steps were taken inside the National caucus towards expelling Peters. The driving force in the campaign was Chief Whip Jeff Grant. Government research unit head Wayne Eagleson was also an important player. A petition was drawn up stating caucus members had no confidence in Peters and inviting him to resign from the party. Junior whip John Carter took the petition around, collecting the signatures of around 40 MPs out of a caucus of 65. Not all of those who refused to sign were supportive of Peters; some preferred to wait and have their say in caucus the next day. In caucus the petition was presented by Graeme Reeves to Bolger, who afterwards passed it on to the party president. The petition was effectively a request from caucus to the national executive to review Peters' membership. If the executive decided to move against Peters it had a number of options. It could expel Peters directly from the party. Or it could take the more indirect route of waiting until the following year and then vetoing Peters' nomination for the Tauranga candidacy. As for Peters, he was his usual defiant self, invoking the 1689 Bill of Rights.

Naturally the businessmen named in Parliament by Peters denied they had been associated with any offer of money. Bolger even apologised to Cushing on behalf of the National Party. The quality media generally treated Peters' performance with the scepticism it deserved: Bolger was regarded as having won a key tactical victory over Peters. With the general public, however, sentiment was very different. They had not had to sit through Peters' tangled performance in Parliament. Nor would many go through a transcript of what Peters had actually said, examine its inconsistencies, and compare it to other statements he had made. But the public did hear talk of dramatic accusations, and see some great television sound bites of Peters holding forth in the House. Shortly afterwards came a deeply depressing opinion poll. According to an NBR-Mattingly survey, 81 per cent of New Zealanders believed there was corruption in New Zealand politics.

The multiple untruth had started, was making its way, and would gather force.

CHAPTER ELEVEN

A New Zealand McCarthy

June 1992–August 1992

*E*VEN before the poll on corruption had come out Peters was attempting to focus attention back on to the BNZ; he promised to reveal more facts to support his demand for an inquiry. Peters also reminded National that Bolger himself had promised an inquiry into the BNZ back in 1989. Bolger had indeed made such a promise: it had happened as a standard piece of political grandstanding at the time of the first BNZ bailout, but the promise did not appear in National's election manifesto. Once in government there had been no reason to hold an inquiry, although there would have been good politics in holding one immediately after the election. Rather than play politics and look backwards the National government had concentrated on improving the taxpayer's value in the bank. Richardson had walked into the next board meeting and thumped the table. 'I was *appalled*,' she said, 'at having to pay $620 million to bail you out in our very first week in office.' To be fair to the directors, by that stage most of them had firmly received the message. If they had not, they very soon did. The bank's performance improved rapidly.

If holding an inquiry in November 1990 would have had little point, holding one in June 1992 would have had even less. An inquiry at that stage would not even have made good politics for National. An inquiry into the BNZ would have been an expensive diversion which could only have reduced the taxpayer's value in the bank. It would also have adversely affected financial market confidence. In the face of Peters' demands Bolger once again ruled out an inquiry.

Two days later Peters walked into the House for question time carrying a pile of documents. It was on his supplementary question to Richardson that they came into play:

> Peters: I want to ask the minister whether she has seen documents — and, if not, why not — that show a massive breach of the bank's loans-to-value ratios, which were then set at 50 per cent, and a serious breach of section 190 of the Companies Act by Sir Michael Fay; and these documents are a certificate of title, mortgage . . .

> Mr Speaker: Order! The question has been asked.

Richardson pointed out that as a shareholder in the bank it was not her role to see such material. The documents were tabled. They concerned a loan made by the BNZ to a Fay, Richwhite company Foenus Investments; the loan was used to refinance the Fay, Richwhite building in Auckland. An angry Fay challenged Peters to make his accusation of illegality outside the House. Peters did not take up the invitation. BNZ chairman Syd Pasley rejected Peters' allegations. A few days later, three independent valuers cited in the documentation denied they had valued the Fay, Richwhite building in the way Peters claimed. Attorney-General Paul East, after examining the documents, declared they showed no evidence of irregularity; East challenged Peters to take any suspicions he had to the appropriate authorities.

It was a pattern that was repeated over and over again in the coming weeks. There was a dramatic Peters claim under Parliamentary privilege alleging illegal dealings. There was a flourish of tabled documents. There were denials. There were challenges — not taken up — for Peters to repeat his accusations outside the House. Independent parties reviewed the documents and found no evidence of illegality. The government invited Peters to take his concerns to the appropriate authorities. Peters did not do so. By the time the denials and refutations had all trickled in, Peters was attacking on a new front, producing more material, and his new accusations were dominating the headlines.

That June weekend Peters, the embattled fighter, champion of the common citizen, was feted in his Tauranga electorate. He and Louise were piped down the street from his electorate office to a public rally where 2000 awaited him. He told the crowd that New Zealanders were fighting to retain their democracy. He repeated many of his lines about the BNZ, and challenged the board to make public documents on the Fay, Richwhite building loan. He was at his populist best:

Accountability should apply at all levels in our society. There should not be one set of rules for the élite and another set for ordinary New Zealanders.

The following week Peters was attacking again. He attempted to table in the House more details on the BNZ loan to Fay, Richwhite, claiming it showed further irregularities. Richardson prevented him from tabling the documents. Peters also attacked the underwriting fee paid to Fay, Richwhite in the 1990 bailout arrangement, saying it involved 'white-collar theft and bogus invoices'. The accusation was nonsense, as Richardson's detailed reply showed; she challenged Peters to repeat his accusation outside the House. Responding to government demands to take his concerns to the Securities Commission, Peters claimed the commission did not have sufficient resources to do its job properly.

Television New Zealand had been resisting strong public pressure to screen the *Four Corners* programme on New Zealand television. This caution was understandable given how expensive McLaughlin's previous effort had proved. But *Four Corners* was not without an audience: some radio stations were playing it, there were public screenings, and the programme was circulating on video. At the Auckland Town Hall Peters addressed a crowd of over 1000 which had gathered to see a screening. The next day Peters attacked Fay again in the House, saying Fay had been present at two meetings where the loan for the Fay, Richwhite building was discussed. As Fay was also a director of the BNZ, Peters claimed there was a conflict of interest, and that Fay was using the BNZ as a 'piggy bank'.

In response Fay once again challenged Peters to repeat his

claim outside Parliament, but made no comment on the specific allegations. Peters challenged Fay to say whether he had been at the two loan meetings, adding in sinister tones that 'silence could easily be misinterpreted'. Perhaps it was a different Winston Peters from the one who for years had talked about the assumption of innocence and the fundamental principles of British justice. Perhaps too it was a different Peters from the man who in 1989 had strongly objected to a clause in the Serious Fraud Office Bill removing from suspects the right to remain silent. So strongly had Peters objected to that clause he even threatened to cross the floor if his colleagues voted in favour.

The 1992 Peters may have been happy to put the burden of proving his innocence on Fay. But when it came to his own private battle with the National Party he would be doggedly insistent on every conceivable right and principle of British justice, both real and imagined. Already he had complained that comments by Bolger meant he would not get a fair hearing from the national executive. Now Grant, as Chief Whip, lodged to the national executive his own protest over Peters' behaviour. Grant put down a substantial list of charges against Peters: repeated absence from the House without leave; repeated missed votes without leave; inhibiting free caucus discussion because of his colleagues' lack of trust in him; general failure to co-operate with the whips; and extravagant and repeated criticisms of colleagues. Grant recommended either cancelling Peters' party membership or censuring him, adding that if censure were chosen the party should still consider vetoing Peters' renomination for Tauranga.

A short Parliamentary recess put a temporary halt to Peters' BNZ campaign. During the recess the latest *One Network News*-Heylen poll came out. Peters' rating as preferred Prime Minister had surged nine points to 23 per cent. Not only was he the most popular politician in New Zealand, it was his highest ever score in a Heylen poll. His pleasure at this turn of events was soon be tempered by less welcome news that the BNZ was about to be sold. Unless he prevented the sale, he would soon be chasing a target at one remove from the government, with reduced political impact.

Richardson had for a long time been hoping to clinch a sale of the BNZ. Not only did she believe the bank would be best placed for future development in the private sector — it was a political millstone around the neck of the government. Peters' campaign against the BNZ simply underscored the political risk the bank had become. The sales process had progressed to the point where an offer from National Australia Bank lay on the table. A ministerial committee consisting of Bolger, Birch, Richardson and Burdon met to consider the offer.

At the start of the meeting Bolger was very sceptical about the idea of selling the bank. Birch and Burdon both supported Richardson. In the end, after a long discussion, Bolger was talked around by his colleagues. The next day Cabinet accepted National Australia Bank's offer, and the sale was announced almost immediately. There was still a hurdle for the sale process to go through: the small shareholders had to accept the offer in large enough numbers. For those shareholders who had bought into the bank in 1987 at $1.75 a share and were now selling for only 80c a share, it was a big loss to take. In the end, after a long period of angst, enough small shareholders agreed that the price was a reasonable one.

Naturally Peters slammed the sale announcement, calling it the third bailout of the bank. He also promised the media more disclosures under Parliamentary privilege to support his calls for an inquiry. Peters' next attack in Parliament did not strictly concern the BNZ, though it did concern two of the directors of the bank — Robin Congreve and Geoff Ricketts. Both men were partners in the firm Russell McVeagh McKenzie Bartleet and Co., Peters' old law firm. Peters accused Congreve and Ricketts, plus a third partner, Paul Carran, of tax fraud over the financing arrangements for the film *Merry Christmas, Mr Lawrence*. Though the details of Peters' allegations were hard to follow, he claimed Congreve, Ricketts and Carran had 'defrauded innocent investors, defrauded the revenue and defrauded the people of New Zealand'. According to Peters, a letter from the Inland Revenue Department in 1988 had declared the transactions to be a 'sham'; and in his typically understated manner he declared:

That information has been with the Inland Revenue Department for some time. Why has it not acted on what is clearly massive, criminal, fraudulent activity? What immunity from prosecution do those perpetrators of fraud have in this country? Is not the law in New Zealand to be applied in the same way for everybody? I know that this matter has been with a government department for some time, but because of inaction — inexplicable inaction — I have referred this matter to the Serious Fraud Office.

Another pile of documents was tabled.

Russell McVeagh vigorously denied the accusations of fraud. The Commissioner of Inland Revenue, David Henry, pointed out that the letter referred to by Peters had later been withdrawn by his department. After examining Peters' material, Henry said it contained nothing causing him to revise his view of the transaction. Russell McVeagh talked of taking libel action against Peters, not over the speech in the House, but for comments made afterwards at a press conference. Despite Peters' prediction that Russell McVeagh would not take action, a defamation writ was eventually filed against Peters by each of the three men named, and by the law firm itself. The case has yet to come to court.

With tension between Peters and his colleagues already running high, the issue of Quality Inns again reared its head. Quality Inns had recently been sold to Australian interests, prompting Peters to once again bring up the subject in caucus. He charged, with some justification, that the common fund had been improperly used as bridging finance to the benefit of Australian and Hawaiian interests. Peters infuriated Bolger by bringing out his old accusation that Bolger had endorsed the deal, and Peters demanded that ministers give an account of their actions over the affair. Peters even refused to yield the floor when told to sit down by Bolger, called the PM a liar, and advanced from his seat towards the front of the room. The atmosphere grew seriously ugly. There was a cascade of shouting, with many of Peters' colleagues telling him to get out. Though there were some in caucus who shared Peters' concerns over Quality Inns, none were brave enough to support him at such a moment.

It was the most torrid message of contempt Peters had ever received in a caucus meeting. The incident had the usual degree of effect on him — none at all. After the meeting Peters put out a novel version of history. He was reported as telling the media he had promised an inquiry into Quality Inns 11 months ago. As we saw, Peters had actually said that he would *consider* an inquiry. Peters also told the media, with more drama than plausibility, that he had been sacked from Cabinet in order to prevent an inquiry. A few days later at question time Parliamentarians had one of their typically objective and reasoned discussions on Quality Inns:

> Bolger: I repeat the advice that I gave to the House a few moments ago that, following representations from the parties proposing the arrangement for the Quality Inns deal, I took a paper to Cabinet that recommended giving no support. Cabinet concurred. I believe the honourable member for Tauranga was in Cabinet on that occasion — he may have been asleep, I am not sure.

> Peters: I raise a point of order, Mr Speaker.

> Moore: That is mean and small. Everyone sleeps when the Prime Minister speaks.

> Mr Speaker: Order! The House must settle down. I am on my feet.

> Peters: My point of order relates to part of the answer given by the Prime Minister. It is out of order from a Parliamentary point of view, and — more importantly — we know who was asleep and who let the deal go ahead. He is responsible.

An hour later Peters was leading off for the government in the weekly general debate, gaining a jump on the designated National speaker, John Falloon, who was slow to his feet. Peters returned to his film fraud allegations, giving a textbook example of how to widen a conspiracy theory in the face of new facts:

> This is what has happened: the Inland Revenue Department was told to lift the claim, to change it, otherwise the company would bring every Inland Revenue Department case it had and would paralyse the department; it would paralyse that

department's operation. Either the department was to change its '87 view that there was a sham, or the firm would paralyse the department's operations. What does one call that? What is the name for that?

Cullen: Blackmail

Peters: That is right; that is what it is . . . I want to know from this Parliament what happened to change the mind of the Commissioner of Inland Revenue . . . Who was the minister involved? And why did he do it?

Henry rejected any suggestion he had been subject to political pressure. As for Bolger, he reacted in the manner proper to what was a serious charge against his Cabinet, albeit one made without any evidence. He and McKinnon between them asked each minister whether they had brought pressure to bear on Henry. All denied it. Bolger made a statement in the House to that effect, adding that if the allegation were true a ministerial resignation would have been required. Peters chipped in to say that he had lodged a complaint with the Serious Fraud Office 'of a conspiracy to conceal a fraud, and it is laid against the Commissioner of Inland Revenue, Mr Henry'.

'It is always a shame,' Peters had once said, *'to see members hiding behind the privilege of Parliament when they seek to attack somebody who is not in the House. That behaviour is characteristic of the lowest of the low.'* In a few short weeks Peters had attacked under Parliamentary privilege: Selwyn Cushing, Alan Gibbs, Doug Myers, Charles Bidwill, Peter Masfen, David Richwhite, Michael Fay, Robin Congreve, Geoff Ricketts, Paul Carran and David Henry. He had also slurred groups ranging from the New Zealand Cabinet to a law firm. The following day the Serious Fraud Office cleared Henry of any wrongdoing over the film allegations. But Peters was far from finished.

By now there was only one word to describe the tactics Peters was inflicting on the New Zealand body politic. That word was 'McCarthyism'. After long being a New Zealand populist Peters had now become a New Zealand McCarthy.

Peters, like McCarthy, was a populist and an anti-establishment figure. Peters and McCarthy each exploited a

157

potent mixture of anxiety and distrust among ordinary citizens. McCarthy seized on the fear of communism and the distrust felt by many Americans for the Washington élite. Peters was seizing upon deep public disillusionment with politicians and a feeling that the needs of the common citizen had been taking second place to the needs of big business. In conducting his campaign Peters, like McCarthy, was employing tactics at once contemptible and an affront to civilised values, overriding many of our most basic assumptions about a free society and the rule of law.

Like McCarthy, Peters was making extensive use of Parliamentary privilege — or congressional immunity. Like McCarthy, he was dealing in guilt-by-association, fomenting suspicion against whole classes of people. Like McCarthy, he was placing reliance on unnamed informers. Like McCarthy, he was elevating simple differences of view into charges of conspiracy, drawing much of his strength from the atmosphere of fear that he generated. Like McCarthy, he struck a deep chord with many ordinary citizens. Like McCarthy, he had a success rate of virtually zero in uncovering significant proven illegality.

Both men unleashed their campaigns out of nowhere, tapping with uncanny skill a well of resentment and fear. McCarthy was a little known senator before he made his speech about the '205 communists'. Peters, though already a national figure, had not used McCarthyist tactics in anything resembling a sustained campaign. Both Peters and McCarthy made their initial startling accusation away from the capital: McCarthy made his '205 communists' speech in Wheeling, West Virginia, while Peters' dramatic gesture came on an Australian television programme. Both Peters and McCarthy then faced demands to front up with evidence backing their claims. In response, each made a speech in his respective assembly thought to be woefully inadequate by press and peers. Both men surprised the pundits by the degree of popular support they rallied for their campaigns. Both men continually shifted their fire, burying responses to previous accusations in a welter of new charges.

Both Peters and McCarthy made repeated and telling use of

the 'multiple untruth' — a term coined by one of McCarthy's earliest critics, journalist Richard Rovere:

> The 'multiple untruth' need not be a particularly large untruth but can instead be a long series of loosely related untruths, or a single untruth with many facets. In either case the whole is composed of so many parts that anyone wishing to set the record straight will discover that it is utterly impossible to keep all the elements of the falsehood in mind at the same time. Anyone making the attempt may seize upon a few selected statements and show them to be false, but doing this may leave the impression that only the statements selected are false and that the rest are true. An even greater advantage of the multiple untruth is that statements shown to be false can be repeated over and over again with impunity because no one will remember which statements have been disproved and which haven't.

The multiple untruth, in other words, places a quite unreasonable burden of proof on those who would challenge it. Refutation is boring and confusing, and cannot match in the public mind the excitement and colour of an accusation.

Even the backgrounds of Peters and McCarthy show similarities. The two men even seem to share a common confusion over their date of birth, with several different dates floating around. Both Peters and McCarthy were the middle child in large families, brought up in rural poverty far from the centres of power. Each put himself through law school and worked as a lawyer before entering politics. Each was an outsider without connections. Each made it into their country's most prestigious political assembly in their mid-thirties. Each spent some years in that assembly in relative obscurity, probably underrating the latent powers they possessed.

Both Peters and McCarthy grew to be extremely skilled in using the media. Both knew how to use a story to make repeated headlines. Both were master conspiracy theorists. Both revelled in flourishing around documents to accompany accusations, though the documents rarely if ever fully backed up their claims. Both invested a great deal of time in drinking and socialising with the media, so that many in the press gallery could not help liking them personally, even if 'underwhelmed' by their political tactics.

Both Peters and McCarthy were cunning tacticians rather than strategic thinkers; their ride was an exhilarating one but the planning of the route haphazard. Just as McCarthy was surprised at the response to his Wheeling speech, so Peters probably did not anticipate the demands to front up following his *Four Corners* appearance. The Cushing accusation was probably given reluctantly; his main target was the BNZ. Both Peters and McCarthy were skilled at keeping one step ahead of the chaos they habitually created. Both appeared to live largely for the moment. Both were agents of destruction. McCarthy's career as an inquisitor was short, ending in a sudden and unexpected fall. Peters' career is still alive, but has been marked by a series of strategic mistakes.

There were also important differences between Peters and McCarthy. McCarthy was known for his roughness and directness of manner. He cultivated the image of an ordinary, plain-speaking man who retained his hard edges and the unaffected instincts of the common citizen. Being a street-fighter was part of McCarthy's appeal. In Peters the bully was less overt, more hidden behind a veneer of civilisation. Paradoxically, Peters' appearance and dress would suggest he was attempting to join the very establishment that he was attacking. There may also be differences of motivation between the two men. The evidence suggests that McCarthy lied consciously, repeatedly and blatantly, though some would still argue that he was merely an enthusiast who became carried away. Peters, by contrast, may well believe his own conspiracy theories. Motivation is the hardest factor to pin down with any certainty. In the end it is not intentions but actions that make the impact felt by others. It mattered little to the victims of Peters' attacks whether he was cynical or merely misguided, just as it mattered little to McCarthy's victims whether he was a pathological liar or just a blundering patriot.

McCarthy was the greater and more powerful demagogue than Peters, though Peters may yet surprise us. McCarthy was more widely feared and exercised more effective influence. But Peters in his classic McCarthy months rocked the New Zealand body politic in a way that should not be underestimated. A New Zealand McCarthy on the rampage was a sight both frightening and disturbing. Mob rule did not seem too far away, because that is where the logic of Peters' tactics led. The rule of law was being replaced by denunciation and summary judgement. Peters was cruelly fanning many of the baser instincts of the New Zealand psyche: envy, suspicion, retributive justice, mistrust of the successful and a relish in seeing the mighty fallen.

The effect of Peters' campaign on the government was debilitating, not least in morale. Just a little more pressure and the government may well have bowed to the Peters' demand for a full public inquiry into the BNZ. Holding an inquiry would have been a concession to mob rule — an admission that one man, simply by employing the most odious of tactics, and devoid of any evidence, could force the government to do his bidding. An inquiry would have provided Peters with an enlarged stage on which to perform, given him scope for bold new conspiracy theories, and set a precedent for future demands. Bolger, to his credit, never wavered in his view that an inquiry should not be held. Some others in caucus and even in Cabinet were more inclined to appease Peters. In Cabinet both Graham and Creech would at various times be in favour of an inquiry.

After McCarthy's fall there was soul-searching in many quarters of American society. How, it was asked, could such an obviously destructive force have dominated public life for four years? Which institutions had let America down? Some, like the clergy, came out of the self-examination well. Others, like the Republican Party in the Senate, came out badly. Yet in the end the Senate did decisively reject McCarthy, and his reign came to an end.

So far, Peters is still with us. In his classic McCarthy months, when he was posing a serious danger to the workings of a free society, many New Zealand institutions were found wanting. There were organisations that should have opposed Peters more strongly, and organisations that failed to oppose him at all.

The weakness started with the government itself. Cabinet did not have a strategy for dealing with Peters. It was reactive and defensive, hoping the problem would go away. Responses were certainly made to the various accusations whenever responses were required, but, by confining itself simply to that, the government was fighting the campaign on Peters' terms. Each round of accusation and denial could at best end in a draw for the government, and usually ended in a loss. The government needed to go heavily on the attack against Peters, his style of operating, and his record of almost total failure to substantiate his charges. Richardson was more than willing to go into battle in this fashion, as was Shipley. But they were not the right people to lead the charge. Bolger was the man who needed to front an attack. To be fair to the Prime Minister, his instincts told him to do that; it was his handlers who persuaded him that going on the attack would be too risky. So the government boxed on, looking weak and growing increasingly demoralised.

But what of Parliament? Peters had abused Parliamentary privilege repeatedly, and not just during his classic McCarthy months. The number of people Peters had attacked under privilege in the course of his career was over 20 and climbing, and he had also slurred whole groups of people. The abuse of privilege was overriding some of the most basic tenets of a free society. It should not have been beyond the capacity of our House of Representatives to pass a censure motion, deploring Peters' tactics.

There was, and had long been, an ample measure of hypocrisy and party political opportunism in the attitude of both major parties towards Peters. Bolger had promoted him to National's front bench back in 1987, despite Peters' shallowness and liking for unsavoury personal attacks. In that action Bolger was putting the pursuit of power over the integrity of the political process, and was now reaping what he had sowed. Labour, long the target of Peters' attacks, had for some time been enjoying the sight of Peters turning on his own party. Though many of Peters' attacks in his classic McCarthy months concerned the period of Labour's stewardship of the BNZ, Peters' campaign was far worse in its impact on National than on Labour. The Opposition tut-tutted at Peters' tactics, while often aiding and abetting him.

If Parliamentarians did not acquit themselves well, the business sector was also more conspicuous for its silence than for its resistance to McCarthyist tactics. The Business Roundtable denounced Peters. Michael Barnett of the Auckland Chamber of Commerce also spoke out. But where was the Bankers' Association, one of whose members was the subject of a long series of attacks? Where were the Employers' Federation, the Manufacturers' Association and Federated Farmers? Where was the Accountants' Society? All appeared to be keeping their heads down, hoping Peters would send nothing in their direction.

Stronger condemnation of Peters from within Parliament and from the business sector would certainly have been welcome. But it could only have been of limited value. Parliamentarians stood extremely low in public esteem, while business was one of the very parties being attacked by Peters. It was above all independent parties prepared to stand up for the rule of law that were badly needed. Yet such people were hardly anywhere to be found. New Zealand has a Council for Civil Liberties; it might as well not have existed during Peters' classic McCarthy months, saying not one word. University academics, whose job security gives them an obligation to speak out on behalf of their society, were scarcely more vocal than the Council for Civil Liberties. New Zealand has church groups who have often entered the political debate arguing for higher taxes on the wealthy and more social spending. Church groups are perfectly entitled to join in that debate, but they cannot then claim that secular affairs are not their concern. There was not a word from our churches regarding Peters. They did not denounce him as American churches had denounced McCarthy.

The worst failure to stand up and be counted undoubtedly came from our legal profession. Lawyers, if anyone, should be concerned to see the rule of law upheld. The emergence of a New Zealand McCarthy was not a party political issue; it was an issue that went to the heart of the country's legal and constitutional integrity. The New Zealand Law Society certainly should have condemned Peters' tactics in very strong terms; so should have retired judges. They failed to do so.

And what of the media? Many of the quality newspapers acquitted themselves well. They kept most of Peters' accusations to the inside pages, and treated him with appropriate scepticism in their editorials. For instance the *New Zealand Herald* soon had this to say about the call for an inquiry into the BNZ:

> The call of Mr Peters' supporters has an artless ring: 'What harm an inquiry if the companies and individuals concerned have nothing to fear?' That is the most chilling argument of all. Star chambers throughout history treated fear as evidence of guilt. The victims of Mr Peters' campaign have acted entirely within commercial law yet have good reason to fear an inquiry conducted inevitably in a climate of political passion.

The Press in Christchurch took a very similar view:

> His [Peters'] success is not in driving accusations home but in sustaining his attack by making new accusations. To initiate an official inquiry on this ragged bill of indictment would be pusillanimous. As the Prime Minister said, it would be to give in to what can be regarded as McCarthyism. That is, the investigation of individuals on the basis of innuendo, unsubstantiated accusations, and the assumption of a conspiracy.

Unfortunately few New Zealanders read editorials, but vast numbers are tuned into the tabloid journalism of *One Network News*. There they saw, night after night, a breathless Linda Clark recounting uncritically the latest Peters accusation, interspersed with vivid soundbites of the man himself. It was sobering to think that for hundreds of thousands of New Zealanders *One Network News* was virtually their only source of information on current affairs. The poor journalism of the TV news programme was one of the most influential elements working for Peters.

In all, it was a dismaying catalogue of failure and compromise. Every free society has its defence mechanisms against threats to the rights of its members. Peters' continuation in his campaign, virtually unchallenged, showed that the defence mechanisms in our society were not working strongly enough. Peters would go on, and on, and on.

There was, however, one group not prepared to put up with Peters any longer — the National caucus.

CHAPTER TWELVE

Exile

September 1992–March 1993

*I*N his next attempt to prod the public psyche on government and big business, Peters at first seemed on splendidly fertile ground. The initial reports of the affair would have made a fine opening to a thriller movie. A 26-year-old man had died mysteriously in the early hours of the morning in a car crash on the Auckland harbour bridge. The police were investigating stories that the death was linked to information the man had obtained on computer disk from a multinational bank. The dead man was known to have been negotiating with the bank, who earlier that day had given him a thick wad of money in cash. But the money was not in the crashed car. There were even reports of SIS involvement. New Zealand's own Perry Mason — the fearless, good-looking backbencher in the double-breasted suit — was on to the story. He had been seen more than once in the company of the dead man.

Sadly for Peters the plot did not develop in the fashion promised by that opening sequence. The dead man, Paul White, had been drinking in a number of Auckland bars and nightclubs on the night of his death. There was no evidence his car had been tampered with. White had earlier bought a job lot of office and computer disks from Citibank for $525. When he realised he had been accidentally given confidential commercial information, he had apparently offered to sell the disks back to Citibank for $50,000. Citibank had laid a complaint of extortion with the police, who raided White's premises and seized 86 of the disks. After a legal negotiation between Citibank and White, an out-of-court settlement had been reached. White had agreed to hand back the two remaining disks and some written material. In return White received $15,000 as a contribution towards his legal costs. White was given the money in cash, because he claimed he had immediate debts to pay. As it turned out, White's biggest debt was to his maker: he immediately went out to celebrate with a night on the town that lead to his death.

The SIS said they were not involved in the affair. Both the police and the Serious Fraud Office stated that they saw nothing suspicious about the disks. But there was a colourful new angle offered by one Chris Cotton, a computer dealer who had known White. Cotton said White had told him he had discovered sensitive information on the disks. That information apparently included a US$50,000 payment from a multinational to a New Zealand MP through a bank in the Bahamas. There were also memoranda from four government departments to Ruth Richardson.

White's imagination was stronger than his knowledge of the process of government. Departments report only to their own minister. There could not be reports from four departments to Richardson because as Minister of Finance she had only one department — the Treasury. White had told Cotton that he saw the disks as containing evidence of corruption and asked who could help him. Cotton had suggested getting in touch with Peters, which Cotton believed White then did. Cotton's comments led the Serious Fraud Office to begin an investigation into the disks.

All of this led to intense interest in what had passed between Peters and White. Peters was not saying. At first he was reported as denying he had met White in an Auckland bar, then he refused to comment. What White said to Peters will probably never be known. Presumably White was attempting to use Peters as a pawn in his legal battle with Citibank, hoping that threats to get Peters saying things in Parliament would frighten Citibank into making concessions.

The Serious Fraud Office duly reported that the computer disks held no evidence of fraud and contained no mention of any member of Parliament. When asked to comment, Peters deepened the air of mystery by saying, 'What, all 92?'

The Serious Fraud Office had examined the 88 disks known to have been in White's possession. Charles Sturt, Head of the Serious Fraud Office, was angered by Peters' hint that there could have been more disks. He complained publicly that Peters had not co-operated with his office: 'If you asked a question of him he turned it back to a question to you.'

When asked by the media why he had hinted at the existence of more disks Peters simply said 'I said it because I said it.' It was not exactly elucidation. Citibank, for its part, said all the disks were accounted for.

In Parliament, responding to a question on whether Peters had met White, Police Minister John Banks stated:

> The Commissioner of Police advises that the police have received information to the effect that the member for Tauranga met the now-deceased Paul White. The meetings allegedly took place late at night or early in the morning in Auckland pubs and nightclubs. As the member for Tauranga has made numerous unsubstantiated allegations about fraud and corruption . . .

At this point Banks was interrupted for moving away from the question. But in the exchanges that followed Peters at no stage denied he had met White.

Peters' hints about more tapes, and his failure to co-operate with the Serious Fraud Office, were seriously irresponsible. In a splendidly trenchant editorial *The Dominion* advised Peters to take a hard look in the mirror:

> Winston Peters will see a man stripped of all pretence and pretension dedicated ardently and volubly to his own self-promotion. He will see a man who, far from being the champion of all that is open and upright in politics, will exploit half-truth and innuendo to advance his own claims to the moral high ground in any argument . . . Either Mr Peters has information that would throw light on the allegations or he has not. If he has, he should divulge it and not waste police time. If he has not, he should say so and stop playing silly, self-serving games.

But Peters preferred to continue playing games. Later that very day in Parliament, during the 'estimates' examination of the Serious Fraud Office, he asked:

> I have a number of questions about the authority that the Serious Fraud Office used, for example, in respect of disks and files that were held under an injunction, and how it was that that office was able to pass to Citibank those disks and files, about which the question of intellectual property had not been ascertained. I want to know under what authority the office did that, under what surveillance it did that, and with what technological expertise it did that, in order for it to be able to tell the public that nothing on those tapes was touched, changed or altered . . . I cannot believe that it was appropriate for the Serious Fraud Office to hand that information to Citibank, which had every reason — and proved that by the payment of money — not to be independent once the disks temporarily were back in its possession.

Dark hints from Peters of altered disks: it was very reminiscent of McCarthy's claim that State Department files had been rifled. It is a good angle for an inquisitor: it enlarges the conspiracy theory, and it is usually next to impossible to prove disks have *not* been tampered with. Still, Citibank denied any tapes had been handed back to it from the Serious Fraud Office.

While the Paul White affair was going on, forces unknown to Peters were gathering against him in caucus. The informal bankbench committee, which in theory comprised all backbenchers, held a special meeting under chairman Bruce Cliffe at the Te Mata Vineyard in Hawke's Bay. The backbenchers decided that the next time Peters stepped out of line they would move to expel him from caucus. Chief Whip Grant was not directly involved in the meeting, but the backbenchers knew he would support them in any move. There had long been discussion about whether caucus had the legal power to expel one of its own members. Enough backbenchers were now of the view that it had the power, and that it was time to use it.

Peters was probably unaware the meeting had taken place. Laws had stopped attending meetings of the backbench committee and could not have reported to Peters what had gone on. Peters pressed ahead with his next blockbuster series of allegations. His chance to speak in the House came in the general debate. National had given Peters a speaking slot with the intention he speak on the day's topic, which was electoral reform. He gave one-and-a-half sentences to electoral reform before swinging into his favourite subject:

> The BNZ in 1988 provided a false set of accounts to the New Zealand government, the New Zealand people, and overseas institutions that provide the bank with funding lines. That was done by a conspiracy between some BNZ office-holders and executives, the BNZ's auditors, the BNZ's lawyers, and Fay, Richwhite.

It was certainly a large cast this time around. Peters asserted that a financial arrangement entered into by the BNZ in 1988 constituted a conspiracy to conceal $200 million of losses. Because Fay, Richwhite was involved in the allegedly fraudulent arrangement, a particularly surreal theory suggested itself to Peters:

> Fay, Richwhite lied to the previous government and to this government, concealing the truth from the minority shareholders, the public, and overseas financial institutions. Fay, Richwhite knew the truth in March 1988, more than a year before it bought into the bank. I say that it bought into the bank to prevent exposure of what it did and to conceal further the true position of the bank's books and of Fay, Richwhite's position in relation to the BNZ.

How the Labour government of the day allowed Fay, Richwhite to buy into the BNZ while remaining itself outside of the conspiracy, Peters wisely did not attempt to explain. Perhaps for consistency Peters should have brought in Caygill and the whole of the Lange Cabinet. As it was, those in the conspiracy formed a large group: the BNZ's auditors Ernst Young; the BNZ's lawyers Buddle Findlay; Fay, Richwhite; some of the board of the BNZ; and some of the senior executives. Three people were named specifically in terms that would have been actionable outside the House: Fay, Ron Diack of the BNZ, and

Mark Jones of European Pacific Banking Corporation — the company, jointly owned by the BNZ, Fay, Richwhite and Brierleys, that had carried out the reinsurance arrangement.

Also featuring in the documents tabled by Peters were accountants Peat Marwick. Before tabling the documents Peters wound up with a fair rallying call:

> To those of my colleagues and others who say: 'So what?', I give this warning: this growing storm will rage and worsen; we members will not ride it out. By knowing what we now know, and not acting, we become part of the conspiracy. We politicians and other respected members of this establishment aid and abet the conspiracy; we condone it. Thus, we will be guilty. For months I demanded an inquiry. This evidence is irrefutable. It screams for public disclosure and accountability and, backed on this matter by 85 per cent of New Zealand, I will go on making disclosures of this magnitude until we get an inquiry into the Bank of New Zealand.

Peters' allegations were denied from the expected quarters. Pasley would call the allegations 'preposterous'; Fay would call them 'ludicrous'. More to the point Don Trow, a respected accounting professor at Victoria University, would examine Peters' documents and state they showed no evidence to support Peters' claims. Trow warned that an inquiry into the BNZ would erode confidence in the financial community.

While the standard wave of denials, clarifications, refutations and challenges to step outside the House was happening, an event of a very different sort overtook Peters. The government was just concluding its negotiation with Maori tribes over what became known as the Sealord deal. The government agreed to provide $150 million to Maori to help finance a joint Brierley Investments-Maori bid for Sealord Products. The government also agreed to allocate 20 per cent of all new fishing quota to Maori. For their part, Maori agreed that the deal would be the final settlement of all fishing claims under the Treaty of Waitangi. It was an historic deal and, as the negotiations wound to their close, an increasingly emotional one. Maori knew they were signing away for ever their rights under the Treaty; the government knew that — if the deal were successful — they would be able to wipe the slate clean on a major area of Treaty claims with honour to both sides.

On the night of Peters' latest allegations the final details of the negotiations were settled. There was a large Maori contingent in the Beehive, and many had been there for some days. It had been an exhausting negotiation process, and the corks were popping as the two sides were at last able to celebrate. Just before the House was due to rise at 10.30 pm, leave was sought for Graham, as Minister in Charge of Treaty Negotiations, to make a ministerial statement, to be followed by replies from Wetere and Moore. MPs had been pouring into the chamber. The air was thick with a sense of history. Unfortunately Peters, who had not been involved in the deal, was keen to make his mark. He raised a series of purely procedural points of order. Moore had taken a far better reading of the atmosphere than Peters. Stessing the word 'loyal', he said:

> It is true that any one person who is mean-spirited enough, and who is narrow-minded enough, and who is shallow enough, could at this moment stop the minister from making the statement. That is not the position of Her Majesty's loyal Opposition.

The pedantic points of order from Peters continued. Hamish MacIntyre, who often popped up on these occasions as Peters' little helper, added some of his own. Finally Peters' challenges to the chair were so persistent he was ejected from the chamber. But the spell had been broken. Graham's words were brief:

> I am grateful to the House for granting leave for me to make a ministerial statement, but in view of the behaviour of the House — or some members of it — I decline to do so.

The next day Graham got his chance during the general debate, earning a standing ovation from both sides of the House. But as the House broke up for the evening the rancour towards Peters from his caucus colleagues was more virulent then it had ever been. Ian Revell gave Peters a piece of his mind and an ugly row developed. MPs avoided using Peters' lift. It was not because those in caucus were hugely in favour of the Sealord deal; many MPs had reservations about it. But they resented Peters taking away their moment of history.

To most caucus members it was Peters' behaviour over the Sealord deal, not his latest instance of McCarthyism in the House, that proved the last straw. To an outsider that seems puzzling. Peters' string of points of order over Sealord was certainly to be deplored, but it was minor in comparison to the stream of McCarthyist tactics he had been employing for weeks. It says something about the dynamics of group behaviour that Sealord should have constituted such a trigger point for caucus.

Preparations were made overnight to put a motion of expulsion at the caucus meeting the following morning. Bolger was away overseas, and McKinnon was nervous about an expulsion taking place while the Prime Minister was out of the country. At the caucus meeting Bruce Cliffe, the man who had signed Peters up for the National Party 25 years earlier, stood up and read out a motion:

> That this caucus withdraws the whip from Winston Peters and excludes him from caucus meetings and activities as he has lost the trust and confidence of caucus members and cannot be relied upon to act as a responsible member of the caucus, but that this action in no way purports to affect Winston Peters' membership of the New Zealand National Party.

Wayne Kimber seconded the motion. There was extensive debate. McKinnon said that, if they decided to expel Peters, they needed to be absolutely certain they were doing the right thing. Some of Peters' small group of supporters spoke in his favour. There were others who, though quite opposed to Peters, believed caucus did not have the right to expel one of its rank. Some advocated compromise measures. But the bulk of MPs present wanted Peters out.

To Peters the motion had probably come as a complete surprise. He defended himself by pointing up to the photographs on the caucus wall of former National Party leaders: Hamilton, Holland, Holyoake, Marshall, Muldoon and

McLay. Hardly any had stepped down of their own accord. If people wanted to talk about loyalty, Peters charged, perhaps they would like to hear a little history. It was good theatre from Peters, especially with the ghost of Jim McLay staring down from the wall. But few were persuaded by Peters' argument. A preliminary vote was taken, registering a significant majority in favour of Cliffe's motion. But there were many MPs not present. To give all a chance to vote, and to ensure the expulsion move was seen as an act of considered deliberation, McKinnon put off the final vote until a special meeting to be held the following Tuesday.

Peters walked out of caucus as stunned as he usually was on such occasions. It was finally sinking in that caucus may really do what they had threatened they would do. He had been invited to leave at the Picton caucus, been screamed at over Quality Inns a few weeks back, and attacked many other times in the course of the year. Perhaps he had lived for so long in the world of the grandiloquent gesture, the politics of pose, that he imagined his colleagues were just acting. If so, he now knew differently. Unusually, he at first had little to say to the media.

No doubt Peters was still hoping caucus nerves would fail when it came to the final vote. But his chances did not look good. The only thing that might save him was complete and open repentance for past misdeeds and a determination to mend his ways. He was about as likely to do that as he was to change his double-breasted suit for a tutu. He was given hope when party president John Collinge said he doubted whether caucus had the power to expel a member. With the national executive meeting on Wednesday, it was decided to delay National's caucus meeting till the day after, so that MPs knew the results of any executive deliberations. The executive was due to consider a proposal to allow caucus to expel a member on a 75 per cent majority, though few expected the proposal to gain acceptance. There was some typical fighting talk from Peters early in the week. When the national executive met it backed away from addressing the expulsion question, making it clear that the ball was entirely with caucus.

The following morning a tense-looking Peters walked into caucus, knowing it could be the last meeting he would ever attend. There had been times in the past when just walking into caucus had been an act in itself for Peters. In Opposition his route to the caucus room had taken him down a long corridor. He would always be the last into caucus and, if for some reason the television camera was there, he would bask in the glow as he was filmed walking, in his solitary splendour, all the way up to the caucus room. This time there was no camera to greet him; all the media had been banned from the 11th floor of Bowen House. It was a very different Peters now who took his seat.

The atmosphere was not as bitter as at some earlier meetings. Excellent speeches were made, many of them more in sorrow than in anger. Bill English, who seconded Cliffe's expulsion motion, was particularly telling. 'I don't mind people saying they disagree with me,' he said, 'but when I walk down the street in my electorate and people say, "There goes a duplicitous, untrustworthy bastard," I've had enough, Winston. I am *not* going to be seen as duplicitous and untrustworthy in my own electorate.' English looks — and is — as honest as the day is long. It was a potent speech.

For much of the time Peters sat reading, or at least staring at, the newspaper. Was he filled with self-righteous anger at what his colleagues were doing? Or was he wondering how it had all gone so wrong, how he could have thrown away a charmed career that had looked destined to send him to the very top? Perhaps he was thinking back to the day when he first walked into the National caucus, 13 years before. Peters rose and defended himself with some of his old arguments. But there was nothing that had not been heard before and rejected, nothing to stay the executioner's axe.

October had always been the cruellest month for Peters. It was in October 1989 that Bolger demoted him from the front bench. It was in the same month, two years later, that Bolger sacked him from the Cabinet. Now it was again October, but Peters' troubles this time could not be blamed on Bolger. The PM was still overseas; Peters' old flatmate McKinnon was chairing caucus. The motion was voted on. Those against expelling Peters were reportedly Robert Anderson, Cam Campion, John Carter, Christine Fletcher, Marie Hasler, Roger McClay, Peter McCardle, Ross Meurant, Brian Neeson, Grant

Thomas, Laws and brother Ian. Almost everyone else in caucus supported the motion, including all three of Peters' former flatmates. Support had firmed against Peters over the past seven days. There were three abstentions: Bolger, Speaker Robin Gray, and Peters himself. The motion was carried by 50 votes to 12. Peters stood up and walked out.

Though visibly shaken, Peters was still in fighting mood after caucus. He claimed National's proud tradition of freedom of speech had been trampled on:

> I will not be silenced in this or any other way. I am still the National MP for Tauranga with the overwhelming support of the people of my city. None of my Parliamentary rights can be proscribed. I will go on with my campaign which I am certain precipitated this seventh challenge. I'm taking on part of the establishment that the rest of the establishment have yet to accept were wrong.

There were hints from Peters that National's financial backers had demanded his expulsion, and that Bolger had also been a key player in the move. Peters was adamant he would not be leaving the National Party. His intention was to win reselection for National for Tauranga in 1993. He also said he would seek legal advice on the expulsion.

Most MPs voting for Peters' expulsion had not done so primarily on the basis of a calculation of electoral costs and benefits. There was even considerable nervousness over the possible electoral consequences. Some in marginal seats had even admitted in the final caucus that Peters' expulsion might worsen their re-election chances, but that did not deter them from wanting him out. Most MPs simply found his presence in caucus intolerable, and were not prepared to put up with his self-promotional style of chaos politics any longer. With Peters gone there would be a huge sense of new unity in caucus. There would be a trust and an ability to work together as a caucus that had not been there before. Even one MP who voted against Peters' expulsion later likened the event to a great weight being lifted off the shoulders of caucus.

As expected there was a surge of public support for Peters. Perhaps at no other time did he have the mood of the country more firmly in his favour. The BNZ campaign had made him the people's hero, and now he was the people's martyr. Letters and telephone calls poured into the National Party complaining about the expulsion. Peters arrived back in Tauranga to a welcome befitting the country's most loved, and now martyred, politician. The *Sunday Star* published a poll showing that 80 per cent of New Zealanders disapproved of Peters' expulsion. The same number also wanted an inquiry into the BNZ. Later that week Peters' rating as preferred Prime Minister rose six points to 28 per cent in the latest Heylen-*One Network News* poll. It was his highest ever level of popularity. He was 12 points clear of Moore, with Bolger further back on just 8 per cent.

For the National Party these were morale-sapping statistics. It did little good to complain that the public were schizophrenic over the whole issue of party rebels. MPs who speak out against the party line are lauded by the public as honest, forthright and courageous. Yet the public is just as quick to punish a political party for appearing disunited. And how does a political party appear disunited? By having MPs speak out against the party line in public.

Nonetheless, there were facts about Peters' performance of his duties that National could have tried harder to put before the public. Over the past two years Peters had missed no fewer than 186 votes in the House for which he did not have leave. At the time of his expulsion he was hardly ever turning up to caucus committees. He was the only National backbencher who was not on a select committee. He had spoken constantly of his rights as a National MP, but had seemed to disregard all his responsibilities except those that suited him.

Having by now arrived back in the country, Bolger at his Monday press conference strongly hinted he thought Peters' chances of reselection as a National candidate to be doubtful. Peters had other ideas: he said he was confident he would win selection for Tauranga. Peters' status in the House was now somewhat problematical. Though the Opposition had offered to accommodate him on its speaking lists, Gray ruled that Peters was still a government MP. Peters was promptly relegated to the last government seat in the House — No. 64. For the campaign Peters was running, where he sat in the House was immaterial.

He again used the House to talk about the BNZ reinsurance scheme that had featured in his previous allegations of falsified accounts, and he tabled more documents. For the umpteenth time he demanded an inquiry into the BNZ.

At a public rally in Tauranga Peters promised to 'take the Bank of New Zealand head on'. He launched a public appeal for funds to help him defend law suits lodged against him, and to help him bring legal actions 'to defend my political status'. It was the firmest indication yet that Peters expected to be going into court to do battle against his own party.

If Peters was coming out fighting, so was BNZ chief executive Lindsay Pyne. In a clear change in the bank's strategy, Pyne called a press conference to hit back at Peters' campaign against the BNZ:

> I feel I have no option but to speak out. It's time to say enough is enough. I'm speaking out today because this affair needs to end — and end now. It's debilitating for the bank, and it's debilitating for the country. It's also damaging to the bank's international position and disruptive to the entire financial community in New Zealand.
>
> The 6000 staff in the bank have also had enough. They've worked solidly for more than three years to rebuild the bank.

All of that was true. Pyne itemised and responded to each of Peters' allegations. Unfortunately for Pyne, contests with Peters never seemed to be won on logic. Peters labelled Pyne's press conference a giant public relations exercise.

The Securities Commission met to consider whether in light of public disquiet there was justification for holding an inquiry into the BNZ. The government had made it plain that, if the Securities Commission believed there were grounds for an inquiry, sufficient funding would be made available. The Commission reviewed its eight previous investigations of the BNZ and all allegations by Peters. It concluded there was no reason to undertake a public inquiry into the BNZ, saying 'there is nothing we have seen to date which justifies such an inquiry'.

In the classic McCarthy style of trumping refutation with new allegation, Peters that very night was in the House continuing his attack on the BNZ loan for the Fay, Richwhite building. He read out a long affidavit from one Larry Johnson, late of the BNZ, who had been involved in the loan approval process. Johnson in his affidavit claimed Fay had tried to intimidate him into approving the loan, despite Johnson's reservations. After reading the affidavit, Peters pronounced dramatically:

> For his troubles Larry Johnson was dismissed. His mortgage with the bank was called up instantly and his property was sold within a matter of days; he was made bankrupt.

Well, not quite. The next day Pyne was sure enough of his facts to call another press conference in which he said, 'Mr Peters has based this whole story on the basis of the word of a proven liar.' Johnson was not sacked as a result of any loan argument. He was sacked because he could not be trusted by his employer, and because he had so grossly mismanaged his personal finances that his interest payments on loans totalled $400 a day. Johnson was not bankrupted when he was sacked: bankruptcy happened four months later. At the bankruptcy hearing Johnson wrongly claimed to have been offered half a million dollars by the BNZ for wrongful dismissal. The case for unjustified dismissal brought by Johnson's union to the Employment Court was abandoned after two days.

All in all, American-born Johnson appeared to be not the most credible of all possible witnesses. Television journalist Michael Wilson tried checking up on Johnson's background. The law school where Johnson claimed in his affidavit to have obtained his degree had collapsed 15 years ago and records were not available. Wilson continued:

> Another issue is whether Victoria University ratified his law degree. We couldn't contact the dean of the faculty, but one faculty member said he didn't know what Mr Johnson meant by ratification. There's also the matter of Johnson calling himself an Auckland University lecturer. A University spokesman says he's worked there less than ten hours this year. What adds to the mystery is that Johnson told BNZ employees he fought in Vietnam. That means the sixties and seventies were busy decades for Johnson, earning a law doctorate, building up his international reputation as a valuer and fighting an Asian war.

At his Auckland home today Mr Johnson didn't want to talk, so
the mystery of his background remains.

Fay disputed Johnson's allegations of intimidation, and Pyne
stressed Fay had taken no part in the loan approval process.
Fay's denial of Johnson's allegations had a charmingly old-
fashioned ring to it:

> Mr Peters' behaviour in this matter is vile. The man is a liar and
> a coward. He has lied to the Parliament and people of New
> Zealand, not once but on numerous occasions in his shameful
> campaign to remain in the political spotlight. I challenge him
> to take his lies and false evidence and lay them before a court
> so that I may defend my reputation.

Though Peters stated Fay's response was defamatory, he took
no action. Instead he challenged Fay to debate with him in the
Auckland Town Hall and to let the public judge, with the
proceeds to charity. There was an ugly and bullying aspect to
that challenge, directed at a private citizen from a politician to
whom debate was the stuff of his professional life. No wonder
Peters was no longer talking about British justice. His challenge
to Fay seemed more like trial-by-combat before a paying
audience. Wrong-doing in our system of justice is established
by more sophisticated methods. Like many a Peters statement,
the challenge also contained a rich vein of unconscious self-
parody. Who else but Peters would issue such a challenge?
Perhaps, as in some radio and television panel games, he was
expecting victory to go to the man who received the longest
bout of applause at the end from the studio audience.

In view of the charges that had been made by Peters and
Johnson, the BNZ appointed George Barton QC to conduct an
investigation into the loan. Peters claimed it was 'not a proper
inquiry'. When Barton eventually produced his report clearing
the bank, Peters dismissed it as a 'public relations stunt'. But
there was another angle open for Fay to pursue. Tony Ryall had
prevented Peters from tabling Johnson's affidavit in the House.
On the completion of Barton's report Fay filed a defamation
writ, seeking damages from both Peters and Johnson over the
affidavit on the grounds that it was not privileged.

A Parliamentary recess again halted temporarily Peters' efforts under privilege. During the recess the BNZ held its annual general meeting. It was a rowdy affair, with a large audience of mainly elderly people understandably upset at having to sell for 80 cents shares many had bought in 1987 for $1.75. Peters' arrival at the meeting was greeted with applause, and there was a testy exchange between Peters and Pyne. When the final hurdles to the sale of the bank were cleared a few days later, Peters said he would continue his campaign for an inquiry. He slammed the sale and reminded National of Ian McLean's commitment in 1989 not to sell the bank to overseas interests. McLean's commitment was rather like Bolger's promise-on-the-hoof to hold an inquiry; neither had appeared in National's 1990 manifesto.

When Parliament resumed Peters was quickly back into his work. He quoted from an alleged minute from a board meeting of the State Bank of South Australia at the time of the BNZ bailout; the minute expressed some reservations about their relationship with Fay, Richwhite. The minute was moderately titillating but hardly earth-shattering. Potentially more substantive was Peters' speech in the general debate later that day. He picked up on a story that both New Zealand's business weeklies — the *Independent* and the *National Business Review* — had recently been running. The story was the tax avoidance activities of European Pacific Investments, another company part-owned by the BNZ, Fay, Richwhite and Brierleys. European Pacific had been involved in highly aggressive tax avoidance activities involving Cook Islands companies. Allegedly leaked material was finding its way to the two newspapers, and as Peters spoke European Pacific was locked in a legal battle with them over what could be published.

Peters waded into this debate with his usual lack of inhibition. It was not one of his better speeches; his explanation was confusing and hard to follow. He charged that tax evasion had taken place. Tax 'evasion' means breaking the law in order to evade paying tax, as opposed to 'avoidance' which merely means minimising one's tax bill through using schemes that are within the law. Peters accused three companies — Lion Corporation, Magnum and Carter Holt — of using European

Pacific and its associated Cook Islands companies for the purposes of tax evasion. Peters specifically named Pyne as a party to tax evasion. This was unfair, as there was no evidence to link Pyne with any of the alleged tax evasion schemes. After taking over as chief executive of the BNZ in 1989, Pyne had been on the board of European Pacific for only a few months before the BNZ sold its holding. Pyne had reportedly been keen to end the bank's investment in European Pacific.

Peters' attempt to table his documents was prevented by government members. He had also been prevented from tabling the alleged State Bank of South Australia minute. This reflected a new and long overdue policy on the part of the government. They could not stop Peters abusing Parliamentary privilege in his speeches, but they could at least stop him tabling documents. As for Peters' allegations, Lion and Magnum both denied they had broken the law. It is doubtful whether any of Peters' material was new to Inland Revenue.

Peters' next target in the House was Securities Commission chairman Peter McKenzie. A company called Energy Source Television had gone into receivership in 1989 owing money to the BNZ. Peters' supplementary question to Graham drew rather a long bow:

> Has the minister any reports that the amount owing was $5 million; that on the prospectus of that company a Peter Donald McKenzie — the chairman of the Securities Commission — was named as a director; and has the government any position on his obvious conflict of interest in respect of investigating matters involving, and complaints against, the Bank of New Zealand.

Graham pointed out that McKenzie had ceased being a director of Energy Source Television three and half years before the company went into receivership. Any suggestion of a conflict of interest was nonsense. Caygill asked:

> Does the minister happen to have a list of the the number of business people whom the member for Tauranga has attacked in this way, to which Mr McKenzie's name could be added, or, as is likely, has the minister lost count?

With his attack on McKenzie, Peters' classic McCarthy months came suddenly to an end. It had been an extraordinary time. For six months, despite a steadily improving economy, the government had struggled as if in chains. Some of the government's problems were self-inflicted. But the major factor had been Peters' campaign. On the barest minimum of evidence he had managed to spread the odour of corruption in the public mind with an effectiveness that was at once frightening and astonishing. Often enough in the past his antics had proved as exasperating to his colleagues as they were exhausting to counter. But this time he had gone far beyond anything done in the past. Those in government not only had to ward off an unprecedented series of scatter gun attacks. They had to face constant accusations from the public that they were part of a corrupt system of government.

Peters' classic McCarthy period had brought him to his highest yet level of popularity. At the same time it had destroyed any chances he may have had of staging a comeback within the National Party. Early in the new year he would face a new battle to stay as the National candidate for Tauranga. But there was a real puzzle about the ending to Peters' classic McCarthy phase: why did it happen? Peters' tactics had been an enormously successful formula in terms of his main yardstick — public popularity. Peters had continued with his tactics despite the expulsion from caucus. By the end of 1992 he must have had vast amounts of material coming to him from the potty and the disaffected. Yet in the course of 1993 he would use hardly any of that material.

One factor may have been the new demands on his time in the new year. In his classic McCarthy months, he had been doing very little besides running his campaign of accusations. That changed in the course of 1993. Pressure of events, however, can only be a partial explanation for the halt to the campaign. It is possible that a note of caution sounded in his ear. Perhaps mindful of how McCarthy had overreached himself, Peters may have felt that for the moment he had taken his attack on the establishment as far as it could go. If it was caution on his part, it was thoroughly uncharacteristic.

Peters began the new year knowing he would be fighting for

his survival in the National Party. His chances of remaining the National MP for Tauranga after the 1993 election did not look good. A majority of the party in his own electorate were still supporters, but the national executive was due to meet to consider the Chief Whip's complaint against him shortly after final nominations for the Tauranga electorate were received. The national executive could choose to expel Peters from the party, or it could merely veto his nomination. The rules of the National Party provided for both courses of action, and it seemed likely the executive would act in one direction or the other.

In February Peters took his own party to the High Court. Peters sought an injunction on three counts: to prevent his expulsion; to prevent the vetoing by the national executive of his nomination for Tauranga; and to prevent National from requiring him to use its new nomination form. The nomination form was effectively a loyalty pledge; in signing it, a candidate agreed legal action would be taken against them if, having failed to win the party's nomination, they then stood against National's chosen candidate. The party had always had a loyalty rule, but the attempt to make the rule legally enforceable in advance was new. Some argued the rule was unconstitutional and would not be upheld in the courts. It did not need a conspiracy theorist of Peters' scope and imagination to link the attempted strengthening of the rule with a certain member for Tauranga.

In keeping with the theme of the times, Peters used his state-of-the-nation speech to lambast a wealthy and powerful coterie who he claimed were disregarding democracy in an attempt to retain their positions:

> It is not right that a small cabal with temporary authority go unchallenged outside the constitutional law, the proper processes of democracy and freedom of speech. We must never stop considering if other individuals are correct, or if the support of the general public warrants further inquiry and investigation.

The first legal skirmish appeared to favour Peters. Counsel for the National Party gave a commitment that National would not attempt to expel Peters, or enforce the loyalty pledge on him.

Only the national executive's right to veto was now being contested. After two days of hearings, Peters was faced with a nervous wait over the weekend for the court's judgment on Monday. Short of a nasty bout of judicial activism, it was not easy to see his appeal succeeding. And so it proved. Justice Fisher ruled the party did have the right to veto Peters' nomination. Peters' only consolation was Fisher's ruling that the loyalty pledge was unenforcable. Making the best out of a bad situation, Peters declared the result a victory for democracy and justice.

There was now nothing to impede the national executive from ending Peters' Parliamentary association with National. The party was careful to ensure the procedure adopted was fair. All four of the MPs on the executive withdrew from the hearing. Both Peters and Grant were asked to make written submissions to the executive, and invited to make oral submissions on the day of the hearing. In his written submission Peters played heavily on his popularity:

> Scientific opinion polls assessing political personality likes and dislikes at the time leading up to the 1990 General Election found that I attracted many votes for the National Party that would else have gone elsewhere . . . Current polls indicate that, for every one vote I would lose the party, I gain at least 13 to 14 votes, whereas the Prime Minister loses eight for every one vote he gains. Comparative ratings of some other senior ministers are even worse than that of the Prime Minister.

Peters was never one to hide his light under a bushel. Two days before the hearing he spoke to a crowd of 3000 in Auckland's Aotea Square, and was as combative and uncompromising in his speech as ever. There was no tempering of his message with an eye to the hearing. Peters' fate, however, would be decided not in Aotea Square, but in a room at National Party headquarters in central Wellington.

The day in question came — Thursday 4 March. It was grey and overcast. For Peters it was a day of trauma such as he had rarely experienced in politics. He arrived at party headquarters only to find the national executive was not yet ready to see him. The strain showed on his face as he emerged from the building and walked back to his office. On entering the House that afternoon, Peters' humour was not enhanced when he found his seat had been moved and that Cam Campion — recently dumped as the National candidate by his own electorate — had been given Peters' place. Peters had moved down one place. The shift had no connection with what was going on at party headquarters, but the symbolism was brutal. Peters returned to party headquarters for the final stages of the drama. Peters and Grant and their counsel were brought before the executive. The caucus case against Peters was presented by Grant. Peters left the talking to his counsel. A secret ballot was held among members of the executive. Of the 17 members present, only two voted against the veto of Peters' nomination.

It was late in the day. Peters emerged, strain and defeat heavily imprinted on his face. He said the executive's decision was the worst thing to happen to 'democracy and freedom and the constitutional relationship between an MP and his or her constituents' in the history of the National Party'. He said he had been dumped because National was looking after its big business funding. He hinted about Cabinet papers in his possession that he might release. He refused to be drawn on his own future. Then he walked out under the autumn skies, leaving the building as a National MP for the very last time.

CHAPTER THIRTEEN

New Zealand First

March 1993–November 1993

WHEN Peters found himself cut adrift from the National Party, with a General Election due in just a few months time, there seemed two likely courses open to him. He could concentrate on winning re-election in Tauranga in 1993, and then form his own political vehicle to contest the first MMP election. Or he could take the plunge and form a new party to contest the 1993 election. In theory there was another alternative — joining the Alliance, the grouping of minor parties consisting of New Labour, the Greens, the Democrats, the Liberals and Mana Motuhake. To those who knew Peters, his joining the Alliance always seemed unlikely. Even if he were offered the leadership of the Alliance, the political constituencies it represented were not a good match with his own sources of support. The Alliance was a grouping of the forces of the left. Peters' constituencies included blue collar workers, but generally consisted of disaffected elements from middle New Zealand. In addition, wealthy superannuatants had formed an important constituency for him ever since National's broken promise on the surcharge.

Joining the Alliance would also have created major personality problems. Neither Peters nor the recently-elected Alliance leader Jim Anderton would have enjoyed working with the other, no matter who ended up with the top job. Both men had powerful egos and very different political philosophies — a sure recipe for disaster. Peters was a pure populist and Anderton a philosophically-driven socialist. Neither had been noted in the past as team players. The two could never have got on; Anderton must have known that, as Peters did. Both men, however, knew they needed to be seen to make an attempt to explore common ground. There were certainly some in the Alliance who were hoping Peters would join them. Some desultory negotiations took place, mainly for the sake of form.

Peters was in no hurry to inform the world of his plans. There was speculation that his first move would be to resign from Parliament and force a by-election in Tauranga, a contest he would be almost certain to win. There was no constitutional necessity for such an action; it would solely be a means of generating publicity. There was only one problem with the by-election idea. If Peters resigned, the government would not be bound to call a by-election if it could simultaneously announce that the General Election would be held within six months. To choose that option the government would need the support of 75 per cent of Parliament. That scenario seemed unlikely, since Bolger, even if he could obtain the Opposition's agreement, would be loath to cut off election day options so far in advance.

Peters broke his silence by announcing he would resign only if the government promised to hold an immediate by-election. The National leadership were not at first playing his game. They gave no guarantee, though McKinnon did point out that if Peters resigned on 2 April during the Parliamentary recess, a by-election would be automatic owing to a technicality in the electoral law. But that would have been three weeks away. Meanwhile National had got into their own special tangle over whether they would stand a candidate in a Tauranga by-election, if there were one. Bolger had said publicly National would contest Tauranga; most others in the party saw little merit in taking part in a pointless and expensive exercise in which National was certain to be creamed.

After repeatedly calling for — and not receiving — assurances that a by-election would be held, Peters was finally given the nod from McKinnon. Immediately the member for Tauranga was into his resignation speech in the House. It was vintage Peters:

A small élite in the National Party and outside it has sought for more than nine months to contest the right of a member of

> Parliament to represent his electorate in the way that the
> electorate feels it should be represented. That is what the issue
> is about. That small élite bears the total responsibility for the cost
> of a by-election, which is required to restore to the people of
> Tauranga the right that, until 4 March of this year, they thought
> they always had — the right to choose who they would have as
> their National Party candidate . . . To those who speak of the cost
> of the by-election, I ask what price should be put on freedom of
> speech, and what price should be put on proper democratic
> processes — on listening to and consulting the people.

Never mind that the 'small élite' included the 50 democratically
elected National members voting for Peters' expulsion from
caucus, who amounted to over 50 per cent of the MPs in
Parliament. Never mind that a by-election would not restore
anything to the people of Tauranga that they did not already
have. Never mind that Peters' freedom of speech was not under
threat, nor, if it were, could it possibly be restored by his
resigning and holding a by-election. Never mind all of that: like
many a Peters speech it *sounded* good, if you were prepared not
to overstrain your critical faculties. Peters challenged National
to stand a candidate against him in Tauranga.

He was to be disappointed. First the Alliance, then Labour,
then National announced they would not be contesting the 17
April by-election. But Tauranga was not without its candidates:
a bumper field of 11 lined up for the starter's pistol. They
included McGillicuddy Serious, who had already challenged
Peters to a wrestling match in a vat of porridge (declined);
Blokes Liberation Front (fielding a woman for suffrage year);
Independent HEMP (Help End Marijuana Prohibition); an
unemployed man hoping to obtain a job by becoming an MP;
the Natural Law Party; a man from Waipukurau who was
standing because he thought the by-election was a waste of
time; and the Christ's Ambassadors' Union candidate, who
could only improve on the one vote he scored in the Wellington
Central by-election. Perhaps if all the minor parties had joined
forces and fielded a marijuana-smoking, levitating, female,
Scottish, unemployed evangelist — if one could be found and
brought down to earth — they might have had a chance. As it
was Peters' opposition was to be hopelessly fractured.

Sensing victory by this stage, Peters was in a confident mood at his campaign opening, telling his audience that the forthcoming Securities Commission report on the BNZ would be bad news for the government. He had not actually *seen* a copy of the report, he later admitted. But he had *heard* that it was bad. There followed a fortnight of campaigning, during which Peters became increasingly unhappy at his press coverage; unsportingly, not all of the media were perpetually glued on Tauranga to watch one man's brave fight against the system. At a rally late in the campaign, Peters turned sharply on Television New Zealand, criticising a *Holmes* programme as 'the most biased, disgraceful and unprofessional TV report I have ever seen'. Peters tried some bully tactics, threatening to look into TVNZ's expenditure and funding when back in Parliament. At the same rally Peters sharply demanded that a television camera, which had been filming the rally, be turned back on.

Two days before the by-election Peters unveiled his policy for employment. It called for community work and training schemes to be administered at the regional, rather than the central government, level. In retrospect the late release of the employment policy was probably not crucial to the by-election's outcome. After Saturday there was no anxious wait while the specials were counted: Peters collected 11,147 votes, followed by McGillicuddy Serious on 260, the unemployed independent on 187, Health For All on 179, and Silent Majority on 176 (its supporters again having failed to turn up on the day); a host of minor parties followed. Peters' majority was 10,887, the voter turnout a surprisingly high 47 per cent. As Peters bit into the 'tartan' cake brought around by the losing McGillicuddy Serious candidate, he must have been more than happy with his majority.

On the very day Peters was sworn in again as an MP, there was some very encouraging news from a special *One Network News*-Heylen poll. It showed that 31 per cent of the respondents said they would vote for a Peters party compared to 34 per cent for Labour, 22 per cent for National and 11 per cent for the Alliance. The poll was purely hypothetical; as yet Peters had no party, no candidates and no policies. But it did suggest Peters could initiate a viable political party, and it spelt real danger for the Alliance.

Despite the positive messages Peters was receiving, there remained huge obstacles to launching a new party for the 1993 election. The organisational work would be formidable. The party would need to hurriedly select a large slate of candidates, many of them inevitably coming from the ranks of the politically unsophisticated and the frankly opportunistic. The new party would need to bring together policy. It would probably miss out on the publicly-funded television advertising time allotted to political parties, owing to its late formation. And the new party would need to raise funds.

Despite the difficulties of launching a new party, the result of the poll must have settled the question in Peters' mind — if it needed settling. But he did not reveal his hand. He let the suspense build up, allowing all manner of public speculation over his future. This helped him stay in the news while working to bring his new party together. Gilbert Myles offered Peters the leadership of the Liberal Party. Other members of the Alliance were treating Peters with more circumspection, though Anderton issued a public invitation for Peters to join the Alliance. Bruce Beetham offered Peters the leadership of the New Zealand Coalition, an obscure group which included the living ghosts of the Social Credit Political League and the New Zealand Party. Peters was not tempted.

While all this was going on the Securities Commission's report on the BNZ's $200 million bad debt insurance scheme finally came out. The report found no evidence of the fraud, conspiracy or falsification of accounts claimed by Peters. It did, however, criticise the accounting treatment of the scheme as creative. The commission's finding was largely a rebuff to Peters, though typically enough he claimed it as 'a damning indictment and total vindication'. Earlier Peters had criticised the commission for not talking to him in the course of the inquiry, and for conducting its inquiries in secret; the Securities Act, however, required such secrecy. It had not been a good month for Peters' BNZ allegations: the Serious Fraud Office had ruled no fraud had taken place in the financing of *Merry Christmas, Mr Lawrence*.

The Securities Commission report on the reinsurance scheme, however, did leave Peters with one angle to seize upon.

The report noted European Pacific had refused to co-operate with the inquiry, on the grounds that Cook Islands law prevented disclosure of material. Peters claimed the commission only cleared the bank because it had met with a 'wall of silence'. This meant a 'full public inquiry' was needed to get to the truth of the matter. In a speech in the House Peters went further:

> What is worse is this silence from the House. Why is the Opposition saying nothing? Why is the government, like the Minister of Justice, not prepared to do something about it? . . . Every other western democracy has answers from its Parliament, but, oh no, not in New Zealand. Who is in whose pocket? The reason that there is silence here is that somebody is in the pockets of those businesses.

The businesses must have done an extremely good job to have bought everyone on the government side and everyone on the Opposition side, leaving Peters alone struck with horror at the depravity of the reinsurance arrangement. Only Peters remained outside the conspiracy. Soon afterwards Peters was again talking in the House about tax evasion and European Pacific. Peters claimed he had a document discussing how to 'mitigate Australian withholding tax', as if that necessarily meant fraud. Peters was prevented from tabling the documents.

Late in June Peters was telling an overflowing audience in the Auckland Town Hall he 'intended to be part of a political vehicle capable of changing directions'. That seemed a very strong hint that a new political party was on its way. A few days later Peters set a date — July 18 — for the announcement of his plans. Negotiations with the Alliance broke up unsuccessfully. Not surprisingly the two sides had different stories over what had constituted the final stumbling blocks. But it was clearly Peters who had been dragging the chain, failing to negotiate face-to-face and refusing even to discuss policy. Peters had wanted legal discussions on how all parties could be bound to stay within the Alliance after the election. It was a concern that came oddly from a rebel who had already left one party himself, albeit involuntarily. The proposal was never a starter. Throughout the negotiations Peters displayed the unwillingness to work constructively with others that his former National colleagues knew only too well.

Just before his launch Peters found himself further snookered on the issue of television advertising. He had already known his new party would be allocated little or no free air time. Now a last-minute change to electoral legislation removed a new proposal that would have meant political parties could buy themselves additional air time. This left Peters high and dry without any air time at all. Not surprisingly, National, Labour and the Alliance had all supported the abandonment of the new proposal. Peters was less impressed, saying the move showed 'latent fascistic and anti-democratic tendencies'. He also argued, with some plausibility, that denying the right to buy air time was contrary to the freedom of expression set out in New Zealand's Bill of Rights Act. Whatever the merits of the argument, Peters had been well and truly hoisted with his own petard: the man who had so often thundered against business money buying influence in politics was now arguing that political parties should be able to buy their own air time.

On Sunday 18 July 1993, at Alexander Park Raceway in Auckland, Peters formally announced his new party — New Zealand First. He said that the party would 'support' candidates in all 99 seats. There was no naming of candidates, and little about the key figures in the party organisation. More details were promised at a press conference on Wednesday. But Peters did spell out 15 policy principles. Some of them were platitudes, such as putting New Zealand first, investing in health and education, and placing top priority on employment. Other principles did give a flavour of where Peters was coming from. He promised new financial institutions and more financial support for business from the government. He promised a halt to state asset sales; 'management by private contracts' — whatever that meant — would be brought in when necessary in place of selling assets. Peters promised a tougher line on immigration, with hints that immigrants were taking the jobs of New Zealanders. He promised tax exemptions for surtax payers investing in capital development. The first objective of foreign policy would be 'good government at home' and being a reliable neighbour.

There was no small measure of populist xenophobia in Peters' address. He told his audience the government had sold assets to people who did not even speak our language. Even the name of Peters' new party — New Zealand First — was implicitly a message of insularity: it was New Zealand *against* the world. Peters was against too many foreigners coming here to live and taking our jobs, against foreigners buying up our assets, against New Zealanders having to rely on foreign funds for capital development and — as far as one could tell — against an internationalist foreign policy.

Peters promised to reduce the number of seats in Parliament from 99 to 80. He also made a commitment to halve the number of consultants in government, undergoing a second conversion on the merits of consultants now that he was no longer spending lavishly on Ka Awatea. Peters said he would establish an independent anti-corruption commission. He would encourage the use of referenda; policies not in New Zealand First's manifesto would be put to the electorate. New Zealand First MPs would not be required to vote with the party except on a vote of confidence; on all other issues their first duty would be to the electorate and the country. This commitment to relax the party whipping system came close to stripping the New Zealand First policy platform of significance: in the absence of a whipping system there was no guarantee New Zealand First MPs would vote in the House for policies carrying through the party's manifesto commitments. Soon Peters would also propose that select committees report directly to the House without reference to party caucuses; this change would make it even more difficult for manifesto policies to be carried through into law. As a final populist offering on the day of the launch, Peters told TV3 he would do the job of Prime Minister for 40 per cent less money than Bolger, and that other top earners in the state sector — including those in SOEs — would also take cuts.

It was already apparent in rough outline where New Zealand First would be standing on the political spectrum. Like the Alliance, it would advocate returning to the more controlled and insulated economy of the pre-Douglas years. In social policy, however, New Zealand First stood somewhere between the Alliance and the government — more willing to spend money than the government but, unlike the Alliance, not desiring a hugely expanded state sector. In a left-right spectrum New Zealand First would be to the left of both National and Labour, but to the right of the Alliance. Like the Alliance, New Zealand First would be a nostalgia party. But while the Alliance would draw its main support from disillusioned Labour voters, New Zealand First's constituency was primarily disillusioned National voters. New Zealand First also had two distinct and almost opposite constituencies — Maori and the wealthy elderly.

If Peters were expecting the new party to make a dramatic impact in the public opinion polls, he was disappointed. In a *One Network News*-Heylen poll taken the day after the launch, New Zealand First was on 12 per cent, just one point ahead of the Alliance. It was not a level at which New Zealand First could expect to win more than one or two seats in the upcoming election. Peters' personal poll rating had fallen, though he remained the most popular politician in the country. Peters was also receiving an unexpectedly hard time from the media. Various amateurish aspects of the launch had been highlighted. His policy was under fire as vague and insubstantial. Nor did the media like having to wait until Wednesday to hear more details. *One Network News* on Monday ran a particularly unsympathetic item on New Zealand First. There was even film of a rattled and irritable Peters being questioned by journalists who had descended on him uninvited. That had never seemed to happen to the old, suave Winston Peters who had had the media doing everything on *his* terms. Worse was to come for Peters on Wednesday when he held his press conference. Billed as the conference in which he would answer questions about the party, it came close to being a disaster.

In the conference, which lasted an hour, Peters seemed to spend most of his time refusing to reveal information. A six-person interim management committee would run the party and select candidates. Peters would not say who they were, or even who had picked them. Peters said he had been selected as leader by the founder members, but would not name the founder members. Key people had approved the 15 principles given at the launch, but Peters refused to say who those people were. Policy committees were working on policy development, but Peters would not say who was on them. Four economists were advising the party but Peters would not give their names. Nine regional committees were being formed but Peters could give no names there either.

It seemed especially strange coming from a self-styled apostle of openness in government. The conference sometimes became heated. Suddenly the media were enjoying putting the hard questions to Peters, and treating him critically. The switch in media sentiment was uncanny. Some members of the gallery who for years had fawned on Peters when he was the scourge of the establishment, were now for the first time subjecting him to the scrutiny they habitually gave other politicians. It was happening because Peters had now crossed that line between opposing and proposing. To oppose was easy and glamorous; it was Peters' natural territory. To propose invites questions, scrutiny, scepticism. From now on Peters would be judged by a higher standard than many of his drinking partners in the gallery had formerly accorded him.

Peters did clear one matter up in the press conference: he stated New Zealand First would stand candidates in all electorates. Some Peters-leaning National MPs had hoped New Zealand First would not stand a candidate in their electorate but would instead formally endorse the National candidate. They were disappointed by Peters' announcement. But no members of the National caucus were tempted to make the jump into New Zealand First. Over the next few days various other names came forward into the public arena. Ian Shearer, a minister in the Muldoon administration, emerged as New Zealand First's candidate for Onehunga. Gilbert Myles, having been in turn a National MP, an independent MP, a Liberal MP, and an Alliance MP, now discovered his true philosophical home as a New Zealand First MP.

For Peters the months running up to the election must have been the busiest in his entire political life. He had an enormous workload: getting a party organisation under way, coming up with policy, keeping tabs on dozens of candidate selections, and still participating in the day-to-day cut and thrust of politics. With these pressures it is not surprising he soon suffered the embarrassment of failing to turn up to support an amendment he had moved to a bill in the House. The amendment sought to cut the size of an MMP Parliament from 120 seats to 80.

Peters eventually gave the names of the six people on his party's management committee. One was Peters himself, though he had previously said he would not be on the committee. Other members were Cheryl Shearer, wife of Ian Shearer; Christchurch businessman Brooke McKenzie; former National Party official Neil Atwood, who had headed Peters' by-election campaign committee; Judith Surgenor, a former National Party worker for Gilbert Myles; and Doug Woolerton, formerly of National's Waikato Division. Woolerton would later become chairman of New Zealand First. All New Zealand First candidate selections were being held in secret, in contrast to the practice of other political parties. The names of the unsuccessful nominees were not even disclosed after the event.

The mishaps surrounding the party launch continued when Peters and Sarah Neems were involved in a drink-driving incident in the early hours of one Friday morning. Peters was the passenger in a car, driven by Neems, that was stopped by police. She was breath-tested and subsequently charged with excess blood-alcohol. News of the story was in the media remarkably quickly, something Peters was understandably unhappy about.

Peters and the police were quickly at odds over details of the incident. According to a statement issued by Wayne Strong of Wellington police, in response to numerous media inquiries, the incident happened at 2.30 am when police stopped a car that was driving south on Taranaki St without its headlights on. The driver was breath-tested and asked to come back to the station for further tests:

She agreed but wished to advise her passenger of what was happening. She spoke to her passenger for three to five minutes. He then approached the constable and advised that he was the driver's lawyer and would be representing her from that point. The constable recognised the male passenger, who explained that the female was driving because he had asked her to drive him home after working late at Parliament.

The passenger then asked that the constable undertake a further breath test on the driver, in front of him. This was declined as it is contrary to the normal breath-alcohol procedures. Further requests were made and these were refused. Throughout the conversation the constable stated that the male passenger's attitude was not of an obstructive nature.

After about five minutes Neems then accompanied the police to the station for further tests.

The female driver was then returned to her vehicle where the male passenger was asleep. The unit was then called away to an urgent incident at a city nightclub.

Peters told the media that the statement about being asleep in the car was 'an absolute bloody lie'. Peters claimed he had stayed in the car because Neems said it could not be locked. According to Peters, after a long wait the police then dropped Neems back at the car with her keys, and told her she could drive. Neems then drove on to their destination. If Peters' version is true it is extremely odd that the police allowed Neems to drive after a positive breath test. The police were shortly to lay charges against Neems, though she would be acquitted on a technicality.

Peters and the police also gave differing accounts of Peters' final destination. According to the police Peters had told them Neems was driving him home from Parliament. But Peters told the *Sunday Star* a different story:

On Thursday my schedule had been set back and Sarah was driving me from a confidential meeting with a businessman to the home of my sister in Wellington who, with her husband and others, have been helping me draft speeches on Maori policy and organise meetings with Maoridom. We were preparing material for a meeting I am holding with the Ratana Church in Wanganui tomorrow. I take total responsibility for asking my secretary to attend those meetings.

I have no car of my own in Wellington and use my secretary to drive me to appointments when I want confidentiality to be maintained. She has worked with me for four years now and is one of only two people in Wellington I feel I can totally trust.

Politics is certainly a lonely life for a conspiracy theorist in a party of two MPs. The list of people in Wellington Peters did not completely trust evidently included at least one of his siblings. But now we had two stories about where Peters was going. If Peters' *Sunday Star* version is true, his family are certainly night owls, as is the businessman who had been seeing Peters in a top secret meeting ending around 2.30 am; either that or the business was extremely urgent. To complete the confusion, the *Sunday Star* reported a taxi driver as saying he had seen Peters and a young woman taking a taxi from the rank outside Parliament at around midnight that night.

There were a number of loose ends to the story. But Peters was exasperated by the extent of the media interest. He told *The Dominion*:

> My theory is if it was a man there would be nothing in it. If it was the BNZ the media would not be interested and that is all I am saying.

It was a damaging incident for a party that — unlike the other three main parties — was built almost entirely around one charismatic leader.

Peters did make a speech on Maori policy. He attacked the Treaty settlements process, saying it had been captured by a small élite and had done little for the average Maori. He called this process 'the brown version of trickle down'. Peters made it plain Ka Awatea would form the basis of New Zealand First's Maori policy. Late in August the government, Labour and the Alliance announced that a multi-party accord had been reached on superannuation. All three parties were now committed to keeping the surcharge in one form or another. Peters, who had refused an invitation for New Zealand First to join in the talks, labelled the accord 'betrayal and deceit'. He committed New Zealand First to axing the surcharge.

New Zealand First had now slipped to around 10 per cent in the opinion polls, roughly equal with the Alliance. Only a fraction of the 99 candidates sought by Peters had been selected. Little policy had been released. The nationwide party organisation seemed in a rudimentary state, with little evidence of activity on the ground. Two months out from polling day the Broadcasting Standards Authority confirmed New Zealand First would receive no publicly funded air time, since the party had been formed too late. McGillicuddy Serious, doughty opponents in the by-election, received $50,000 for advertising. No wonder Peters was in a bad mood the following day when he ordered two men from a television comedy show out of a candidate launch in Auckland. Shortly afterwards Peters' ranking as preferred Prime Minister fell to 16 per cent in the latest *One Network News*-Heylen poll, ending his 14-month period as the country's most popular politician.

Peters was at odds with fellow New Zealand First MP Gilbert Myles when Myles tabled in the House the transcript of a taped conversation between two Labour Party members. The transcript purportedly backed up Myles' assertion that former Labour MP Fred Gerbic had accepted money for election expenses from immigrants in return for granting them permanent residence. Myles soon discovered that there was only one person in New Zealand First allowed to table documents obtained from shady characters. Displaying an uncharacteristic sense of propriety, Peters said Myles should not have tabled the tape, but should instead have sent the material to the Attorney-General. Peters *did* call for his mandatory 'full public inquiry'. To Myles the apprentice, it must have been puzzling to find himself so disowned by his master. Gerbic was later cleared of any impropriety.

A fortnight before New Zealand First's campaign launch, Peters was admitting the party may not field candidates in all seats. Two days later Peters was telling a Grey Power meeting that New Zealand owed $67 billion and could not pay it back. He said we should reschedule the debt 'to buy us time to restructure the economy and to get it back on a sound footing'. Peters even suggested that New Zealand use the repayment of its debt as a bargaining chip for gaining market access for its products. Coming from a former minister of the Crown, it was a speech either of the purest ignorance or the crudest and most cynical populism. Only basket-case third world countries propose rescheduling debt; it is usually done in conjunction with organisations like the International Monetary Fund imposing packages of 'orthodox' economics of the type Peters had been vigorously opposing in New Zealand.

Two-thirds of the $67 billion that Peters claimed we could not pay back was in any case private sector debt. The government was quite capable of paying the interest on the remainder. New Zealand's international creditors would not stand any talk of rescheduling — nor should they. Any such proposal would turn New Zealand into a laughing stock, to say nothing of the economic consequences. The government would face higher interest rates when its debt was rolled over, while the private sector would also face a steep increase in borrowing costs. Many credit sources would dry up altogether.

Various formal party policies had by now been trickling out from New Zealand First. The tertiary education and training policy promised to abolish tertiary fees and cancel all loan obligations to students — quite a windfall for some lucky borrowers. There was a commitment to boost the numbers in the training opportunities programme. Many New Zealand First policies were fiscally expensive, and all were uncosted. One policy that met a less than wholehearted reception was the environmental policy on recreational fishing. It proposed to ban all commercial fishing within ten kilometres of the coastline in stipulated areas. Commercial fishers adversely affected would be compensated from the proceeds of a special tax on recreational fishing equipment. The 'fishing rod tax' seemed a bizarre idea, though as a keen recreational fisherman himself Peters must presumably have given it some thought.

When the day came for his election campaign launch at an outdoor rally in Tauranga, Peters was struggling with laryngitis. The warm-up men had a lot of work to do; Peters exceeded even his own standards of tardiness by arriving 45 minutes late. Peters' speech hit the usual notes, but with his voice often tailing off he lacked his normal fire. The New Zealand First schools policy was announced at the launch. Though the party had set itself the target of selecting candidates for all electorates by this stage, 30 electorates were still without a candidate. Two days later the party conceded for the first time it would be unable to field a full slate.

The campaign saw Peters into a hectic schedule averaging three rallies per day, all around the country. It was a style of campaigning in marked contrast to that of his opponents. Bolger and Moore held few public rallies, concentrating instead on informal meet-the-people events and photo-opportunities. Only Peters could draw the crowds in public rallies, even if his audiences were mainly elderly. His campaign themes were familiar ones: the small élite who had sold out ordinary New Zealanders; corruption in government; broken promises. But now there was a new element in his conspiracy — the media. According to Peters there was a plot between the media and 'monied élite from certain big business interests'. He particularly singled out the *Herald*, *The Dominion* and Television New Zealand. He complained that New Zealand First was always covered last of the four main parties on the television news. The falling out between Peters and the press gallery was virtually complete.

Peters released an old Cabinet paper saying there were no major impediments to the sale of New Zealand Post. He used the paper to question Bolger's assertion that the government would not be selling New Zealand Post. Not until 24 October — two weeks out from polling day — did Peters release New Zealand First's economic policy. Anyone inclined to give him the benefit of the doubt on economic issues would be well advised to plough their way through the six pages of that remarkable document. No mere description of its contents can convey its unique confusion, obscurity and illiteracy: it is hard enough even to understand half of the sentences.

Naturally there is a long section on monetary policy and the Reserve Bank Act, unfathomably headed 'fiscal policy'. The claim that the 0-2 per cent inflation target is set down in the Act, along with many other misconceptions and half-truths, suggests that Peters may never have actually read the Reserve Bank Act that he has so long excoriated. The section giving New Zealand First's economic policies is brief and vaguely worded, but broadly represents a return to the 'Fortress New Zealand' policies prevailing until 1984. Foreign investment would be restricted and in its place an attempt would be made to provide a pool of domestic savings for investment purposes. There would be tax breaks for business investment. Import protection would be increased. A new banking institution would be set up to improve access to capital for small businesses (already announced in the small business policy). On the basis of such policies New Zealand First claimed growth rates in excess of 6 per cent were achievable.

New Zealand First's taxation policy, released with the economic policy, was scarcely more reassuring. It promised to lower taxes for those on very low incomes, and to abolish the superannuation surtax. It also spelt out a raft of tax breaks for job creation, capital investment, new export markets and specific industries. Nowhere, in either the economic or taxation policy was there any serious discussion of overall fiscal policy, i.e., the implications of individual spending and taxing policies for aggregate government spending, taxation and the deficit. New Zealand First's spending commitments and tax breaks, even on a conservative estimate, could only have been funded through a substantial increase in tax *rates* or much higher government borrowing. Nowhere is that fact admitted. One searches New Zealand First documents in vain for any discussion whatsoever of the fiscal trade-offs that would need to be made. New Zealand First was the only one of the four major parties whose fiscal policy did not even *begin* to engage with reality. Even the Alliance were honest enough to admit their policies required tax increases.

New Zealand First's employment policy was already in the public arena. Many of its sentences had syntax so tangled they read like clues to cryptic crossword puzzles:

New Zealand First will encourage a partnership between government and local government and any institution or public enterprise with a proven record of work placement to the full amount of the unemployment benefit plus ten per cent.

There were other sentences the plausibility of which dissolves after a moment's thought:

New Zealand First will forgo for two years the taxation

component of any wages, in favour of the employee, of any
registered unemployed placement in new employment.

In other words, you escape having to pay income tax for two
years if you use the New Zealand Employment Service — a
great way to make periodic returns to the dole queue popular.
The employment policy also promised a homemaking rebate
or allowance to encourage one parent to stay at home, adding
that 'this would then free up jobs for unemployed sons and
daughters'. That approach incorporated one of the most fatal
fallacies about the labour market — the idea that there is a
fixed stock of 'jobs' out there, and that if one person stopped
working it would free up a job for somebody else. A
homemaking allowance would shrink the size of the labour
force, increase the tax burden on those in work and reduce
gross domestic product, but not necessarily lower
unemployment.

The final elements of the New Zealand First policy were
released in a rally in the National stronghold of Te Kuiti. The
party promised publicly-funded community service work for all
parental welfare recipients who could not find work in the
private sector. Those on the schemes would receive an income
10 per cent higher than their current earnings, with guaranteed
child care and health care.

With all policy now out in the public arena, Peters plugged
on with his campaigning. But it was not to be his year. Instead,
it was the Alliance that was steadily gaining in support. Many
factors were leading to the strengthening of its vote. In an
attempt to counter National's claim that Labour would put up
taxes, Moore and finance spokesman Michael Cullen were
shifting as close as possible to the government on taxation and
government spending. This move shored up Labour's support
in the centre, but it meant Labour was losing support on the left
to the Alliance. Anderton was performing surprisingly strongly
in the campaign, successfully projecting an image of strength,
wisdom and sweet reasonableness. The Alliance had a much
more developed party structure than New Zealand First for the
campaign work on the ground. And New Zealand First were
missing their free advertising time. One poll just before the

election showed Peters trailing all three of the other main party leaders as preferred Prime Minister.

At least in his own electorate Peters knew there would be few problems. National in Tauranga had started the year with low membership and morale, and with a sizeable debt to the Waikato Division. The electorate had been weakened further by defections to New Zealand First, and had then spent much of the next few months on infighting. The selected candidate, John Cronin, had to survive persistent attempts by factions in the electorate to persuade him to stand aside. There was a strong view in the electorate that Cronin was not a dynamic enough candidate to cope with Peters. The divisional chairman, Lindsay Tisch, had been forced to come into the electorate and bang heads together.

By election day all barometers were indicating a comfortable National victory. New Zealand First would win Tauranga, it was agreed, but no other seats. But 6 November turned out to be a night of the unexpected. National's confidently planned victory celebration in Te Kuiti turned into a tense and very long evening. Though National was gaining the largest number of seats, no clear victor was emerging. By night's end New Zealanders were faced with a hung Parliament. Although Peters had taken Tauranga by well over 7000 votes, the performance of his party nationwide must have disappointed him: New Zealand First captured just over 8 per cent of the total vote through its candidates in 84 out of the 99 seats. The Alliance had captured over 18 per cent of the vote. New Zealand First had performed surprisingly strongly in the three Maori seats it contested. And in the biggest upset of the night, New Zealand First candidate Tau Henare, possessor of the most prestigious surname in Maoridom, was leading Labour's Bruce Gregory in Northern Maori by over 300 votes. It looked as if Labour's 50-year stranglehold on the Maori seats was over. Henare looked as surprised as anyone.

CHAPTER FOURTEEN

Wineboxes and
Swine Boxes

November 1993–June 1994

A number of explanations can be made in retrospect for Henare's win. Labour had been divided in Northern Maori, Bruce Gregory having seen off a challenge to his nomination earlier in the year. Henare's name had sure selling power in Maoridom, and he was an articulate candidate in his own right. And there was a strong sympathy vote for Peters from Maori.

Henare's election may have come as a shock to Peters, as well as a surprise. Peters may even have regretted taking Henare on as a candidate. Henare was ambitious, having reportedly written to both New Zealand First and the Alliance to test their interest in having him. Henare would be able to share Peters' Parliamentary workload and he would also shore up New Zealand First's support among Maori. But that was the problem: Henare had strong views on Maori issues, and on the Treaty, that were well outside the co-ordinates of middle New Zealand. New Zealand First's 1993 Maori policy had scarcely mentioned the Treaty; Peters did not want his party to have a Maori flavour that would consign it to the fringes of political life. There is bound to be tension between Peters and Henare, particularly on Treaty issues, and perhaps a political parting of the ways further down the track.

Peters was little in the spotlight on election night or on the days immediately following. Anderton, however, was constantly in the news and continued his rise in public esteem. The provisional result had seen National taking 49 seats, Labour 46, the Alliance 2 and New Zealand First 2. MMP had won a narrow victory over first-past-the-post. New Zealand politics was clearly in a radically new environment. For some days the media, who are professionally subject to sudden viruses, suffered a chronic attack of the word 'consensus'. Consensus was everywhere and everything, displaying an almost historical inevitability. In this environment, Anderton's shrewdly-projected image of reasonableness and moderation fitted precisely the public mood. Peters said almost nothing. His glowering, defiant face seemed for a moment almost like yesterday's image. A TV3-Gallup poll taken the week following the election showed Peters' rating as preferred Prime Minister down to 13 per cent.

The post-election atmosphere in which the two Jim's — Bolger and Anderton — carried out their mating dance, was a pointer to the challenges Peters will face in joining a power block under MMP. It was towards Anderton, not Peters, that Bolger instinctively made his overtures. This was partly because Bolger had no personal animosity towards Anderton. But there was a deeper reason than that. Bolger is nothing if not a realist when it comes to his own political survival. Bolger turned to Anderton because he knew he could predict Anderton's responses with a reasonable degree of certainty. Anderton was a known quantity who had shown himself capable of negotiation. Peters, by contrast, had defined himself almost entirely in terms of what he was against, and had shown himself incapable of working with anyone. He was a chaos politician. Bolger's flirtation with Anderton was a warning to Peters that when the basis for any trust is destroyed, he was not likely to be the first invited into a coalition.

As it turned out, the media orgy of consensus had a short life. The seat of Waitaki turned back to National on the special votes, leaving Bolger with 50 seats in a Parliament of 99. National were now confirmed in office, though barely in power. From now on it was safety first from Bolger. Richardson was axed as Finance Minister because the economic recovery was now so strong he could afford to rid himself of her. For the next 18 months almost no significant new policy initiatives were undertaken. National became a ghost of a government: the talk was not about what National would do, but about how long the government would last and what the future shape of Parliament would look like under MMP.

When Peters arrived back in Wellington after the special votes had been counted, he fired a broadside at 'consensus' politics. He stressed that New Zealand First would not be 'talking about deals and wheeling and dealing'. Politics had not essentially changed, he said, but there was a paramountcy about Parliament that had not been there over the past ten years. When the government announced that Labour MP Peter Tapsell would be the next Speaker, Peters slammed the move as an attempt to set aside the will of the electorate. He promised New Zealand First would oppose the appointment when Parliament opened. He also warned that New Zealand First might not participate in the multi-party employment talks unless the terms of reference were acceptable.

Four days before Christmas, Parliament sat for its largely ceremonial opening day. There was a conspicuously empty seat next to Henare, as the MPs went up in turn to be sworn in. Peters' taste for dramatics had not left him. Four minutes before it was his turn to be called, Peters finally arrived in the chamber. After all members had been sworn in and the new Speaker was proposed, Peters countered by proposing the previous Speaker Robin Gray. Peters also tried without success to gain a place on the finance and expenditure select committee, and to gain third party representation on the Parliamentary services commission, the body that allocates funding for support services to MPs.

Little was heard from Peters in the early weeks of January. After a year of almost constant pressure, he must have more than usually relished his summer holiday. If he had not already known that heading a small party in Parliament is extremely hard work, he did now. No longer could he just sit back and pick off the issues that he wanted to run with, as he had done for much of his career. With minimal research support, Peters now had to form a view on almost every issue, vote in Parliament, wait around attempting to get the call from the Speaker in Parliamentary debates, and keep up an attack on the government. Anderton could have told Peters a thing or two about the demands of leading a minor party. And Anderton possessed important advantages over over Peters: he was brighter and had a better sense of strategy.

The 12 months following the 1993 election were not vintage ones for Peters. Instead, Anderton took the Alliance to a remarkable lead in the opinion polls over Labour, who had made the electorally catastrophic decision to dump Moore for Helen Clark. Peters' own rating as preferred Prime Minister would fluctuate around 10 per cent, with New Zealand First ranking between five and 10 per cent. There was one major flare-up of the old McCarthy tactics from Peters, but nothing like the heady days of his classic McCarthy months. There was much of the usual populist rhetoric, but without a great deal of focus. He even missed obvious opportunities to score political points. He seemed to be struggling for direction. For some reason, the edge seemed to have gone off his performance.

In February New Zealand First surprised no one by withdrawing from the multi-party employment talks. Peters complained that the scope of the talks was too restrictive, that the government had ruled out urgent action in the 1994 Budget, and that the New Zealand First nomination for the employment task force — Ian Shearer — had not been accepted. Peters claimed the government wanted 'the illusion of action for cheap political gain'. Neither Labour nor the Alliance shared Peters' position that no progress could be made.

In March Peters assiduously rubbed various populist itches of the body politic. He told a crowd of militant superannuatants exactly what they wanted to hear: that the government's policy of asset testing of geriatric hospital patients was splitting 'part of the fabric of the family'. In Parliament Peters sought an apology from the government over its aborted legal challenge to the election result in the Onehunga electorate. Along with Laws and Napier MP Geoff Braybrooke, Peters launched a petition to hold a referendum on reducing the number of seats in the MMP Parliament from 120 to 100.

Peters also attempted to introduce a private members bill to include employment along with low inflation as one of the objectives of the Reserve Bank. This idea had been missing from New Zealand First's 1993 policy, which had talked only of aiming for an inflation rate slightly below the average of our trading partners. In 1994 Peters also changed his stance over the Employment Contracts Act. In 1991 Peters had voted in favour of it. The 1993 New Zealand First policy had not mentioned the Act at all, though 'a spokeswoman' had told the media that New Zealand First supported the Act. Now in 1994 Peters criticised the Employment Contracts Act and supported an Opposition bill aiming to set up a council to draft new legislation. Since in 1989 Peters had been both for and against 'labour market deregulation', perhaps it should not surprise us that he could be both for and against the Employment Contracts Act.

In March Peters embarked on what would prove to be by far his biggest story of the year — Cook Island tax avoidance deals. Not for the first time, his allegations were based on documents allegedly taken from the European Pacific group of companies, which had been owned in the late eighties by the BNZ, Fay, Richwhite and Brierley's. Late in 1992, during his classic McCarthy months, Peters had talked in Parliament about international tax avoidance schemes. On that occasion he had not done a good job of explaining the issue. Now he returned to the subject with a vengeance. It was the first time in his career where an allegation of illegality under privilege would draw support from a significant number of independent experts — though not necessarily a majority. Because of this fact, and because of the typically scattergun manner in which Peters launched his attacks on this occasion, it is important to keep in mind some key principles.

New Zealand, like most countries, has a substantial tax avoidance industry. Many of the more aggressive practitioners are without doubt low life forms, for whose business ethics few excuses could be made. Assisting corporates and wealthy individuals to avoid paying tax through schemes often going to the edge of the law — and contrary to the spirit of the law — is one of the least edifying of occupations, though the pecuniary rewards can be extremely high. Tax avoidance is not illegal. However, the Commissioner of Inland Revenue does have the power under the Income Tax Act in certain circumstances to effectively set aside the avoidance mechanism and require tax to be paid.

Sometimes tax planning schemes break the law and become tax *evasion*; in those cases the Commissioner can prosecute the offender in court. Because tax evasion is a criminal offence, prosecutions must be proved to the criminal standard of proof, i.e., beyond reasonable doubt. Sometimes schemes fall into the grey area between avoidance and evasion, and it is up to the judgment of the Commissioner, and ultimately the court, to make a determination. Like other arms of the state with the power to bring prosecutions — such as the police — the Commissioner has complete operating independence from politicians. The Commissioner applies the law; Parliament makes the law. This separation of functions is crucial to our constitution. As with the courts, if Parliament is unhappy at the way the Commissioner is applying the law, the proper response is to change the law to make Parliament's intentions more explicit.

European Pacific was formed in the late eighties primarily, it appears, to take advantage of opportunities for international tax avoidance opening up in the wake of the abolition of exchange controls by Roger Douglas. Others in the business sector were at a similar time moving to exploit these opportunities. When the Labour government appreciated the erosion of the tax base that was taking place, it moved in 1988 to introduce international tax legislation to counteract avoidance activity. All the transactions talked about by Peters date from the time before the law was tightened.

European Pacific's activities clearly included some highly aggressive avoidance schemes which pushed to the edge of the law. There was one in particular — termed the 'Magnum' scheme — that would prove to be of most interest. Its full details emerged only slowly over a number of weeks. The Magnum scheme was an extremely complex chain of transactions, but in essence the avoidance occurred because tax was paid to the Cook Islands Tax Department on a transaction in the Cook Islands, while simultaneously a benefit was received from a different branch of the Cook Islands government. The benefit came from a European Pacific company selling a promissory note to the Cook Islands Government Property Corporation, and then buying it back for a large profit later that day. The profit virtually matched the tax paid to the Cook Islands government. The scheme generated Cook Islands tax certificates which could be used to offset tax in New Zealand, even though tax had not in substance been paid.

Plainly this scheme raised serious questions about possible corruption in the Cook Islands government. Whether or not New Zealanders involved in the scheme had broken the domestic law was far more problematic. The scheme appeared to fall into the grey area, and it would take the wisdom of Solomon to be certain how it should be viewed. The Commissioner of Inland Revenue viewed the scheme as tax *avoidance*, and we can assume he imposed tax on it for that reason. However, the Commissioner judged it was not tax *evasion*, and so there was no attempt to prosecute.

In Peters' first attack in Parliament, he claimed 'high-powered tax lawyers and merchants of greed in this country, and crooked officials and politicians in the Cook Islands' had combined to defraud taxpayers. Peters gave a description of the Magnum transaction, but did not name any New Zealanders. He also described another European Pacific scheme, known as the 'JIF' transaction. Peters called on the Cook Islands government to hold a full public inquiry and the New Zealand government to withhold future aid to the Cooks. He was in full conspiracy mode:

> If one has read the *Independent* and the *National Business Review*, and has followed the court cases, one knows that it has been going on for much too long. Why is this government protecting those people? . . . My explanation is this: they have a hold on some people in New Zealand politics; they have some New Zealand politicians in their pockets.

Catching the government off guard, Peters tabled the 'winebox' full of documents that he had tried unsuccessfully to table 16 times before.

The next day the Speaker ruled that Peters' tabled documents could not be distributed to MPs, as was the usual practice; one copy only would be held in the Office of the Clerk of the House for inspection by MPs. The Speaker's ruling was given in order to respect a court order against the publication of material contained in the winebox papers. European Pacific had obtained an interim injunction against TVNZ (who had prepared a *Frontline* documentary on the Magnum and JIF transactions), and against the two business weeklies, blocking the publication of confidential material. The relationship between the courts and Parliament had long been an uncertain area of constitutional law; Tapsell's ruling was bound to be controversial. Peters strongly opposed the ruling. He argued, with a hazy grasp of constitutional law, that Parliament was the highest court in the land.

Peters succeeded in spurring the Cook Islands government to initiate an inquiry. But in New Zealand the head of the Serious Fraud Office, Charles Sturt, stated his office had already seen the documents tabled by Peters and had found no evidence of criminal fraud. Peters called for a full public inquiry to match the one happening in the Cook Islands. He also said he would make further disclosures in Parliament.

He was not joking.

I name the guilty men in this transaction as the following: David Lloyd, Managing Director, European Pacific; David Richwhite, Chairman, European Pacific and Managing Director of Fay Richwhite; Paul Collins, Director, European Pacific and Managing Director of Brierley Investments; and Peters Travers, director, European Pacific and formerly of the Bank of New Zealand (BNZ). I also accuse the following employees of European Pacific: Peter Brannigan and Anthony McCullagh, now partners in Horwath, Brannigan, McCullagh and Co., Auckland; Geoff Barry, Chief Executive, European Pacific; David Lilly, now with Tip Top foods, Auckland; Mark Jones, whereabouts unknown; Robert Hay, European Pacific Hong Kong; George Couttie, thought to be in Auckland; and Trevor Clarke, Rarotonga.

I accuse the following lawyers and outside accountancy firms who gave approval to this criminal fraud on the New Zealand and Cook Islands revenues: Russell Florence, KPMG Peat Marwick, Auckland, and Jonathon Flaws of the legal firm of Bell Gully Buddle Weir . . .

212

If the Serious Fraud Office cannot find enough evidence in the Magnum Corporation transaction alone to put a number of these men behind bars, then the Serious Fraud Office should be immediately suspended from operating, pending an inquiry into possible corruption of that office . . . If the Commissioner of Inland Revenue stands by his press statement of last Friday and today, and continues to claim that all of this — including the use of fake tax certificates — is legal, he should be fired immediately and charged with conspiring to pervert the course of justice in New Zealand.

Later in the speech, Peters added Jan Dawson of KPMG Peat Marwick to his list. It was classic McCarthy: the enlargement of a conspiracy theory by including the authorities who cleared the accused; the elevation of differences of view into charges of criminality; and the wholesale attacks on individuals under privilege. This occasion was especially ugly, since Peters had attacked the integrity of two law enforcement officials — Henry and Sturt — in whom it was important the public had confidence.

Peters received a second chance to speak in Parliament's address-and-reply debate. In a speech peppered with virulence Peters claimed the government was actively sheltering fraudsters from their just desserts'. Peters also challenged the Prime Minister:

Will the Prime Minister deny now — in this House, tonight — that there was the other day a secret meeting between the Prime Minister's department and others, in which it was agreed to get the documents back to Mr Henry and Mr Sturt with the intention of a whitewash in mind.

The Prime Minister promptly came down to the House and denied the allegation.

There was the standard round of denials after Peters' speech. But the virulence of Peters' attacks, his repeated use of the multiple untruth, was forcing the government on to the back foot. Revenue Minister Wyatt Creech was refusing to rule out the public inquiry demanded by Peters. An inquiry would, needless to say, have been a serious over-reaction. All that had been presented so far was one marginal deal occurring under a legislative regime that had subsequently been changed. New Zealand's prosecution and enforcement agencies often make borderline decisions on whether someone has, or has not, broken the law; not infrequently those decisions displease people. If the government believed Sturt or Henry were interpreting the law in too lax a fashion, the proper course would be to strengthen the law.

The following week reports by both Sturt and Henry were presented to Parliament. Both men stated they had gone through the documents tabled by Peters and had no reason to revise their earlier conclusions. Henry's report noted that an 'independent barrister of extensive commercial, criminal and taxation experience' had looked at the 'best documented' scheme, i.e., the Magnum transaction, and confirmed no tax evasion had taken place.

A long Parliamentary recess halted for some weeks Peters' use of privilege. He reverted to feeding the electorate the usual populist scraps that were its diet when there was no big inquisition under way. He criticised the Treasury for its large overestimation of the fiscal deficit (which by then had turned into a surplus), asserting that poor forecasting had added to New Zealand's interest bill. He also claimed that the government had no mandate to go ahead with further asset sales. Meanwhile European Pacific continued locked in its legal battle with the media. Finally the court injunction was lifted solely as it applied to the Magnum and JIF material, enabling the *Frontline* programme to be screened. In view of that new development, the Speaker ruled that the Magnum and JIF material could now be made public from among the papers tabled by Peters.

The screening of the *Frontline* programme made quite an impact. Though it did not assert that tax evasion had taken place, its detailing of the transactions spoke volumes for the business ethics of those involved. *Frontline* was followed by a special edition of *Fraser*, in which Peters, Creech and Henry were among those interviewed. The impact of the programme was eloquent — some might say frightening — testimony to the power of television to influence political debate. The world of highly aggressive corporate tax avoidance was new to many viewers. Had the programme screened at a different time, it would have performed a useful public service. It would have been especially useful coming in 1992 when Richardson, who had consistently wanted a tough line on tax avoidance, was locked in a Cabinet battle on international tax policy. As it turned out, the *Frontline* programme served to fan one of Peters' McCarthyist witch hunts.

Following the programme some of the government's more fringe backbenchers made calls for an inquiry. Creech told the House there was no need for an inquiry, but Peters was keeping up the pressure:

> Sturt and Henry should be suspended immediately. An inquiry should hear evidence linking these men to a criminal conspiracy involving Michael Fay, David Richwhite, Paul Collins, Peter Travers, and Lindsay Pyne, formerly of the Bank of New Zealand. This conspiracy involved secret agreements by the Inland Revenue Department and Serious Fraud Office not to prosecute European Pacific.

The speech was a vivid example of how deeply into fantasyland Peters' conspiracy theories could take him. The *only* evidence for Peters' shocking charge against Sturt and Henry is that, over one deal already several years old, they had taken a borderline decision with which *some* — not all — tax lawyers disagreed. A thousand other conspiracy theories could be spun with equal ease. One could easily invent conspiracy theories about Peters himself. Peters had entered Parliament through a misreading of the Electoral Act by a judge appointed by the National government. A conspiracy involving Peters, the Chief Justice, the other presiding judges, Muldoon, the Attorney-General and the Governor-General would have made a vivid speech in Parliament. It was no less plausible than Peters' own effort.

Peters added to his conspiracy some more names, both familiar and unfamiliar, pushing his total of individuals attacked under privilege to over 40:

> The conspiracy also involved Robin Congreve, Geoff Ricketts, John Lusk, John King, Geoff Clews, and Richard Green, all

lawyers from Russell McVeagh McKenzie Bartleet and Co. and all either one-time directors of European Pacific — associated companies and/or designers of these tax frauds.

The next day the government introduced the Taxation Reform (Companies and Other Matters) Bill, which had been in the pipeline for some time. It was a typical omnibus taxation bill dealing with a range of areas - including international tax. Among its measures it made it illegal to claim a foreign tax credit where in substance the tax had not been paid. The bill further strengthened the law against the Magnum transaction occurring again. By that evening, however, Creech was stating that the finance and expenditure select committee, which would be considering the bill, would 'examine the practices that were going on' back in 1988.

This indicated some type of 'inquiry' by the select committee, beyond a normal examination of the bill before it. Clearly the government had buckled to the pressure to be seen to be doing something. Yet a select committee was precisely the wrong forum for an inquiry. This was to become even more apparent when Labour offered one of their places on the committee to Peters. A select committee, like Parliament itself, is protected by privilege. It looked ominously as if another parallel between Peters and McCarthy would be played out before our eyes: McCarthy had employed a senate committee as one of the most powerful weapons in his campaign. The government's move bore every sign of a panic decision.

While it was now clear that some type of inquiry was due to take place, it was far from clear precisely what the select committee would be examining. Several weeks of confusion followed. Richardson, who was now chairing the committee, was attempting to narrow the focus of the inquiry as much as possible; she did not want the committee to become a kangaroo court. Opposition committee members were understandably wanting a much wider investigation. Even government member Max Bradford, who had not been noted for his toughness on tax avoidance while a member of the committee, was wanting a wide inquiry. It was just this type of playing to the gallery which had seen Bradford, once a close friend of Bolger's, passed over for promotion after the 1993 election.

Shortly after the select committee 'inquiry' had been announced, the privileges committee, which had been considering whether to release the remaining 'winebox' documents tabled by Peters, unanimously agreed that the papers should finally be released. Since very little in the legal situation had changed, it was hard to avoid the conclusion that the decision reflected the new political winds blowing since the *Frontline* documentary.

In July Richardson announced her resignation, putting the government in a substantial quandary over the inquiry. Bolger had been relying on her to keep tight control over the rest of the select committee. With Richardson gone, Bradford was the natural person to take on the job of chair. But ministers were not confident Bradford could prevent the inquiry degenerating into a circus or a star chamber. It was ultimately up to the committee members themselves to decide who should be chair. Bradford wanted the job badly, resisting strenuous attempts by Bolger, Birch and Creech to persuade him to stand aside.

By now key members of the government were growing seriously concerned. They had become a victim of their own wimpishness, and were looking for a way out. Geoffrey Palmer helped by making an excellent speech highlighting the potential for the inquiry to turn into a 'political and media circus', in which natural justice was overruled. The Solicitor-General also came to the government's rescue with advice that the select committee was not an appropriate vehicle for an inquiry. In August the government made its second sharp change of direction over the 'winebox' affair. Bolger told Parliament the select committee would not be an appropriate forum, citing both Palmer and the Solicitor-General. Instead Bolger announced an inquiry by a retired High Court judge. The judge was Sir Ronald Davison — the Chief Justice who had presided over the Hunua electoral petition 15 years before.

The terms of reference of the inquiry were as follows:

- to report on whether Henry and Sturt had acted in a lawful, proper and competent manner in dealing with the winebox documents.

217

- to indicate what, if any, changes needed to be made to the criminal or tax laws, to protect New Zealand's tax base from fraud, evasion and avoidance arising from the type of transactions detailed in the winebox documents.
- to refer any matters relating to specific taxpayers to the appropriate authorities.

It is one of the ironies of the government's double shuffle that, from a starting point of saying no inquiry was warranted, *two* concessions were then made to Peters, each of which may provide him with a platform for grandstanding. One is the Davison inquiry. The other is the select committee on which Peters was given a place. One thing seems certain: we have not heard the last of the 'winebox' affair.

Cook Islands tax allegations were the one bright spot in an increasingly gloomy year for Peters. Opinion polls continued to show New Zealand First hovering at between 5 per cent and 10 per cent in public support. The media seemed not inclined to take New Zealand First with much seriousness. They were even less inclined after the Selwyn by-election, occasioned by Richardson's resignation.

New Zealand First's candidate for the by-election was none other than Tim Shadbolt, a man impossible to dislike but hard to take seriously in the context of national politics. Shadbolt had joined New Zealand First the very day that he won selection — an event which upset many in the local party organisation. Shadbolt's selection was perhaps not as baffling as some in the media — and party — portrayed it. His was a very well-known face. And his sunny, populist style had brought him success in local body politics out of all proportion to his achievements. In a normal by-election, where the result did not greatly matter, Shadbolt may well have harvested a large number of votes. But the Selwyn by-election was not a normal by-election — it was a mini-General Election which would decide whether or not the government retained its majority in Parliament.

Cartoonists had a field day with Shadbolt's selection. Commentaters gleefully remembered Shadbolt's recent appearance in a television advertisement for cheese, in which he had proclaimed, 'I don't mind where as long as I'm mayor.' He was the very caricature of the political carpetbagger. The by-election quickly turned into a three-horse race, and then — as Labour's campaign went from bad to worse — into a straight fight between National and the Alliance. Peters campaigned solidly in Selwyn, at one point promising large subsidies to the possum industry. The thought of a possum-led economic expansion did not have Selwyn voters jumping out of their skins. New Zealand First collected just over 5 per cent of the vote. Still, Peters could hardly have been more unhappy than Labour, whose vote collapsed to just 10 per cent. National won the contest narrowly.

Shortly after the by-election the first major sign of tension between Peters and Henare opened up in public. Henare told *The Dominion* that he favoured a coalition between New Zealand First and Labour, rejecting the Alliance as too 'wacky' and National as less compatible than Labour. In theory a Labour-New Zealand First coalition does indeed look plausible. It is also the option most likely to place Henare at the Cabinet table as Maori Affairs Minister. Peters was understandably annoyed by Henare's public speculation, and was careful to distance himself from his statements. There is little doubt Henare is more inclined by instinct to do deals with other parties than Peters. Interestingly, however, when Labour's economic policy came out a month later, Peters called it a 'victory for commonsense over blind ideology', suggesting that he too may be thinking seriously about working with Labour.

But the problems with Henare were as nothing compared to the messy falling out with Ian and Cheryl Shearer. Ian Shearer, a former Cabinet minister, had been one of the few figures in the party with significant political experience. His wife Cheryl worked in Peters' Parliamentary office. Both had been important figures in setting up the party. In the space of two days Cheryl Shearer left her job and Ian Shearer resigned from the party. Both had concerns about the running of Peters' Parliamentary office. Ian Shearer walked out with all guns blazing: his allegations about the office had Peters threatening legal action. Shearer also labelled Peters a poor organiser, and lazy. 'I am no longer prepared to watch Mr Peters demand of others an accountability that he was unwilling to demand of himself,' he declared. In a parody of Peters' own operating methods, Shearer responded to Peters' talk of litigation by threatening to release a 'swine box' of documents backing up his concerns over the office.

The heart of the argument was whether taxpayers' money intended for Peters' Parliamentary business was instead being spent on party business. The dividing line between 'Parliamentary' and 'party' is somewhat fuzzy and — if truth be told — is often enough stepped over by MPs. Peters vigorously denied any wrongdoing. In the end an inquiry by the Speaker cleared Peters, but not before the incident had brought very bad publicity for New Zealand First. As Peters knows better than anyone, perception counts for a great deal in politics. The self-appointed scourge of New Zealand's élite, and condemner of those feeding at the public trough, had been forced to do some explaining of his own.

In an attempt to deflect attention from the Shearer incident, Peters released a 'second winebox' of documents on Cook Islands tax schemes. None of the material in it incriminated New Zealanders. However, the documents were not without their colour. Max Raepple, who had entertained the nation as one of the key players in the Maori loans affair, was among the cast in the second winebox; his career as a loan raiser for the Cook Islands government came to an end in the wake of that affair. According to Peters, the second winebox demonstrated that the notorious — and now collapsed — British-based Bank of Credit and Commerce International (BCCI) was involved in Cook Islands deals. However, the documents did not themselves bear out a BCCI linkage.

The year ended with few signs from Peters that he possessed a strategy capable of lifting New Zealand First into the big league of political parties. The early months of 1995 were little different. Peters continued with essentially the same populist lines he had been plugging since the formation of his party. The Davison inquiry was proceeding slowly, amid considerable procedural wrangling among the parties.

Foreign investment was a theme Peters was now pushing

especially hard. He chose ANZAC Day of 1995 to launch the New Zealand First policy on foreign investment, playing heavily on the symbolism of the occasion. He said that the sacrifices of earlier generations in war had not been undertaken so that we could become 'strangers in our own backyard, serfs in our own country'. New Zealand First undertook to limit foreign ownership in New Zealand companies to 24.9 per cent, while completely banning land sales to foreigners. Foreign investors could keep their existing holdings but, if they sold, would be required to sell to New Zealanders. Peters promised stricter regulations on 'essential services' already under foreign ownership. The largely elderly audience gave Peters an enthusiastic reception, proving that he still had the ability to play the Messiah at public meetings. It remains to be seen, however, how much nationwide political traction he can muster on the foreign investment issue.

In June Peters announced that he and Louise were separating after 22 years of marriage. He blamed the split on the stresses of political life.

Conclusion

PERHAPS Peters has been right all along. Perhaps Hugh McCarthy *did* work for Malcolm Douglas. Perhaps Russian submarines *were* plotting the seabed of Cook Strait. Perhaps Judge Casey *did* take his riding instructions from the Labour Party. Perhaps it *was* a Russian submarine reportedly sighted off Great Barrier Island. Perhaps the *Mikhail Lermontov was* carrying spying equipment and there was a cover-up between the New Zealand and Soviet authorities. Perhaps Ann Hercus *did* rack-rent a property and lied to Parliament about it; perhaps Phil Goff *was* addicted to property speculation and lied to Parliament about it. Perhaps Richard Prebble *had* been reading a newspaper while driving a car and lied to Parliament about it. Perhaps Roger Douglas *was* attempting to run monetary policy to help property speculators, and that he was a speculator himself. Perhaps Rod Deane *was* a political hack who had been given a $750,000 payoff for whitewashing the government in two inquiries.

Perhaps Helen Clark *did* intervene to see that Labour Party cronies were given a lucrative Area Health Board contract. Perhaps Colin Curruthers *was* appointed a QC in lieu of being paid for acting for the Labour Party, and Lange lied to Parliament about it. Perhaps Bolger *was* responsible for the Quality Inns deal going ahead. Perhaps Selwyn Cushing *did* try to bribe Peters; perhaps Cushing *was* secretly working for the Roundtable, and his offer of money was a very late follow-up to a meeting with Roundtable members Peters had attended nine months before. Perhaps the government *did* pay Fay, Richwhite $190 million commission in the 1990 BNZ bailout, and then covered it up — though it was rather a large lump of money to shove under the carpet. Perhaps the government *did* secretly sell its shares in the BNZ, though it must have repurchased them in order to sell them again for the final time a few weeks later. Perhaps there *was* a cover-up undertaken to hide a dodgy loan made by the BNZ to Fay Richwhite, a cover-up that must have included the Attorney-General, three valuers and a compliant QC. Perhaps it *was* always a shame to see members hiding behind the privilege of Parliament, but never a shame when Peters did it.

Perhaps two BNZ directors *had* been involved in tax fraud over the funding of a film, and David Henry had suspiciously failed to prosecute over it. Perhaps Henry *was* sat on by a Cabinet minister who did not want to see his business mates prosecuted. Perhaps extortionist Paul White *had* accidentally received 92 computer disks from Citibank, rather than the 88 examined by the Serious Fraud Office. Perhaps the Serious Fraud Office *did* pass disks back to Citibank and perhaps they *were* altered. Perhaps it was a whitewash. Perhaps the BNZ's reinsurance arrangement attacked by Peters *was* fraudulent. Perhaps Fay, Richwhite *did* buy into the BNZ so that the conspiracy would avoid detection, even though the government — who did the deal with Fay Richwhite — were apparently outside the conspiracy. Perhaps the Securities Commission, along with academic Don Trow, were *wrong* in pronouncing the reinsurance arrangement legal — or were themselves part of the conspiracy. Perhaps other politicians *were* in the pockets of big business, which is why they failed to share Peters' horror at the deal. Perhaps Larry Johnson *was* dismissed from the BNZ for opposing the loan to Fay, Richwhite rather than, as claimed by the bank, for getting his personal finances into a spectacular mess.

Perhaps a dozen or more people *should* be locked up over the Magnum deal. Perhaps the Prime Minister's department *was* secretly plotting to have Sturt and Henry whitewash the Magnum transaction, and the Prime Minister told a barefaced lie to Parliament in saying no meeting had taken place. Perhaps the government was actively sheltering fraudsters. Perhaps there *was* a criminal conspiracy involving Henry, Sturt, Michael Fay, David Richwhite, Paul Collins, Peter Travers, Lyndsay Pyne, Robin Congreve, Geoff Ricketts, John Lusk, John King, Geoff Clews and Richard Green. Perhaps all these men *should* be locked up. Most intriguingly of all, perhaps on 29 March

1986 a Cook Strait ferry *did* briefly touch the bottom, at the entrance to Tory Channel, causing paint scratches but no buckled plates.

All things are possible. But none of the accusations are proved, many are manifestly absurd, and for the vast majority there is not even a scrap of evidence, let alone an arguable case.

Peters set out in 1992 to show there was corruption in government. If anything, he has come close to proving the opposite. For at least eight years he has had a reputation as a promising recipient of a leak. For all of that time he has been associated in the public mind with the glaring denunciation, the call for an inquiry, and the flourish of mysteriously-obtained documents. Endless threats have been made to 'reveal more'. Almost every person in the country who is something short of the full quid must have written to Peters with their conspiracy theories; his mailbag must be overflowing with the indecipherable and the richly hilarious. Even plenty of sane people must have sent Peters material. Out of all that, Peters has identified only one instance where it is even arguable the law was broken — the Magnum case. It was not even a Peters 'scoop'; the media were on to it, and the *Frontline* programme presented the material better than Peters had done, leading in a few days to the inquiry Peters had been seeking for weeks. Unhappy the country that has a Peters in its midst. But happy the country where a conspiracy theorist can turn up so little.

Peters may one day hit the bull's-eye with an allegation. There is always that chance. It might even happen in the course of the current 'winebox' inquiry. If it did happen, it could never excuse the tactics Peters has been employing for the last ten years, or change our view of him as a New Zealand McCarthy. A major Peters success in uncovering corruption would be nothing more and nothing less than a twofold disaster. The discovery itself would be dismaying in the extreme. And it would give our New Zealand McCarthy an added stature, an unwarranted moral legitimacy. We must fervently hope it never happens.

Peters' positive contributions to New Zealand life are quickly told. He has consistently articulated the view that the road to advancement for Maori is through education and independence, not through ever increasing demands on the state. That has been positive. So too has been Peters' insistence that resurrecting the Treaty is no substitute for an ethic of self-advancement among Maori. As National's Maori Affairs spokesman in Opposition, Peters exposed to public view many of the inadequacies of the Maori Affairs Department. That is one of the roles of an Opposition, and Peters performed it well — even if much of the material was supplied by Laws.

The rest of Peters' career has been a catalogue of waste and misplaced effort. As a minister Peters accomplished almost nothing. Ka Awatea may have impressed Maori, but Peters was an ineffective advocate for his own people within Cabinet. Nor can Peters claim any other substantive policy achievement from his first dozen years in politics. He may credit himself with electoral reform, though on that issue — as with much else — he was more of a follower than a leader of public opinion. National would most likely have embraced electoral reform without Peters' public advocacy. As for Peters' interminable attacks on 'monetarist' economic policies, there is little evidence they have had an impact either on the last Labour government or the current National government. If Peters was ever seriously interested in influencing the outcome of the economic debate, he lost all chance when he neglected caucus forums for an almost exclusive concentration on publicity.

In style Peters is the most negative politician seen in New Zealand for at least a generation. As an 'image' politician devoid of substance, he has contributed to the trivialisation of political debate. He has both benefited from, and encouraged, the tendency of television journalists to deal in image and soundbite to the exclusion of rational debate. As a highly persuasive populist who resisted the new economic realism from 1984 onwards, Peters can only have inhibited the adjustment of New Zealanders to the new environment they were heading into. As a grievance politician, Peters encouraged New Zealanders to view the economic changes as unfairly imposed upon them by a small élite, rather than as necessary adjustments to which they could adapt, and of which they could take advantage.

As a National rebel whose cause was himself, Peters seriously detracted from the policymaking cohesion of the

Bolger administration. The sheer amount of time and energy used up over 'the Peters problem' by senior ministers and their staff, not least by the Prime Minister himself, is something no outsider should underrate. Dealing with Peters was barren time, totally incidental to the needs of running a government. In a sense, caucus fared even even worse. Week after week in caucus was spent, not on discussing policy or political strategy, but on arguments over what Peters had said or done during the previous seven days. Attacks on Peters were the constant caucus diet.

Peters' campaign on the BNZ, and on corruption in government, seriously eroded public confidence in the political system and in the integrity of politicians. A healthy public scepticism about the claims of politicians is one thing, a belief they have their hands in the till is quite another. It was the ultimate achievement of the negative politician that Peters managed to spread this belief in the public mind with remarkable success, and yet with no evidence to back his claims. The close vote in favour of MMP in the 1993 referendum is widely believed to have been a vote *against* the current generation of politicians, rather than for MMP. This seems particularly likely in view of the astonishing ignorance among New Zealanders, even now, over how MMP actually works. It is doubtful MMP would have been chosen — for better or for worse — in the absence of Peters' efforts to sour the public mood. In this indirect sense Peters can claim responsibility for the most important change to our political system this century.

As a New Zealand McCarthy, Peters brings an ugliness to the political scene not remotely matched by any other member of Parliament. The pressure he has placed on men such as Sturt and Henry — both professionally and personally — has been, for a civilised society, quite intolerable. It also risks seriously detracting from the quality of people making themselves available for top law enforcement jobs. Who would wish to be the next Commissioner of Inland Revenue, the next head of the Serious Fraud Office, with Peters still on the scent and having tasted blood? Sadly Peters has injected a climate of fear into public life not seen since the heyday of Muldoon, if then.

Our New Zealand McCarthy is also distorting the responses to allegations of corruption that one would expect from politicians in a healthy body politic. One type of distorted response has already happened: an inquiry is under way into allegations for which there is no evidence at all. A judge has in all seriousness been looking into accusations that Henry and Sturt are corrupt, merely on the basis that Peters has repeatedly asserted it in the House, and that some people have started to believe it. No one in government has any doubts as to the integrity of either man — yet an inquiry is under way. It is a most unwise precedent to be setting — a form of appeasement to the forces of anarchy and mob rule. On the same premise, if another MP repeated loudly enough, and often enough, and was believed by enough people, that the Police Commissioner and the Governor of the Reserve Bank were running a money laundering racket, that would justify holding an inquiry. There is no end to the number of possible inquiries because there is no end to possible conspiracy theories.

The other type of distorted response has thankfully not yet happened, but could occur. If an Opposition politician, not necessarily Peters, does get the sniff of a serious case of corruption, there could be a heightened temptation in government to cover it up. On top of the usual pressures not to deal with the issue openly, there would be the added pressure of not wanting to appear to vindicate Peters' long campaign. That temptation, if it ever occurred, would be the most melancholy of all Peters' legacies.

Peters has been written off in the past; it would be a foolish commentator who predicted with confidence that Peters will in the new MMP Parliament be confined to the margins of political life. The political mood is nothing if not volatile. Any number of events could propel Peters on to centre stage.

There remain, however, some formidable difficulties in the path of New Zealand First becoming a coalition partner in government, or entering into formal co-operation with the governing parties. With the exception of the new element introduced by Henare, New Zealand First remains largely a vehicle for its leader. That leader, among his peers, is probably the most mistrusted man in Parliament. Other parties know that Peters would be an unstable element in a coalition because his driving motivation — promotion of himself — is inherently unstable. The whole of Peters' career stands as a warning for anyone wishing to do business with him. He has shown no ability to work with other MPs. He was unable to fit within a National Cabinet, and then unable to work within a National caucus. Since being cast out by National, his track record has been no better.

The absence of a whipping system in New Zealand First further suggests the party would be an unstable coalition partner in an MMP Parliament. Peters has repeatedly said New Zealand First MPs would not be required to vote for manifesto policies, and the same presumably applies to any deal made between New Zealand First and another party. Under those rules, there can be no guarantee New Zealand First MPs would provide a stable voting block in the House.

More seriously for Peters, the political product promoted by New Zealand First may have increasingly less appeal. New Zealand First's constituency has mostly comprised those who believed the Douglas/Richardson reforms were wrong in theory and disastrous in practice. This group remains sizeable, but its numbers are steadily diminishing. 1994 was a year of buoyant economic growth, and even saw falling unemployment. Many individual aspects of the reforms remain highly unpopular. But fewer New Zealanders would deny that the economy is now stronger, or would genuinely prefer a return to pre-1984 policies.

Certainly there is a mood shift in the electorate towards softer *social policies* — a desire for a 'kinder, gentler' Rogernomics which looks after more of the casualties of the system. This mood is strengthening as the government's fiscal position continues to improve. Both National and Labour have shifted slightly to the left on social policy since the 1993 election, largely in response to the new mood. The great beneficiary of this shift in sentiment, however, has been the Alliance. In theory New Zealand First could plug into the new mood, since it has a softer social policy than both National and Labour. But Peters has so far pitched little of his rhetoric in that direction.

Another mood shift is the apparent preference for 'consensus' politics, as New Zealand moves ever deeper into an MMP environment. How serious this mood really is, and how long it will last, are open questions. But there is no doubting its existence. The language of consensus is now a standard weapon in the armoury of most politicians. Yet Peters himself has changed little. He remains the negative, take-no-prisoners politician he has always been. More than anyone, Peters epitomises the adversary political system that conventional wisdom says we are leaving behind. It is one of the many contradictions of Peters' career. The destroyer who did so much to discredit the old first-past-the-post system, and who campaigned so publicly for MMP, now himself almost looks like a hangover from a previous era.

The most likely scenario is that Peters will continue in the role of political spoiler he has been playing for years. His support level, along with that of his party, will rise and fall in line with the juiciness of whatever scandal he happens to be peddling. Obviously Peters' support will also be influenced by how the public views the more 'establishment' political parties. A populist is highly dependent on popular disaffection with those perceived as sitting at the top of the pyramid. That disaffection will dwindle, if the economy continues to perform strongly. Or it may grow if the opening manoeuvres under MMP, or the time leading up to it, present a picture of weak, erratic or self-serving government. It is possible that Peters, by sitting out the opening rounds under MMP, may successfully project an image of strength and incorruptibility.

The unbridled right of an MP to use Parliamentary privilege will be an important factor in Peters' future success. That right is currently under active discussion. It was during Peters' classic McCarthy months that it was first mooted that those attacked under privilege should be given a right of reply. The idea died, but with a new bout of Peters McCarthyism in 1994, and a review of Parliamentary standing orders under way in the context of MMP, the subject of privilege came on to the political agenda again. A private members bill has been introduced by David Caygill, seeking to give anyone attacked under privilege the right of a reply to be read out in Parliament.

The bill also requires an MP intending to use privilege to receive clearance in advance from the Speaker.

The right of reply is a welcome initiative and may well become law. But of itself it will do little to combat the problem posed by Peters and other MPs who abuse privilege. Those attacked already possess a right of reply through access to the media, and generally use it. Having their reply read out in Parliament may raise its status. But it cannot combat the in-built advantage of the multiple untruth uttered under privilege.

There is a great deal of preciousness in the attitude of Parliamentarians to the whole question of privilege. They rarely attempt to explain why MPs should be above the law in the first place, other than pointing out that privilege has existed since the Bill of Rights in 1689. If there were instances of privilege having been used to right demonstrable wrongs, it would be more plausible to argue for its retention. Yet few if any such instances have occurred in New Zealand, at least in recent times. Whatever the ideal may be, MPs in our Parliament abuse privilege far more often than they use it wisely. That is true even if Peters' behaviour is put to one side.

Abolition of Parliamentary privilege is most unlikely to happen. The debate will centre on what might be done to rein in the worst abuses. Having the Speaker or the privileges committee vetting an MP's use of privilege in advance, as suggested by Caygill, might provide a check, but only by politicising the Speaker or the committee to a perhaps untenable extent. A better alternative might be to give the Speaker, or perhaps the privileges committee, power to withdraw for a set period the protection of privilege from an MP who has repeatedly abused it. This would still politicise whoever had to take that decision. But it is generally easier to be certain abuse of privilege has occurred after repeated events, rather than attempting to make a judgement in advance. In truth there is no tidy solution that retains privilege yet guards effectively against it abuse. Most probably the problem will defeat Parliamentarians and no fundamental change will be made.

This book has tried to describe Peters' public career and relate him to his times. It has said little about the inner drives of the man himself. Yet how close can we get to the centre of Peters' personality? Few politicians have had an outward career so spectacular and yet so full of mistakes and apparent contradictions. Writing in *North and South*, Rosemary McLeod aptly described Peters in politics as 'a man who seems much of the time to know all the moves but not the game itself'. Yet what is Peters' own game? Does he even know it himself? Has he chosen to play the game, or has the game chosen him? It would take a far subtler student of human nature than the present author to answer these questions with any certainty.

Though a gregarious man in one sense, Peters' personality contains a reserve that is hard to penetrate. One of the most acute descriptions of Peters came from Tony Reid writing in the *Listener*. Fascinated by Peters' famous lopsided grin, he wrote:

> Somehow it manages to be both self-deprecatory and arrogant; relentless charm uneasily coupled to relentless aggression. That's part of the Winston Peters contradiction — one reason why observers have such difficulty in focusing on the centre of the man's character, why they are inclined to mistrust. Always, you suspect, there might be another Winston Peters who is quietly present and not saying a word.

One useful approach to analysing Peters may be through what is termed 'Narcissism' by psychologists. The name derives from the Greek myth of Narcissus, recounted most memorably in the *Metamorphoses* of the Roman poet Ovid. Narcissus was a youth stubbornly in love with his own beauty. He was impervious to the imprecations of a number of would-be lovers, including the nymph Echo who pined away until only her voice remained. The goddess Nemesis, resolving to punish Narcissus, caused him to fall in love with his own reflection seen in a pool of water. Narcissus stayed entranced, gazing enraptured into the pool, until ultimately he, like Echo, gradually wasted away. In the end Narcissus died, after which his body was transformed into the flower that bears his name.

The Narcissus myth tells of an individual trapped in his own self-absorption, lacking empathy towards others, worshipping his own image even as it brings him to ruin. As analysed by modern psychology, Narcissistic personalities display an exaggerated self-importance, a tendency towards perfectionism, grandiosity, exhibitionism, feelings of entitlement, and the pursuit of others to obtain admiration. Because of their self-involvement, Narcissistic personalities tend to lack true interest in others, and are exploitative in their personal relations. The front presented to the world by a Narcissistic personality may well be a defensive facade hiding feelings of inferiority, emptiness and unsatisfied desire.

This description may make Narcissistic personalities sound thoroughly unpleasant to know, but in fact Narcissistic personalities often have no shortage of friends or admirers. One writer on Narcissism, Jason Aronson, comments:

> Patients with Narcissistic personalities may not appear disturbed in their surface behaviour and may function well socially and show good impulse control. Their great need to be loved and admired by others, their inflated concept of themselves, their shallow emotional life, and their minimal or lack of empathy for the feelings of others may only manifest itself on careful examination. These individuals may attain high offices and even be elected President of the United States.

Nonetheless, the development of the Narcissistic personality often runs into uncomfortable collisions with the real world. Another psychologist, James F. Masterson, has written:

> The fantasy persists that the world is his oyster and revolves about him. In order to protect this illusion, he must seal off by avoidance, denial and devaluation those perceptions of reality that do not fit or resonate with this narcissistic, grandiose self-projection. Consequently, he is compelled to suffer the cost to adaption that is always involved when large segments of reality must be denied.

It is beyond the present author's competence or intention to assert that Peters has a Narcissistic personality. But many of the traits of Narcissism are readily recognisable in him. There is the strong egocentrism in Peters' speeches, right from his earliest days in Parliament. There is his well-documented fixation with the opinion polls. There is his obsession with his personal appearance, his love of the television cameras. There has been his careful building of his own image, in ways guaranteed to infuriate many of his colleagues in the National caucus. Perhaps there is a fundamental inability in Peters to empathise, which saw him failing to appreciate just how angry his colleagues would become when called crooks and sychophants. Perhaps Peters' various career setbacks have constituted painful adjustments as the real world has intruded into the fantasy world.

Perhaps the suave, aggressive façade Peters projects to the world is a screen behind which lurks emptiness and insecurity. Perhaps behind the authoritative voice, the flourish of documents in the House, lies a vulnerable man, a Maori, born in the sticks, uncertain of his status, uncertain of his academic ability, desperate to gain the applause of the world.

In the middle of his classic McCarthy months, Peters gave an interview in which he admitted that he was gradually becoming a pariah to many around Parliament Buildings. But he commented:

> I knew this was going to be bad. But I'd be really worried if I walked down the street and people spat on me, and I needed police protection, and everyone called me a liar when I was on the radio. That's when I'd feel pretty bad. Being hated and despised by a few special-interest groups who don't mean a damn in this country is not a cause to be worried about.

No one other than Peters would stand up in Parliament and say:

> Out there in New Zealand tonight there are probably about 45,000 people — and now that I have started, 55,000 to 70,000 people — listening to this debate . . .

It is tempting to hypothesise that it is the drive for adulation in Peters which is overwhelming. That would explain why Peters repeatedly used tactics that brought him public adulation yet cut off his route to power. Yet the true picture is more complex. Many who have been close to Peters insist that he badly wanted power. Some believe he wanted power for its own sake, while others believe he saw power and adulation as two sides of the same coin. It is clear Peters displayed no sense of strategy for obtaining power. He may have been genuinely weak on strategy. Or it may have been that, at whatever level of consciousness, the drive for instant adulation was just too strong.

The fascination of Peters is that he is still on the political stage. He may not belong there, he may have no place in public life in a civilised democracy of the late 20th century. But whatever the pundits may think, he is still there. He may rise to new heights of McCarthyism. He may find new populist causes that he can champion, new disturbances in the political psyche that he can play on. Or perhaps, tired of the life outside, he may begin to manoeuvre for power. Peters' next move may well bring us clues to the enigma of his character.

Index